Gandhi

PROFILES IN **POWER**

General Editor: Keith Robbins

. . . .

GANDHI

David Arnold

An imprint of **Pearson Education**

Harlow, England · London · New York · Reading, Massachusetts · San Francisco
Toronto · Don Mills, Ontario · Sydney · Tokyo · Singapore · Hong Kong · Seoul
Taipei · Cape Town · Madrid · Mexico City · Amsterdam · Munich · Paris · Milan

Pearson Education Limited
Head Office:
Edinburgh Gate
Harlow CM20 2JE
Tel: +44 (0)1279 623623
Fax: +44 (0)1279 431059

London Office:
128 Long Acre
London WC2E 9AN
Tel: +44 (0)20 7447 2000
Fax: +44 (0)20 7240 5771
Website: www.history-minds.com

First published in Great Britain in 2001

© Pearson Education Limited 2001

ISBN 0 582 31978 1

British Library Cataloguing in Publication Data
A CIP catalogue record for this book can be obtained from the British Library

Library of Congress Cataloging in Publication Data
A CIP catalog record for this book can be obtained from the Library of Congress

10 9 8 7 6 5 4 3 2 1

Typeset by 35 in 10/12pt Janson
Printed in Malaysia by LSP

The Publishers' policy is to use paper manufactured from sustainable forests.

CONTENTS

LIST OF PLATES

LIST OF MAPS

. . . .

PREFACE

Mohandas Karamchand Gandhi, India's 'Great Soul' or Mahatma, has been one of the most written-about individuals in modern history. Since his South African friend, the Reverend Joseph Doke, wrote the first life of Gandhi in 1909, when he was only forty years old, there have been more than four hundred biographies of Gandhi and an almost countless number of studies of different aspects of his political, religious, social and economic ideas. This book, however, is not intended to be a standard biography, nor, primarily, does it attempt to provide a guide to Gandhi's religious ideas or his moral and political philosophy. Its aims are twofold. Firstly, it seeks to situate Gandhi in the context of his own times and thus to assess his place in the history of India and the modern world. Secondly, it seeks to use the growing, and in many respects increasingly critical, literature about Gandhi to examine anew the nature of his often unconventional and controversial 'power'. Did he derive his power from his role as a nationalist leader and his unswerving commitment to India's struggle for freedom from British colonial rule? Or was it rather from the force and originality of his political ideas, his advocacy of non-violent action, and his pioneering techniques of non-violent resistance and mass civil disobedience – all of which had an appeal far beyond the shores of India? Was his power perhaps derived less from his ideological stance than from his political astuteness and pragmatism, or from his remarkable willingness, even in old age, to embark on new 'experiments with truth'? Was his power a consequence of his singular energy and his exceptional organisational skills, or, less determinately, from an inner saintliness, from personal charm and charisma? With Gandhi there are no simple answers, but these are the underlying issues that this book seeks to address and to answer.

This book has been a long while in the making. I began to think about Gandhi, about his meaning and impact, when I first went to India in 1968, met old Gandhians and stayed for a time, in 1969, the Gandhi birth centenary year, at his Sevagram ashram. I have particularly benefited since 1988 from teaching an undergraduate course on Gandhi and Gandhism in the History Department at the School of Oriental and African Studies in London, and I am grateful to all the students who have taken that course for the very different ideas they have brought to their understanding of Gandhi and their quest for his meaning and relevance. I am indebted, too, to other members of the Subaltern Studies group – Ranajit Guha, Shahid Amin, Partha Chatterjee, David Hardiman and Gyan Pandey – for what they have written about Gandhi. I hope to have captured something of that critical enterprise in this work without doing injustice to their different approaches and interpretations. I am particularly appreciative of David Hardiman's informed, critical and constructive reading of an earlier version of this book. I am grateful, too, for the intellectual companionship of Sumit Sarkar and Sudipta Kaviraj, who have helped me to see many aspects of Gandhi and his significance that would otherwise have been lost to me. I would also like to thank the general editor of this series, Keith Robbins, for a number of helpful suggestions and his support for this work, as well as Heather McCallum at Pearson Education for helping to develop the book in its present form. And lastly, on a more personal note, I owe a great debt to Juliet Miller for her encouragement in writing this book and trying to put my ideas about Gandhi on paper. Without her it would certainly not have been possible.

David Arnold
November 2000

Chapter 1

INTRODUCTION: THE IDEA OF GANDHI

The life and legacy of Mohandas Karamchand Gandhi (1869–1948) are full of irony and fraught with contradiction. It is not just that Gandhi, a renowned man of peace, an exponent of non-violent action for more than forty years, died a violent death, felled by an assassin's bullets, nor that his greatest aim and achievement, India's independence from colonial rule, was marred by the bloody episode of Partition that left perhaps a million people dead and sparked one of the largest mass migrations of modern times. It was also expressive of his contradictory presence in Indian politics and on the international stage that Gandhi, one of the most influential and powerful figures of the twentieth century, never served as a prime minister or president, or even as a member of government. Within the Indian National Congress, the nationalist party he helped to lead and inspire over several decades, he only briefly held the office of president. Gandhi, as one biographer has put it, was 'a completely unofficial man'.[1]

And yet, without holding high office, Gandhi was in many respects a remarkably public individual. He spent more than fifty years of his life in political activity in South Africa and India. Apart from *Hind Swaraj*, a short tract on Indian nationalism published at the height of the South African struggle in 1909, Gandhi made little attempt to present his political ideas systematically in print. But he did write an often revealingly intimate autobiography, *The Story of My Experiments with Truth*, which remains the principal source for his early life and characteristically merges his public life with his personal experiences, and his letters, newspaper articles and speeches fill the ninety volumes of his *Collected Works*. In many respects his life is extraordinarily well documented. Apart from all the speeches and writings, Gandhi's personal and political evolution is recorded through the large number of photographs of him, spanning his life from the age of 7 to his death at the age of 78. Gandhi must surely be one of the most photographed, as well as one of the most written about, individuals in history. It is ironic (but an irony not untypical of the man) that Gandhi, in many ways a traditionalist, sceptical of the need for industrial technology, should in this sense have lived such a modern life, so fully in the eye of the camera – and, further, that his life should have become more widely known to millions around the world through Richard Attenborough's 1982 film *Gandhi*. But the many photographs of Gandhi, which seem to make his life so open and accessible, should also alert us to the fact that Gandhi became, even in his own middle age, a kind of icon, an image that might conceal as much as it revealed of the inner man and that might acquire a power and meaning beyond that of Gandhi himself to command and control. The idea of Gandhi, though so differently construed by so many different people, has ever been as powerful as the man himself.

Gandhi remains an enigma, but the wealth of different interpretations of his life, work and legacy is only one factor in this, for his own personality remains, despite all the photographs, the speeches and the biographies, surprisingly difficult to pin down. As one of his Western biographers, George Woodcock, observed, Gandhi revealed himself in action, in speech, in print, even on radio, and yet 'as incessantly his inmost self eludes one and perhaps eluded him'.[2] Or, as another biographer remarked, Gandhi 'wore many public masks and many private ones'.[3] It can even be asked how far his mahatmaship was itself a kind of mask, a saintly persona he consciously constructed the better to communicate his message to others, to efface the contradictions and inconsistencies in his own thinking, or simply in order to protect his own intense inner vulnerability. But, if this were the case, Gandhi also experienced the difficulties and frustrations involved in being a mahatma, a saintly figure more commonly revered rather than understood.

In seeking to analyse Gandhi's power it is necessary to look beyond many of the conventional notions of political power. Not only did he shun high office, he never contested an election or sat in a parliament and after his early years in South Africa was generally averse to constitutional politics. Although his language was singularly full, for a man of peace, of the rhetoric of combat, the only battles he ever fought were of a non-violent kind. Gandhi was never a commanding orator, even when he began to speak through another modern invention, the microphone, and yet many thousands of people would turn out at railway stations or flock to beaches, fairgrounds and other open spaces to see and hear him. While Gandhi was a tough campaigner, an astute political organiser and a shrewd publicist, his appeal in India and internationally relied far more upon his perceived spirituality, his saintliness, and his apparent ability to represent India's masses. Many of those closest to Gandhi were unimpressed by his formal writings: some had not read *Hind Swaraj*, the nearest Gandhi came to a political manifesto, or, like Jawaharlal Nehru, his long-term lieutenant and India's first Prime Minister, shared few of its sentiments. And yet they were captivated by Gandhi's charisma, swayed by his charm, inspired by his courage, awed by his capacity for self-sacrifice and self-denial, touched by his impish sense of humour. Personality counted for much in the constitution and exercise of Gandhi's power and it is often only through the eyes of his associates and followers – Krishnadas, his secretary during the heady days of the Non-Cooperation Movement, Mirabehn (Madeleine Slade), the daughter of an English admiral who joined Gandhi at his ashram in Ahmedabad in the 1920s, and Nehru himself, the impetuous prince and heir apparent of India's nationalist movement[4] – that one can get a real sense of the power Gandhi held over others.

It is also all too easy (in India as in the West) to see Gandhi as a timeless figure, an individual whose saintliness elevated him above the petty politics and mundane concerns of his age. The reality is rather different, and indeed to understand Gandhi's importance, it is essential to understand how he was moulded by the times and the places in which he lived and how he reacted to (and brought his influence to bear upon) the politics, the moral issues, the economic and technological challenges of his day. It is worth noting that while Gandhi lived to see the end of the Second World War, the beginning of the dissolution of the British Empire (in which India's independence was a vital first step) and the dawning of the nuclear age, he was, in terms of chronology if not of outlook, a Victorian. He was born in the same year, 1869, that the opening of the Suez Canal brought colonial India measurably closer to imperial Britain, and was already well into middle age at the outbreak of the First World War in 1914.

Gandhi is naturally thought of mainly in terms of his contribution to India's nationalist struggle and his adversarial role in Britain's imperial politics, but it should be recognised that, especially by the

1930s, he was a figure of international significance, aware of, and responding to the spread of communism and the rise of Soviet Russia, the global spread and growing influence of American technology and culture, as well as the emergence of fascism in Europe and East Asia. It should be borne in mind that Gandhi was a close contemporary of Lenin (born a year after him in 1870) and of two British prime ministers, the Labour leader Ramsay MacDonald (1866–1937), whose 'Communal Award' in 1932 sparked Gandhi's most momentous fast, and the Conservative Winston S. Churchill (1874–1965), who over several decades was among Gandhi's leading imperial antagonists. Gandhi was already 50 in 1919 when the Treaty of Versailles cast its long and fateful shadow over Europe, and over the next twenty-five years, when his power was at its zenith, Gandhi shared world attention with men younger than himself – Josef Stalin (1879–1953), Benito Mussolini (1883–1945), Franklin D. Roosevelt (1884–1945), and Adolf Hitler (1889–1945), whose violent credo *Mein Kampf* was published the same year, 1925, that Gandhi embarked on his autobiographical 'experiments with truth'. Was the Mahatma, the 'Great Soul', out of place in the age of the 'Great Dictators', or was his advocacy of non-violence in the troubled years between two cataclysmic world wars remarkably timely?

Opinions about Gandhi have always been divided, often sharply so, and it is not surprising that his ideas about the state, about class, gender and religion should recently have been subjected to fresh and more exacting examination. For many of his critics, Gandhi's saintly image is a fraud, even a calculated illusion. He has been branded an agent of class domination, the prophet of non-violence who became a 'mascot of the bourgeoisie', the man of religion who subverted India's search for secularism and modernity and who, however unwittingly, helped to precipitate India's holocaust, the Partition of 1947. His standing as a social reformer is increasingly challenged, not least his role as the supposed champion of India's most oppressed people, the *dalits*, the untouchables, or as he called them (patronisingly some would say) the Harijans or 'Children of God'. On a more personal level (though with Gandhi public and private life are not easily separated), his sexual attitudes and practices continue to arouse controversy, fuelled by a new readiness to question Gandhi's credentials as a liberator of India's women. And yet, Gandhi, execrated or exalted, refuses to go away. Each generation finds something new in Gandhi, to rediscover or to recreate for itself the Mahatma – as the inspiration for the civil rights movement of Martin

Luther King in the United States, as a source of inspiration and courage for Nelson Mandela in a South African prison, for nationalist movements and non-violent agitations across the globe, or as the pioneer and prophet of the 'green' movement and 'sustainable' development.

Interpretations of Gandhi have varied widely but they have followed three main lines of discussion. Firstly, Gandhi is represented as a saint in politics, a man who exercised the power of a saint rather more than that of a politician. For some Gandhi belongs so self-evidently to the category of saint that he remains almost beyond the bounds of historical scrutiny. As the scientist Albert Einstein remarked in 1944, 'Generations to come, it may be, will scarce believe that such a one as this ever in flesh and blood walked upon this earth.'[5] Gandhi is seen not only to have had a deep spirituality, but to have possessed great moral and physical courage and an unwavering commitment to non-violence that transformed the lives of those around him. It is this saintly idea of Gandhi that has proved the most enduring image of him in India, as in the West, and although his saintliness might seem in some ways peculiarly Indian and Hindu, it has served as a bridge between cultures, making his methods and ideals accessible to others outside the Hindu fold, especially Christians. Particularly in the 1920s and 30s, comparisons were frequently made in the Western world between Gandhi and St Paul, St Francis of Assisi or even Christ.[6] His saintly adherence to non-violence and self-suffering is seen as having enabled Gandhi to transform India's nationalist struggle from a narrowly focused and elitist political campaign into a mass-based moral crusade, enabling him to take on, and ultimately undermine, the authority of the British Empire, still in the interwar years one of the most powerful empires the world had ever seen.

It has been pointed out, though, that Gandhi was by no means unique in the context of modern India in adopting and utilising a 'saintly idiom', even in political life.[7] Indeed, since the middle of the nineteenth century, it has been one of the most common and influential roles taken up by (or bestowed upon) not just religious teachers, but by a wide variety of peasant leaders, politicians and social reformers. Gandhi both inherited a saintly tradition and, through his own influence and eccentricity, gave it new credibility in the modern world. Whether the aura of saintliness arose as it were naturally from Gandhi's spirituality and his unique blend of

ideals and actions, or whether Gandhi in the course of his struggle
for Indian rights in South Africa deliberately assumed the mantle of
saintliness the better to advance his cause and consolidate his leadership, remains a source of controversy, and we will return to the
issue in Chapter 3.

The idea of Gandhi as a saint in politics is, however, more ambivalent than might at first appear. Saints, many of his critics have argued,
have no place in politics. As Bal Gangadhar Tilak, a prominent
nationalist from an earlier generation of leaders, advised Gandhi
before he embarked on his career in Indian politics, 'Politics is a
game of worldly people, and not of *sadhus* [holy men]'.[8] The converse
of this was the view, expressed thirty years later by Lord Wavell, the
penultimate Viceroy of India and no admirer of the Mahatma, that
Gandhi was 'a very tough politician and not a saint'.[9] His sainthood
could further be seen as having a distinctly Hindu flavour and as
such alienating (among others) the Muslims of India, who feared that
the swaraj, the self-rule or independence that Gandhi advocated, and
sometimes called Ram Rajya (God's rule), in effect meant a Hindu
Raj (state). Penderel Moon, a former civil servant in India and at the
more critical end of the spectrum of Gandhi's biographers, dubbed
him 'a Hindu to the depth of his being'. In remodelling the Congress
Party, Gandhi 'imparted to it his own Hindu bias'. Even though
Gandhi personally 'failed to see the danger', Moon believed, this
'Hinduising of the national movement, which Gandhi's leadership
promoted and symbolised, was injurious and ultimately fatal to
Hindu-Muslim unity'.[10] Others have argued that to be a saint was to
be naive, peddling an idealised vision of the pre-colonial past and of
village society, a golden age which had never existed and to which
modern India could not possibly return, or it meant misjudging the
masses and their ability to adhere to a rigorous programme of non-
violence. One Indian historian, R. C. Majumdar, thus argued that
Gandhi was 'lacking in both political wisdom and political strategy'.
Far from being infallible, he 'committed serious blunders, one after
another, in pursuit of some utopian ideals and methods which had
no basis in reality'.[11] At times, too, to the fury and bewilderment of
Nehru and others, Gandhi invoked God in support of his own
actions and beliefs, but would provide no rational explanation.
Especially in later life, he was prone to acting according to the
dictates of his 'inner voice' or conscience, declining to explain his
reasons even to his closest associates and verging on the frankly
dictatorial. Saints seldom make good democrats.

Second only to the saintly image of Gandhi is his reputation as the 'father' or 'maker' of modern India. Such an idea was common during the later stages of the Indian nationalist movement and has been widely held in India and elsewhere since Independence. Jawaharlal Nehru was one of those who, despite his own personal and political differences with Gandhi, did much to promote this idea, but it has been taken up by many Western writers, historians and journalists as well. Such an idea rests on Gandhi's perceived centrality and dominant role in the anti-colonial struggle from 1919 onwards, the unique style of his leadership and especially the manner in which he was seen to give the nationalist movement a mass (essentially peasant) base, and the attribution of India's independence to the several non-violent civil disobedience (satyagraha) campaigns that Gandhi led against British rule between 1919 and 1942. Perhaps even more than his political leadership, Gandhi's wide-ranging programme of social reform might be said to have stamped an indelible mark on modern India. His campaigns against untouchability, his pursuit of gender equality, his efforts to revitalise India's villages and encourage hand-spinning, his opposition to the coercive power of the state – in these, as in many other respects, Gandhi would seem to have set the social and economic agenda for India for decades to come.

And yet here, too, Gandhi's reputation seems increasingly in jeopardy. Not all Gandhi's ideas and activities are now seen to have promoted national unity or to have advanced the cause of national independence. Other political leaders, reformers and intellectuals have been seen as having a clearer and worthier vision of what modern India might be. Nehru, for instance, with his ideal of a modern state and secular society, in which the benefits of science, technology and education were to be available to all, might equally be regarded as a 'maker of modern India'. Recent historical scholarship has also raised considerable doubts about some of the more sweeping claims for Gandhi's foundational role and inspiring leadership. We now know much more about the peasant and other popular struggles that preceded Gandhi's 'rise to power' and can see how Gandhi was able to latch onto existing movements and grievances rather than mobilising a hitherto inert peasantry almost single-handedly. It can be argued that peasants had good reasons of their own for being attracted to Gandhi, making him a mahatma in their own image and attributing to him ideas and aspirations that were close to their outlook and experiences but far removed from his own programme. In a nationalist movement spread over many decades and involving a wide variety of different personalities and approaches, including constitutionalism, terrorism and mass protest, Gandhi and his political techniques can hardly be credited with having had more than a partial share in wresting India's independence from the British. Emphasising the contribution made by others to India's anti-colonial struggle before and during Gandhi's own period of leadership, Majumdar remarked that 'It would be a travesty of truth to give him the sole credit for the freedom of India, and sheer nonsense to look upon *satyagraha* (or *charkha* [the spinning-wheel]) . . . as the unique weapon by which it was achieved'.[12]

Increasingly, too, questions are raised as to how far Gandhi, often praised as much for his role as a social reformer as a political leader, was genuinely able to break free of his own caste background or to shrug off the Victorian moral universe with which he grew to maturity in London and South Africa. While not denying Gandhi's ability to innovate and experiment, it is important not to lose sight of his nineteenth-century, small-town, middle-class and relatively high-caste origins. Born into a family that had served the petty princes of Gujarat in western India for generations, in a region where in his childhood the bullock cart was a more familiar sight than the railway train, how far was Gandhi able, or even willing, to keep pace with an India which, by his death, stood on the brink of the nuclear age? To what extent did the ideas which he brought to the problems of labour, of caste or of the status of women reflect an outlook that was by the 1930s already outmoded and which reflected the views of a member of India's more privileged classes?

Thirdly, the idea of Gandhi has constantly moved between the perception of Gandhi as a revolutionary and as a traditionalist, even a downright reactionary. Certainly, Gandhi was not a revolutionary in the conventional sense. He did not believe in the violent overthrow of the existing order, or even view violence as an acceptable vehicle for political and social change. Nor did he believe in overthrowing one state (the British colonial regime in India) simply in order to replace it by another (the nation state). Gandhi's revolutionary impulse lay elsewhere – in his use of the non-violent methods for which he coined the name 'satyagraha', not just to resist oppression and injustice but also to seek to convert his opponents to his beliefs; in his reorientation of the nationalist movement in India away from an essentially middle-class membership and towards mass participation; and in his rejection of modern industrial society in favour of rural crafts and self-sufficient, self-governing villages. In seeking to ameliorate the position of the poor and to remove the widespread discrimination against Hindu India's lowest stratum, the untouchables, Gandhi in theory posed a fundamental challenge to the established hierarchy of caste authority and social power. The unconventional nature of his political and social philosophy – hostility to the state, espousal of the poor – held out the promise of a radical relocation of power within society, while satyagraha provided the dynamic agency through which to achieve it. By combining social with political change and by devising new means to reach these goals, Gandhi might appear to deserve the title of revolutionary which many of his enthusiasts have awarded him.[13]

And yet it can be argued that the 'people' Gandhi empowered in India, as latterly in the West, were not in fact the lowest of the low, but those who, for all their grievances, were more comfortably ensconced in the social hierarchy and for whom Gandhi's non-violence conveniently bypassed more threatening forms of revolutionary upheaval. In an India in which factory workers numbered in excess of a million by the end of the First World War and two million by the end of the Second, Gandhi virtually turned his back on the industrial working class, and only in one solitary and not entirely successful campaign (in Ahmedabad in 1918) did he attempt to apply his satyagraha techniques to their grievances. Even in the countryside, although many of the poorer and landless peasants looked to Gandhi for inspiration and leadership, it was the wealthier peasants who provided the main basis for his support and who benefited most from his political campaigns. Poor peasants in revolt against Indian landlords, against colonial revenue demands and forest laws, were sternly lectured by Gandhi and his followers on their duty to adhere to non-violence at all costs or to abjure thoughts of class struggle in favour of a more moral way of life.

Sometimes early in his Indian career denounced as a 'Bolshevik' by the British, Gandhi never showed any interest in Marxist thought (and hardly read Marx at all until his closing years). Talk of class war was for him anathema. He believed in harmony, one reason why an idealised image of village society so enthralled his imagination. Gandhi's doctrine of trusteeship, developed over the course of the 1920s and 30s, but arguably betraying his origins among the Banias (merchants and moneylenders) of Gujarat, seemed to favour a paternalistic status quo in which those who held wealth and power were expected to exercise it benevolently on behalf of those in need. Gandhi also drew substantial financial support for his campaigns from some of India's leading industrialists and business-men, including G. D. Birla, one of the country's leading capitalists. So often hailed as a great peasant leader, Gandhi at times appeared more in the guise of a patron-saint of the middle classes. No wonder that the Communist R. Palme Dutt attacked Gandhi as a 'mascot of the bourgeoisie'. Here was 'the prophet who by his personal saintliness and selflessness could unlock the door to the hearts of the masses where the moderate bourgeois leaders could not hope for a hearing', and yet whose leadership, compromised by his close alliance with the propertied classes, was 'the best guarantee of the shipwreck of any mass movement which had the blessing of his association'.[14] Even more moderate writers have seen Gandhi's prin-cipal contribution to the political economy of India as a form of class conciliation that linked mass mobilisation through the nation-alist movement to a party organisation dominated by the business classes and landowning castes, thus precluding violent upheaval and revolutionary social change.[15]

The class struggle in India is not, however, the only measure by which to assess Gandhi's revolutionary impact. Some writers would argue that the true test of his power was not so much what he did for India as to the imperial power itself. While Gandhi is principally thought of as one of the principal architects of modern India, his impact on twentieth-century Britain should not be overlooked. From his South African days virtually until his assassination forty years later, every British Cabinet had to reckon with Gandhi. As Geoffrey Ashe puts it, he was, in a sense, 'a British politician himself, and among the greatest'.[16] By steadily eroding the moral authority as well as political power of the British in India after 1918, Gandhi and his fellow nationalists helped bring about the demise of the British Empire in India and, once that had been achieved, its dissolution in other parts of the globe became almost impossible to prevent. As the British Labour politician Tony Benn remarked on the death of Jawaharlal Nehru in 1964, 'It is sometimes said that Britain liberated India. In fact the reverse is the truth. Gandhi and Nehru liberated us. By winning their freedom, they freed us from the ignorance and prejudice that lay behind the myth of Britain's imperial destiny.'[17] While noting that Gandhi strengthened an anti-imperial tradition that had never been entirely extinguished in Britain itself, Ashe also concluded that it was, nonetheless, largely in response to Gandhi that Britain 'resigned a world mission which had outlived whatever rightness it had, and turned back to a humbler and saner quest for self-realisation'.[18] Gandhi's revolution was a revolution as much for Britain as it was for India.

Whatever interpretation we bring to his life, Gandhi brings us face to face with the problem of the individual in history. Reading about Gandhi's work in South Africa and in India, reflecting on his influence on the course of the nationalist movement in India and the wider fate of European imperialism as it teetered to its fall, it is hard not to see his life as a telling illustration of the power of the individual to affect the course of history. Gandhi, like Napoleon, Lenin, Hitler and Mao, might well be considered as one of those exceptional men and women who have done most to change the course of history, to stamp their personality on modern times. And yet many historians remain uncomfortable with such a notion. Was Gandhi's 'power' really his own? Or did it derive from intellectual and social movements to which Gandhi was himself heir, to circumstances over which he had scant control? Was Gandhi in fact responsible for freeing India from the yoke of British colonial rule, or was his leadership merely one factor among many that brought about that momentous dissolution?

There are no easy answers to such questions, and historians are notoriously reluctant to be drawn into hypothetical questions about what might have been. While it is all too easy to exaggerate his role, there is no denying that Gandhi did enjoy a remarkable personal ascendency over the course of events in India, especially in the interwar years, and imposed his mark alike on the history of the subcontinent and on the empire whose demise he helped bring about. It would be rash to dismiss out of hand Woodcock's view that 'if one had to choose any individual as more responsible than others for the death of the Empire, it would be Gandhi'.[19] And yet one pressing reason for looking again at Gandhi's life is to see him less as an exceptional figure in history, as someone who made history, than as a 'colonial subject', as someone who endured one of the great transforming tides of history. Gandhi's experiences of, and attitudes to, the overwhelming presence of the West, its vast material strength, its immense coercive power, and its cultural hegemony, sometimes strident, sometimes subtle, were, for all his undoubted idiosyncrasies, shared by many of those who came under the awesome sway of the imperial powers in the nineteenth and twentieth centuries. Like countless others in Asia, Africa, the Americas and Oceania, he sought to wrestle with the profound difficulties, experienced at both a personal and a wider cultural and political level, of trying to preserve valued elements of an indigenous identity while finding ways of negating or accommodating the aggressive, self-confident civilisation of the West. Perhaps one of the reasons why Gandhi remains a figure of such enduring interest is precisely that in a post-colonial world his experiences, attitudes and putative solutions retain a remarkable resonance for those who find themselves engaged, if only at a personal level, in comparable struggles for identity and self-expression.

But this parallelism brings us to one of the most intriguing aspects of Gandhi's life and legacy. Where did his ideas come from? Or, to put it another way, to whom does he *belong* – to the East, to the West, or perhaps, in this age of cultural pluralism and globalisation, to some hybrid mixture of the two? Here, too, understandings of Gandhi have been widely divergent. A number of scholars have endorsed the idea, understandably prevalent in India itself, that Gandhi was incontrovertibly and essentially Indian. Not only was he born and brought up there, but his ideas of non-violence have been firmly ascribed to Jain and Hindu philosophy, to techniques of protest prevalent in western India in his youth and to his own family background and early experiences. Many of Gandhi's ideas and practices – from vegetarianism to celibacy – seem to belong strongly, even if not uniquely, to an Indian, and more specifically Hindu, tradition. On the other hand, Gandhi was never an uncritical upholder of Indian traditions. His attack on untouchability was clear evidence of this. In his views on health and medicine Gandhi was as sceptical about the claims made for traditional Indian medicine as he was for those of orthodox Western medicine, relying instead on his own experiments in diet and self-medication and unorthodox European practices, like hydrotherapy. His belief in the dignity of labour – a central tenet in his vision of social harmony and a revitalised rural India – is far more Western than Indian and owes much to Victorian writers like John Ruskin. There is no doubting, too, that Gandhi was greatly influenced, even in his self-styled understanding of Hinduism, by his protracted engagement with Christianity.

It might then be argued that Gandhi was at least as much a product of the West, especially as a result of his years as a law student in London (1888–91). It was there, at the very heart of the

Empire that ruled India, that Gandhi was stimulated to think about his own culture, about vegetarianism and Hinduism, and to acquire some of the philosophical tools and political skills that were to sustain his later life of struggle. Equally, Gandhi's subsequent visits to London, in 1906, 1909 and 1914, and again in 1931, seem to mark significant turning points in his political career and personal evolution. More frequently, however, historians have looked to his South African years (1893–1914) as the single most formative phase in his life. This was the period in which he encountered racism in an extreme form and was goaded into direct action, when his sense of national identity was strengthened by the combined struggle of Indians from different religions, regions and classes, when he devised his satyagraha technique and deepened his acquaintance with Hinduism as well as Christianity, when he first experimented with communal living and jail-going, when he adopted celibacy and began to lose faith in the British Empire. South Africa may have been responsible in large part for the 'making of the Mahatma', and yet in certain respects Gandhi was still an incomplete figure when he returned to India in 1915. It was only then that he began to identify himself wholehearted with the peasantry and village life, to defy the Empire openly, and, by committing himself to the nationalist cause in India, become a leading figure within the Indian National Congress. Many of the aspects of his career that have come to be most emblematically associated with Gandhi – the Salt March of 1930, the campaign against untouchability, the doctrine of trusteeship – belong emphatically to his later, Indian years.

It can only reasonably be concluded that Gandhi was never too old to learn or to experiment, and that he was too complex a figure to belong, in his day or ours, simply to either East or West. Gandhi lived for most of his life at the critical intersection between two different regimes of power, represented at one extreme by colonial power in India and South Africa and by Indian (more especially Hindu) tradition on the other. At times these worlds collided, but at others they converged to a remarkable and surprising extent. Part of Gandhi's enduring appeal, and one reason why he continues to excite interest, admiration and anger is that he was such a versatile and eclectic figure, able to combine an intense fervour for selected aspects of India's cultural traditions with a critical (but also at times appreciative) engagement with the West. Gandhi belongs to everyone – and yet to nobody.

. . .

NOTES AND REFERENCES

1. George Woodcock, *Gandhi*, London, 1972, p. 6.
2. Ibid., p. 28.
3. Robert Payne, *The Life and Death of Mahatma Gandhi*, London, 1969, p. 13.
4. Krishnadas, *Seven Months with Mahatma Gandhi*, Ahmedabad, 1951; Mirabehn (Madeleine Slade), *The Spirit's Pilgrimage*, London, 1960; Jawaharlal Nehru, *An Autobiography*, London, 1936.
5. Geoffrey Ashe, *Gandhi: A Study in Revolution*, London, 1968, p. xi.
6. Notably by the French novelist and anti-war writer Romain Rolland, whose *Mahatma Gandhi*, published in an English translation in London in 1924 and in several other European languages, helped establish the saintly or 'Christ-like' image of Gandhi in the West. See also C. F. Andrews and others in S. Radhakrishnan (ed.), *Mahatma Gandhi: Essays and Reflections on His Life and Work*, London, 1939.
7. W. H. Morris-Jones 'India's Political Idioms', in C. H. Philips (ed.), *Politics and Society in India*, London, 1963, pp. 140–1.
8. S. P. Aiyar, 'Gandhi, Gokhale and the Moderates', in Sibnarayan Ray (ed.), *Gandhi, India and the World: An International Symposium*, Philadelphia, 1970, p. 103.
9. Penderel Moon (ed.), *Wavell: The Viceroy's Journal*, Oxford, 1973, p. 236.
10. Penderel Moon, *Gandhi and Modern India*, London, 1968, pp. 275–6.
11. R. C. Majumdar, *History of the Freedom Movement in India*, III, Calcutta, 1963, pp. xvii, xviii–xix.
12. Ibid., p. xxiii.
13. For this view, see Ashe, *Gandhi*.
14. Ibid., p. xii.
15. Francine R. Frankel, *India's Political Economy, 1947–1977: The Gradual Revolution*, Princeton, 1978, chapter 2.
16. Ashe, *Gandhi*, p. vii.
17. H. J. N. Horsburgh, *Non-Violence and Aggression: A Study of Gandhi's Moral Equivalent of War*, London, 1968, p. 155.
18. Ashe, *Gandhi*, p. 391.
19. George Woodcock, *Who Killed the British Empire?*, New York, 1974, p. 330.

Chapter 2

A *DIWAN'S* SON

However we see Gandhi – traditionalist, reformist or revolutionary – it is essential to begin with his family, caste and religious background. Guided by his own autobiography, and more than has commonly been the case with many other leading figures in the modern world, historians, biographers and others have sought, sometimes to excess, to locate the origins of the mature Mahatma's ideas, methods and beliefs in his home environment and early experiences. While this can give us a basic understanding of the India in which Gandhi grew up, the distinctiveness of the region in which he was raised, and the social and religious influences to which he was exposed, it should also be clear that his background was only one of the many influences that moulded him. The second phase of his life, from the age of 18, as a student in London, has at least as great a claim to being among Gandhi's most formative episodes and the period when, in struggling to reconcile East and West, many of his political beliefs and social ideas were first formed.

. . .

THE INDIA OF THE PRINCES

Mohandas Karamchand Gandhi was born on 2 October 1869 in the town of Porbandar on the southwest coast of Gujarat. One of the dozen main linguistic regions of India, Gujarat is today a state of the Indian Union, but at the time of Gandhi's birth the area of western Gujarat then known as Kathiawar or Kathiawad (and now called Saurashtra) was among the most politically fragmented in India. It was divided between outliers of the Bombay Presidency, one of the main provinces of British India, and more than two hundred semi-independent states ruled by Indian princes. Despite coming under British paramountcy between 1802 and 1822, following the defeat of Maratha forces by the armies of the English East India Company, Kathiawar in the nineteenth century was virtually a province apart from the rest of India and, in the minds of Kathiawaris, distinct even from the rest of Gujarat. It was, and still is in many respects, an isolated region, cut off to the north by the extensive creeks and salt marshes of the Rann of Cutch, by the Gulf of Cambay to the south and east, and by the deserts of Rajasthan (or Rajputana) to the north-east. Despite this apparent isolation, Kathiawar was never inward-looking. Before the colonial period, it had been a dynamic region in its own right, its traders visiting the ports of the Arabian Sea and the Indian Ocean and crossing the deserts of Rajasthan and Sind into northern India. Although the colonial era tended to increase Kathiawar's isolation, the merchants of Porbandar, a town of 15,000 people in the 1860s, maintained a brisk trade along the coast of Western India and the Persian Gulf. They also ventured further afield, particularly to South Africa, a link that was to prove vital to Gandhi's decision to go there in 1893. Apart from its merchants, Kathiawar was princely but poor. This was a more backward and feudal part of Gujarat than the well-watered, fertile plains and prosperous towns and villages of eastern Gujarat with which Gandhi later became closely associated.

The eastern ports of Gujarat, led by Surat and Cambay, had also for centuries been thriving havens for coastal and Indian Ocean trade, and, despite profound economic changes, were better able than Kathiawar to adapt to the new order colonialism brought. Ahmedabad, the largest and grandest city in Gujarat, had long been a prominent commercial centre. Lying close to cotton-growing districts, it had a flourishing trade and, until British imports began to take their toll in the early nineteenth century, it was renowned for the quality and variety of its textiles. In the nineteenth century Surat, and to some extent Ahmedabad, declined as Bombay, further south, began to expand aggressively. In 1853 India's first railway line began to operate from Bombay, the following year its first textile mill commenced production, and with the opening of the Suez Canal in 1869, the city became a thriving nexus for regional and international trade and the principal administrative and manufacturing centre of western India. The rapid rise of Bombay city also eclipsed Poona to the southeast, until 1817 the capital of the Peshwas (or prime ministers) and the main seat of the Maratha power.

The fortunes of Ahmedabad and the surrounding districts began to revive as the railway reached the city from Bombay in 1864, but western Gujarat remained largely unaffected. In the mid-nineteenth century the Kathiawar peninsula was one of the most conservative areas of India. Apart from a fierce but localised uprising among the Vaghers of Okhamandal, the Mutiny or Great Revolt of 1857–8, which brought the reign of the Company to an end and ushered in rule by the crown, passed Kathiawar by. It had a reputation for being one of the last strongholds of female infanticide, and not long before Gandhi's birth the Thakur, or ruler, of the small state of Rajkot had been heavily fined by the British Resident or political agent for allowing the death of his infant daughter. It was also one of the places where vaccination, introduced by the British to curb the scourge of smallpox, was most stubbornly resisted. In 1869 there were no major industries, no large towns or cities, not even that potent symbol of Victorian ideas of progress, a railway. The slowness of communications was indicative of the general backwardness. Before the coming of the railway, a journey by camel from Ahmedabad to Rajkot in the centre of Kathiawar took eight days, and Gandhi records in his autobiography how it took him five days in the 1870s to travel the 120 miles from Rajkot to Porbandar by bullock cart. Until the founding of a college in Rajkot for the sons of Kathiawar's rulers, Western education had little impact on the region, and the nationalist sentiments that had just begun to stir among the new middle classes of India's principal port cities – Calcutta, Bombay and Madras – had not begun to infiltrate the region. Some Christian missionaries, Irish Presbyterians, tried to evangelise in Kathiawar, but they were driven out of Porbandar in the mid-1840s by the hostility of the Rana, the Hindu ruler, and retreated to Rajkot, where they enjoyed the protection of the British political agent and the garrison but gained few converts from their attempts at proselytising.[1]

Porbandar was one of six hundred princely states in India, of which roughly a third were located in Gujarat. Across India as a whole these states varied widely in size and character. Some, like Travancore and Mysore in south India and Baroda in eastern Gujarat, acquired a reputation for being 'progressive' states, encouraging industry and economic development, promoting education and social reform; but many others were feudal relics, too small and autocratic, too riven by faction and intrigue, to have much truck with progress. Porbandar, occupying 600 square miles and with a population of just over 72,000 in 1872, was one of the more substantial states in Kathiawar; Rajkot, despite its central location, its rapidly growing cantonment and extensive civil station, was smaller, a 'second-class' state with a population of barely 37,000. Until the Rebellion of 1857–8 the British had steadily conquered or absorbed the Indian states, and under Lord Dalhousie as Governor-General of India from 1848 to 1856 an annexationist policy was pursued with such vigour and determination that the days of the remaining states seemed numbered. But the uprising, the greatest threat to colonial rule in India for more than fifty years, caused the British to believe that the annexations had helped to provoke the revolt and goad the last of the princely order into rebellion. Thereafter they sought to preserve the remaining states and looked to their rulers as loyal supporters of British power as well as decorative, or merely curious, vestiges of India's feudal past. In actuality, the states retained only nominal independence and the British, through their political agents, kept close watch on their internal affairs, allowing them little genuine freedom of action.

The young Mohandas Gandhi grew up in a family with a long tradition of service to the rulers of Kathiawar and in 'an atmosphere steeped in local politics'.[2] Although born into a community traditionally identified with trade (but also with helping to finance the region's princes), his grandfather, uncle and father all served as *diwans* (chief ministers and advisers) to local states. His grandfather, Uttamchand Gandhi, was a celebrated and widely respected *diwan* of Porbandar in the early nineteenth century, though he later fell out with the Rani. Gandhi's father, Karamchand, also served at Porbandar and was later employed by the states of Rajkot and Vankaner from 1875 until shortly before his death in 1885. Mohandas Gandhi's father and grandfather were both, in Romain Rolland's words, 'leaders of the people', though both 'met with persecution because of their independent spirit'.[3] Apart from seeing his father and grandfather as models of integrity and courage, the significance of this princely milieu for Gandhi's own attitudes has attracted less comment from his biographers than might be expected, but it was surely far-reaching.[4] Gandhi grew up with the idea of Indians as rulers in their own states, however small they might be, not mere subjects of the British, but ministers in their own lands, albeit under the watchful eye of the British political agent. The states of Kathiawar, for all their backwardness, represented the survival of an alternative political, even moral, order, one that comfortably predated the British Raj and kept alive ancient traditions of Hindu kingship and the obligations that were seen to accompany it. Apart from brief encounters with European school inspectors and a few other officials, Gandhi was not exposed in his early life to a substantial British administrative presence and in his youth British rule must have seemed very distant.

Gandhi surely grew up with a more positive view of the princely states, their rulers and advisers than many of his more Westernised, middle-class contemporaries elsewhere in India, though he came to learn, to his cost, how plagued by intrigue, how averse to reform they could be, and how bruising could be the political agent's authority. The doctrine of trusteeship that Gandhi developed in later life, as he tried to grapple with the challenge of socialism, evidently owed something to a sympathetic view of the princes and their *diwans* as the enlightened custodians of the people, representatives of an indigenous tradition of paternalistic responsibility and care. This is suggested by an article in which he argued that it was the duty of the ruler to 'serve his people' and, in return for their loyalty, 'be the trustee and friend of the people'. Elaborating on this reciprocity, Gandhi added:

> The poor man must know that to a great extent poverty is due to his own faults and shortcomings. So while the poor man must strive to improve his condition, let him not hate the ruler and wish his destruction. . . . He must not want rulership for himself, but remain content by earning his own wants. This condition of mutual co-operation and help is the Swaraj [freedom] of my conception.[5]

Gandhi's upbringing as 'the son of the Prime Minister' can be made to sound grander than it was, but it may also have been of greater importance that he himself realised or acknowledged. Gandhi is quoted as saying of his childhood, 'I roamed about the villages in a bullock cart. As I was the son of a *diwan*, people fed me on the way with *juwar* roti and curds and gave me eight anna pieces'.[6] There was about Gandhi in later life, as there was about Nehru and many other Indians of broadly comparable background and status, a remarkable presumption of power, an inner conviction that, for all the bitter trials and humiliations of colonial rule, they were men fit to rule or at least, like Gandhi, to be the power behind the throne as India's *diwans*. For such men to experience as Gandhi did, especially in South Africa, the total denial of all such authority (to which had by then been added the status of a highly anglicised, London-trained lawyer), to be treated as a mere 'coolie', was a deeply galling experience, but one that ultimately confirmed Gandhi even more strongly in his defiance and inner self-belief.

Possibly no less important a part of Gandhi's background and his political apprenticeship as the traditions of kingship and *diwan*-hood in Kathiawar were those of resistance. It has been shown that, especially among the Banias and other merchant and moneylender castes of the region, there existed various techniques of protest and self-suffering that were used to enforce the payment of debts or to protest against injustices by rulers and others. Some of these techniques took a violent form, including self-inflicted wounds, to coerce a friend or client into meeting legitimate demands. These are unlikely to have appealed to Gandhi, but others may have done, including fasting or what was known as 'sitting *dharna*', that is, sitting outside a palace or in some other conspicuous place until the aggrieved individual's suffering stirred the ruler's compassion and remorse or attracted public attention to his cause. Occasionally used by groups, these techniques were mostly employed by individuals and relied to a large extent on the fact that the states of Kathiawar were relatively small and political relationships 'personal, face-to-face, and not bureaucratised'. This was the kind of encounter and dialogue between ruler and protestor at which Gandhi was later to try his hand many times in South Africa and in India, despite the generally more impersonal and highly bureaucratised nature of the colonial political order. It has been argued that Gandhi's own techniques of non-violent protest drew their inspiration, in part at least, from this source, though there is little evidence that Gandhi consciously drew upon his Kathiawari heritage in this way.[7]

But even in the 1880s princely India did not stand still. The Gandhi family recognised the need for change: the family's wealth and social standing had slipped since Uttamchand's day. Karamchand, who moved with his family from Porbandar to Rajkot when Mohandas was 7, had received little formal education and knew hardly any English, but he had high expectations of his youngest son. For all his apparent timidity, and the weaknesses and self-doubts he describes in his autobiography, Mohandas Gandhi proved more academically able that his two elder brothers, Laxmidas and Karsandas, and was sent first to a primary school in Rajkot, then to an English-medium secondary school, the Alfred High School, and, briefly, for a term, to a college at Bhavnagar on the Cambay side of the Kathiawar peninsula. Although Gandhi was obliged to persevere with English, he grew up in an environment in which Gujarati, not English, was the principal language, and he retained his affection for his mother-tongue throughout his life. Significantly, most of his important works, including the autobiography, were first written in Gujarati and only subsequently translated into English, and the importance of expression through the vernacular was one of the key ideas both of *Hind Swaraj* and Gandhi's reform of the Congress in 1920.

Previously relatively well-to-do, the future of the Gandhi family became a pressing issue after Karamchand's death, following a long illness, in 1885. Mohandas was chosen by family council to rescue the family's flagging fortunes by going to London to receive a legal training, in the expectation that he would return to Kathiawar to become an eminent and powerful modern *diwan*. As Gandhi himself later put it rather naively in a letter to Laxmidas, 'the object of sending me to England was that we . . . might thereby maintain the status of our father more or less, be well off and enjoy the good things of life'.[8] In sailing from Bombay on 4 September 1888 to qualify as a barrister in London, Gandhi was shifting from one extreme of India's middle-class social spectrum to another – from the family tradition of the *diwans* of Kathiawar to the career of a London-trained lawyer.

. . .

CASTE AND THE BANIAS

Gandhi's background, it has been aptly said, was 'middle caste and middle class'.[9] His family came from the Modh Bania caste. Conventionally each caste had its own hereditary occupation and customary status within the hierarchy of Hindu society. The Banias were by tradition traders, moneylenders and grocers, though Gandhi's family had long since moved away from this occupational niche to become administrators in the princely states. Hindu society has often been represented schematically as consisting of four *varnas* or divisions – descending from the Brahmins (the priests and literati) at the top, through the Kshatriyas (rulers and warriors) and Vaishyas (traders), down to the Shudras (cultivators and artisans) at the bottom, with a fifth category, that of the Panchamas (or untouchables), lying outside the *varna* hierarchy altogether. Like his family background among the *diwans* of Kathiawar, the concept of *varna* was of great importance to Gandhi's evolution and identity. In many respects a critic of caste in the narrow sense, and especially of untouchability, he constantly returned to *varna* because it represented to him a distinctly Indian answer to the question of how society should be ordered and what attributes and responsibilities should characterise each section of society and relations between them. However, as Gandhi could not but be aware whether he approved of it or not, caste was (and is) also an extremely elaborate system of social power. An individual's standing is represented not just by his or her personal attributes, or even by personal wealth, but by what the conventions of his or her caste require. Caste conventionally dictated not just the kind of trade or occupation individuals might undertake and where they stood in the overall social hierarchy, but also whom they could or could not marry, the rituals and ceremonies they followed, with whom they could share food or water (and what kind of food and drink was permitted to them), in which section of a town or village they might reside and even, in Gandhi's day, how men and women might dress or wear their hair. It could even fashion the very vocabulary they used, the manner in which they addressed others and the physical distance and posture to be adopted in their daily contact with other castes. Gandhi grew up in a world in which social power was elaborately encoded in everyday life, even in the seemingly trivial details of dress, diet and speech.

The Bania caste to which Gandhi belonged by birth fell within the Vaishya *varna* division, though in Gujarat the Banias held a higher status than was common among Vaishyas across India as a whole. Despite the manner in which Gandhi later identified with the peasant masses as the real people of India, it is significant that he did not come from a peasant caste, nor even from a rural background. India was still in Gandhi's youth an overwhelmingly rural society, with more than 80 per cent of the population living in the countryside, but it also had a long urban history and much of the cultural as well as commercial life of the country revolved around its towns and cities. The young Gandhi was a product of Porbandar and Rajkot, two out of many thousands of small towns scattered across India. Neither priests nor peasants, but as Banias and as members of a slightly down-at-heel family of *diwans*, as men of the middling sort, the males of the Gandhi household enjoyed relatively high status in Hindu society yet without occupying its commanding heights.

There is, however, a sense in which Gandhi, in his eclectic re-working of Hindu tradition, in his search for self-identity, and in his quest for social harmony and national unity, identified himself with every one of the *varnas*, or at least with the properties they ideally represented. Bania merchants and moneylenders were conventionally far removed from Kshatriya warriors in the Hindu tradition (though as *diwans* the Gandhis served several of them, including the Rajput rulers of Rajkot), but there were times, especially in the early 1920s, when Gandhi thought of himself as a kind of non-violent Kshatriya and exhorted other Indians to find in the example of the Kshatriyas the physical courage and defiant spirit to confront the British. Thus in a speech in October 1920 he declared:

> I claim to be one of the greatest Kshatriyas of Hindustan . . . I am a true Kshatriya when I give up my life in defence of myself, my wife or my country. The physically weakest man – and a woman also – can cultivate in himself the spirit of a Kshatriya, [and] can say to the enemy, 'here I stand as firm as a rock. Do your worst.'[10]

Gandhi seemed less willing to take on the role of the Brahmin, perhaps because his inclinations were more practical than philosophical, or because he was (as we will see shortly) brought up in a devotional or *bhakti* tradition that largely eschewed the brahminical priesthood. Perhaps, too, he was conscious of his lack of formal training in Sanskrit, the language of the high Hindu tradition. Gandhi learned a little Sanskrit during his school days in Kathiawar but mostly acquired it in later life through his own efforts, in order, for example, to read the *Bhagavad Gita* in the original, and as a result of his own restless spirit of enquiry. He thus approached the Hindus' sacred texts more as an outsider, an individual seeker after truth, than as wisdom received from his elders or learned by rote and recitation. In terms of the multiple strands of the Hindu religious tradition, Gandhi opted for the style of the *sannyasi*, the religious mendicant who renounces everything including caste and convention, rather than the status and refinement of a learned pundit. It is perhaps significant, though, that many of those close to him in political life, including Jawaharlal Nehru, Rajendra Prasad and C. Rajagopalachari, as well as his long-serving secretary Mahadev Desai, were Brahmins, and so brought to his inner coterie something of the status of the Brahmins and the traditions of Brahminical learning. But, like priestly ritual, abstract intellectualism was not something Gandhi ever particularly valued and, while others despaired of his apparent utopianism, he emphasised the practical nature of his methods and goals.

In this pursuit of practicality, Gandhi identified himself more closely with the Shudras, the peasants and artisans, seen as the embodiment of service to others and the necessity of labour. But here, too, Gandhi was departing from caste and *varna* conventions. Gandhi learned from the West, not from his caste and family background, the idea of the dignity of physical toil, that 'the life of labour was the life worth living'. In India bodily labour was associated with low caste status. It was not something Gujarati Banias would normally consider either praiseworthy or desirable, though in his idealisation of both Kshatriyas and Shudras Gandhi was reacting against the perceived physical (and hence moral) weakness of his caste and race that was so central to disparaging colonial stereotypes of 'cowardly' and 'effeminate' Indians. At the bottom of the social hierarchy, Gandhi also identified himself with the Panchamas, in a bid to free Hinduism of untouchability, in his eyes one of its greatest blights and a source of inhuman oppression and discrimination. He carried this identification to the extent of taking on the role of a scavenger and cleaner of latrines, to the amazement and disgust of many high-caste Hindus, for whom such things were utter anathema.

Nonetheless, Gandhi's social and cultural ideas owed much to his Bania origins. As traders and moneylenders, Banias were reputed to be intelligent but also 'shrewd' and 'wily'. If in the popular imagination they were seen as grasping and cold-hearted, the Banias prided themselves on being sober, hardworking and thrifty.[11] They had, of necessity, a practical approach to life and, as many biographers (and critics) have remarked, it is not hard to see Gandhi's own mind-set as being deeply influenced by his background. It has often been noted, for instance, that Gandhi, for all his personal self-denial and asceticism, was an assiduous and effective fund-raiser and was methodical and scrupulous in handling money entrusted to him. He introduced into the Indian National Congress in the 1920s 'book-keeping practices that accounted for the last anna received and spent'.[12] The Englishwoman Madeleine Slade, on whom Gandhi bestowed the name Mirabehn, recalled his success on a tour in Bihar in the late 1920s in raising money from rich and poor alike. Gandhi received this 'overwhelming affection' with 'simple, detached gratitude for the sake of the Cause', but he 'treasured every copper as a sacred trust' and insisted on the 'most careful and exact account being kept of all donations'. Every evening those in charge of the collections had to count all the money received that day, much of it in small-denomination copper and nickel coins. The huge pile of money took hours to count, 'but counted it had to be, for Bapu ['father', used as an affectionate name for Gandhi] would not rest content until every detail was reported to him'.[13]

Frugality and practicality were not the only Bania traits attributable to Gandhi. The caste was also renowned for its piety, religious devotion and philanthropy. One does not need to be a cynic to see in this combination of piety and philanthropy a kind of insurance policy through which a community of moneylenders and traders protected itself from critical scrutiny and occasional attack, concealing its wealth behind an unostentatious lifestyle, purchasing public respect and approbation through charity and a reputation for good deeds. Gandhi's later determination to avoid class conflict and to achieve harmony between rich and poor through a doctrine of trusteeship can be seen as having its origins in the conciliatory practices of his caste. The Modh Banias were a socially conservative community, as well as an intensely religious one, and jealously guarded their caste status. It could be argued that Gandhi was something of an exception to this and even in his youth no defender of caste privileges and conventions. When his family decided to send him to London in 1888 he faced a caste prohibition against crossing the ocean or the 'black water'. To judge from his autobiography, Gandhi was unperturbed by this, though technically it made him an outcaste from his own community. He may have felt that, given his family's increasingly desperate circumstances, he had no choice but to go to London. His own ambition may already have been too strong for him to turn back. He chose to ignore the ban, though at his brother's behest he did undergo a ritual of purification on his return in 1891. Even so, in the eyes of the more orthodox sections of the Modh Bania caste, and it would seem his sister, Raliatbehn, he remained an outcaste.

However, while Gandhi rejected the narrow conventions of caste, he was by no means immune to its wider sentiments and mind-set. In his approach to India's lower castes, as to the untouchables and to India's tribals (or *adivasis*), Gandhi tended to adopt a high-caste attitude, calling for the need for moral as much as economic reform. For example, his appeal to them to give up meat-eating and alcohol strongly identified him with high-caste conventions (though in ways that elided apparent differences between East and West; the language of moral reform, especially the abjuring of alcohol and the advocacy of vegetarianism, had a conspicuous place too among the British social reformers and temperance workers Gandhi had encountered in England or whose works he had enthusiastically read). In some respects Gandhi can be seen as an agent of what has been dubbed 'sanskritisation', that is the adoption by low-ranking communities of the practices and lifestyles of the highest castes. While the term is contentious in a number of ways (not least because it suggests Brahmins as the essential model for emulation and upward mobility), it serves to emphasise the extent to which Gandhi was interested in 'uplift', in making the low castes more like the higher ones (including the Banias), rather than in other forms of social and political liberation which might lead to confrontation and the rejection of Brahmin and Vaishya lifestyles and authority.[14] Gandhi's attitudes to the Harijan movement he inaugurated in the 1930s exemplified this reformist, rather than revolutionary, strategy.

. . .

GANDHI AND HIS FAMILY

In the opening chapters of his autobiography, Gandhi discusses in some detail his father (Karamchand) and his mother (Putlibai), as well as his relations with his wife (Kasturbai) and his brothers, Laxmidas and Karsandas (born in 1863 and 1866 respectively). His sister Raliatbehn (born 1862) receives less attention. However, it is important to bear in mind that the book was written in the mid-1920s, largely from memory and in a manner that reflected Gandhi's own moralising concerns at the time, and so needs to be treated with caution as a historical source. Unfortunately, apart from some family reminiscences, there is little other testimony to go by and historians and biographers have accordingly relied heavily on Gandhi's own account of his early 'experiments with truth'.

In his autobiography Gandhi represents Putlibai as a saintly figure and a 'deeply religious' woman. He further remarked to one of his prison colleagues in 1932, 'If you notice any purity in me, I have inherited it from my mother, and not from my father.'[15] She was, by his account, a very pious woman, making frequent visits to the local temple in Porbandar, making solemn vows (Gandhi describes one in which she refused to eat until she saw the sun), and undertaking fasts. Gandhi only received her permission to travel to London in 1888 when, on the advice of a family friend, he took a sacred oath, promising to abstain from wine, women and meat while away from India. Despite having experimented with meat-eating in his mid-teens, and the temptations he records with respect to women in England, this promise to his mother provided a basis for his increasingly stringent regime of abstinence and self-discipline in London. Even Gandhi's use of fasting in his later life might possibly be attributed to the early example of his mother, though it served Gandhi a very different, more public and political, purpose. Unfortunately for Gandhi, his mother died, aged 40, shortly before he returned from London in July 1891, though he did not know about this until his arrival in Bombay. It may well have been a traumatic moment for him, but Gandhi, in the autobiography, attaches less importance to it than the death of his father five years earlier.

Gandhi was also doubtless greatly influenced by his father, Karamchand, not least by his role as a *diwan* and head of the Gandhi household. While his father was clearly religious in his way, Gandhi saw him as far less so than his pious and saintly mother. In the autobiography he represents him as being not only 'truthful, brave and generous', but also 'short-tempered' and 'to a certain extent . . . given to carnal pleasures'. Putlibai was his fourth wife, a fact which Gandhi interprets as meaning that he was over-sexed for a man of his age (Gandhi suggests that he was 'over 40', but he was probably only 38 or 39 at the time). The fourth marriage might, more realistically, be seen as indicative of the pressure on male householders to produce male heirs (Karamchand's previous marriages had produced two daughters) and the high rate of mortality among Bania women, especially in childbirth.[16] His father died when Gandhi was 16, but had been ill for three years, having sustained injuries in travelling from Rajkot to Porbandar for the wedding ceremony in which both Gandhi and his brother were married. Doctors appeared powerless to cure him and Gandhi undertook to help nurse Karamchand in the later stages of his illness. This may possibly have encouraged Mohandas to think, for a while, of becoming a doctor himself, and a number of writers have attached great significance to this episode, including Erik Erikson, in his psychoanalytical account of Gandhi.[17] Louis Fischer refers to Gandhi as having from this time onwards an 'inner compulsion to relieve misery and assuage pain'. It became Gandhi's 'mission' to heal, to be 'India's doctor'.[18] Bhikhu Parekh makes a similar claim, pointing out how Gandhi's thought came to be 'suffused with medical images'. Gandhi never took up a medical training (his brother Laxmidas scotched the idea, saying 'we Vaishnavas should have nothing to do with dissection of dead bodies'), but Gandhi came, nonetheless, to think of himself as a kind of 'doctor', treating an Indian body politic that had become too 'weak' and 'diseased' to be able to resist the attack of 'foreign bodies'.[19]

Sex, like sickness, is a recurring theme in Gandhi's autobiography. To say that he was 'obsessed' with the problem of sex (as Nehru, for one, observed)[20] is not to suggest that he was unable to live without it, for he took a vow of celibacy in 1906 when he was only 37 years old, but the problem of how to discipline his powerful sexual drive was central to Gandhi's personal morality, how he understood himself and society at large. The need to control sex greatly informed his attitude, among other matters, to the role and status of women, to food and health, and even the concept and practice of non-violent action. For many Western writers Gandhi's agonising over sex (and his apparent lack of appreciation for its pleasures even in a stable, loving relationship) presents problems of empathy as well as interpretation. Why did Gandhi take such a negative view of sex (to the extent of regarding it as a form of violence)? To what extent did the experiences of his youth create this attitude and impel Gandhi towards celibacy, or was sexual abstinence an ideal he derived from Hindu tradition? As with so many other aspects of Gandhi's life, there are no simple answers, but it would be as well in this instance not to exaggerate the impact of his experiences in childhood and youth on Gandhi's later attitudes.

Following custom among the Modh Banias, Gandhi was married, in 1882, at the age of 13 to Kasturbai Makanji, a girl of his own age and caste, the virtually illiterate daughter of a Porbandar merchant and family friend of Karamchand Gandhi's. In his autobiography, Gandhi is critical of the practice of early marriage on both physical and moral grounds. It is hard to say what his attitudes were at the time of his marriage – his autobiography suggests a mixture of naivety and bewilderment, followed by an awakening of intense sexual passion, which Kasturbai apparently did not reciprocate. In time Gandhi came to loath his own sexual desire for his wife, and this can in part be attributed to the fact that his father, whom he had been nursing, died while Gandhi was having sexual intercourse with his wife. He had been massaging his father when his uncle relieved him at the sick man's bedside. He went to his bedroom and woke his wife with his 'animal passion'. Within a few minutes there was a knock at the door: his father was dead. The 'double shame' of having left his father at such a time, and having done so in order to satisfy his 'carnal desire' was, Gandhi later wrote, 'a blot that I have never been able to efface or forget'.[21] Kasturbai was pregnant at the time and when the child, too, died shortly after birth, this may have further compounded Gandhi's sense of guilt and shame, cementing his later hostility to sex and his conviction that men's lust stood in the way of their proper conduct and duty. However, there is a danger in reading too much into Gandhi's autobiographical account penned forty years after these events. It was not until twenty years later that Gandhi took his vow of celibacy or *brahmacharya*, though he had been considering it intermittently for several years before that. He and Kasturbai continued to have sex, and between 1888 and 1900 she bore four children, all sons (Harilal, Manilal, Ramdas and Devadas), so it is more likely that Gandhi's remorse and aversion to sex set in only in middle age, in part as a result of his growing commitment to public service and the intensifying struggle for Indian rights in South Africa. Like many other Indian social reformers of the time, Gandhi came to associate early marriage with the alleged physical and moral weakness of the Hindus, but he was somewhat exceptional in carrying this to the extent of advocating celibacy for himself and others.

It is equally difficult to know how much importance to attach to Gandhi's relations with Kasturbai and their significance for Gandhi's wider attitudes to women, marriage and gender roles. Even by his own account he was tyrannical towards the strong-willed Kasturbai, trying to teach her to read when she showed no inclination to do so and being suspicious and jealous of her for no apparent reason. Perhaps Kasturbai bore the brunt not only of Gandhi's sexual frustrations, but also his desire to be an improver of himself and others, and her stubborn disinterest in his ambitions to educate her and make her a more 'modern' wife stood in the way of this. He later said that he learned about passive resistance from her dogged response to his attempts to coerce her. Whatever his aspirations or regrets, Gandhi settled for what was thought of in India at the time as a traditional rather than a companionable marriage in which husband and wife could be intellectual companions (if still far from equal partners). Gandhi used Kasturbai in his own writings (as, for instance, in her entrenched attitude to untouchability) as a convenient symbol of both the negative and positive aspects of the Hindu tradition as he understood it. In later years, he tended to look to other women, Indian and European, as more attractive, if also more problematic, examples of what a desirable wife or female companion might be.[22]

. . .

RELIGIOUS LIFE IN KATHIAWAR

Kathiawar was a predominantly Hindu region. In 1931, 81 per cent of the population of the Western Indian States Agency, which included Porbandar and Rajkot, was recorded as Hindu, and only 14 per cent Muslim. Of the remaining 5 per cent, most were followers of the Jain religion. But statistics do not tell us everything. Ahmedabad, the principal city of the region, had been founded in 1413 by Ahmed Shah, Sultan of Gujarat, and for centuries Kathiawar was ruled over by Muslim princes, often advised by Hindu *diwans*. Significant numbers of Muslims lived in Ahmedabad and towns across Gujarat, and the merchants whom Gandhi followed from Porbandar to South Africa in 1893 were Muslims. The two communities lived side by side in relative amity, and through sects like the Pranamis, to which Putlibai belonged, the two faiths to some extent mingled. This was not, however, an area, like eastern Bengal, on the opposite flank of the subcontinent, where the bulk of the peasantry were Muslims, nor was there as marked an urban, Islamic high culture as existed in Delhi, Lucknow and other cities of the north Indian plain. The absence of a larger and more distinctive Muslim presence in Gujarat may have been important in leading Gandhi to downplay differences between Hindus and Muslims and may possibly explain why, in later life, he failed to recognise the strength of the demand for a separate Muslim state of Pakistan (though this was principally advocated by a fellow Gujarati, Mohammed Ali Jinnah). Equally, Kathiawar was not an area in which Christianity had made much impact. In his early years Gandhi seems to have resented the presence of the few missionaries he did encounter and disliked their abusive condemnation of Hinduism. His negative understanding of Christianity only changed when he went to London and, more radically, when he moved to South Africa in 1893.

Gandhi's Hinduism lay broadly within the *bhakti* tradition. This form of Hindu worship emphasised individual devotion, particularly to the god Vishnu through his incarnations, or avatars, Krishna and Rama. It bypassed the formal Hinduism of Brahmin priests, Sanskrit texts and elaborate rituals and was, in theory at least, open to all castes, high and low, and to women as well as men. In its use of regional languages, in Gandhi's case Gujarati, the *bhakti* movement represented a more popular religious tradition and centred on prayers, individual acts of worship and devotional songs or *bhajans* in which male and female worshippers could participate directly. In Gujarat the *bhakti* movement had developed strongly from the sixteenth century around the Vaishnavite Vallabhacharya sect, which focused on the worship of Krishna, but this had fallen into some disrepute by the late nineteenth century.

In the Gandhi household in Porbandar and Rajkot religious beliefs and attitudes were seemingly more eclectic. Putlibai came from the small Pranami sect, whose eighteenth-century founder had sought, like Kabir, Guru Nanak and the leaders of a number of other religious reform movements across India since the middle ages, to unite Hindu and Muslim beliefs and practices. They combined a belief in the simplicity of living with a distaste for formally structured religion, and it has been argued that the sect had a significant impact on Gandhi's own religious ideas. Thus Robert Payne claimed that the Pranami faith 'deeply influenced the young Gandhi'. It taught 'charity, chastity, peaceful association between the followers of all religions, and a temperate life lived modestly.' The use of intoxicating drugs, tobacco, meat and wine was strictly prohibited. 'Consciously or unconsciously, Gandhi grew up in the beliefs of that strange sect.'[23] The sect may well have contributed to Gandhi's lack of interest in, even positive distaste for, the Hinduism of temples, priests and pilgrimages, though his mother appears to have been a dedicated visitor to at least one of the many temples and shrines in Porbandar. The Pranamis' blurring of Hindu-Muslim distinctions may ultimately have informed Gandhi's own religious stance, but there are many other reasons for this than the influence of his mother. It is worth noting, too, that Kathiawar was not necessarily the home of religious tolerance and inter-denominational mixing that some commentators make it out to be. It was also, for instance, the birthplace of Dayananda Saraswati, a Gujarati Brahmin who founded the Arya Samaj in 1875 in an attempt to revive the 'original' Hinduism of the Vedas and ancient 'Aryans' and to reconvert Hindus who had been lost to other religions.

Nonetheless, the religious life of Gujarat was diverse and further enriched by the presence of large numbers of followers of the Jain faith. This religion dates back to the sixth century BC and its founder Mahavira, and, like Buddhism, it began in part as a revolt against brahminicial Hinduism. As late as the twelfth century Jainism had been the dominant faith in Gujarat, and though in the sixteenth the *bhakti* movement of Vallabhacharya drew many Jains to Hinduism, in Kathiawar a majority of Banias remained Jains. Hindus and Jains continued to associate freely with one another, interdining and even intermarrying. In the search for the origins of Gandhi's thought, and especially in the quest for its indigenous roots, it has been argued that he derived much from Jain influences, including a belief in reverence for all forms of life (the Jains regarded even the accidental killing of insects as a sin) and the extreme asceticism and renunciation practised by Jain monks. But again while Gandhi's adherence to the doctrine of non-violence (ahimsa) can also be seen as having some Jain connections, this did not necessarily arise from his childhood in Kathiawar.[24] Much of Gandhi's religious and social thinking was contingent: it grew out of his own specific needs and 'experiments with truth' as these emerged in later life rather than necessarily being drawn from his family background and childhood experiences. Gandhi's ahimsa, unlike that of the Jains, which tended to be highly formulaic and dogmatic, was much more contextual, part of a dialogic approach to the exercise and constraint of power that Gandhi developed in South Africa and subsequently. He was particularly influenced by Jain ideas not so much in his youth as when, having returned from London in 1891, he met Raychandbhai, a Jain jeweller who was also a man of wide-ranging intellect and deep religiosity. Gandhi continued to correspond with him while in South Africa in 1893–5 and sought his advice over a series of moral and religious issues to which he urgently sought answers. This, as J. T. F. Jordens has shown, came at a crucial time when Gandhi was deeply troubled by missionary criticisms of Hinduism and when he was wondering whether to convert to Christianity. The answers Raychandbhai provided helped draw Gandhi more positively into the world of Jain and Hindu religious philosophy. By his own admission, the Jain jeweller, who died in 1901, was as near as Gandhi ever came to having a religious guru.[25]

Although today Gandhi is often seen, especially in the West, as the embodiment of traditional Indian values and beliefs, his Hinduism was extremely eclectic and idiosyncratic. He was not attracted by the Hinduism of temples, image-worship, and festivals. Nor, despite his idealisation of village India, did he engage with the Hinduism of the peasants, with their many gods, festivals and wayside shrines. Gandhi came late, as part of his personal 'discovery of India' in middle age, to some of the forms and manifestations of Hinduism that he was to find least palatable. Returning to India after several years in South Africa and having previously travelled little outside Gujarat, Gandhi was deeply shocked in 1901 to see 'rivers of blood' flowing from animal sacrifices at the Kali temple in Calcutta. When he visited one of the principal places of Hindu pilgrimage, Hardwar, for the Kumbh Mela festival of 1915, he was disgusted by what he saw, by the hypocrisy and fraud, and by the filthiness of the place: he found it hard to believe that god could be present in such a place of squalor and deceit.[26]

On the other hand, Gandhi was drawn to one of the most powerful symbols of popular Hinduism, the cow, and came to regard honouring and protecting the cow as a central tenet of his Hinduism. He repeatedly drew, too, on Hindu myths and legends, some of which he was familiar with from his childhood, as a rich store of moral guidance and spiritual instruction. He was particularly attracted to the play *Harishchandra*, in which the hero suffers several ordeals in his adherence to truth,[27] and Gandhi in turn equated god with 'truth' (*satya* in Sanskrit). God, he believed, was to be found in the pursuit of truth, especially that truth revealed through one's own 'inner voice' or conscience. Although he appears from his autobiography not to have been particularly familiar with it before he went to London, Gandhi also came to be deeply attracted to the *Bhagavad Gita*, the 'Song of the Lord'. Taken from the ancient Hindu epic the *Mahabharata*, the *Gita* depicts the deep moral dilemma that confronts the warrior Arjuna as he surveys the field of battle at Kurukshetra, where his relatives are drawn up on opposing sides. He seeks the advice of his charioteer, the god Krishna, who urges him to take up his arms: his higher loyalty must be to his *dharma* or duty as a Kshatriya. This is more important than personal bewilderment and grief. He must fight and do so not for personal gain, but in a spirit of non-attachment and truth-seeking. 'Prepare for war with peace in your soul,' Krishna tells Arjuna. Unlike many of his contemporaries, who took a more literal view of the *Gita*'s message, Gandhi saw the battle in which Arjuna was engaged as an allegorical, not an actual, call to arms, a demonstration of the supreme importance of following one's *dharma* through renunciation, selflessness and, in his interpretation, strict adherence to non-violent action.

Gandhi drew in various ways upon Jainism, *bhakti* Hinduism, the Pranamis, and latterly Christianity, to fashion a Hinduism that was essentially a religion of non-violence, duty and truth. It was less an organised religion than a highly individualistic set of beliefs, focusing upon the seeker's personal quest for truth and ultimately *moksha* (salvation). Gandhi turned his back on other aspects of the Hindu tradition, not just the Hinduism of popular pilgrimages and village deities and demons, but also militant Hinduism of the kind exemplified by the seventeenth-century Maratha warrior chief, Shivaji, who harassed the Mughals in western and central India and launched the long career of Maratha power in India. The Hindu religion, like Hindu society, was not, and is not, a homogeneity. Militant Hinduism also had its roots in the *bhakti* tradition, but it took a very different form from that Gandhi identified with. It was particularly associated with the Marathas and their homeland, Maharashtra, lying to the south and east of Bombay, rather than with Gujarat with its pietistic traders and moneylending Banias. Indeed, the competition between these two contrasting strains of popular Hinduism was also a rivalry between Maharashtra and Gujarat, between the Marathas and the Chitpavan Brahmins of Maharashtra and the Gujarati Banias. This rivalry formed one of the polarities in the politics of western India in the nineteenth and early twentieth centuries and one of the underlying conflicts in Gandhi's own life. Some militant Maharashtrian Hindus came to consider Gandhi too conciliatory in his attitudes to Islam and the creation of Pakistan in 1947, and they conspired to assassinate him. He met his death in January 1948 at the hands of a Maharashtrian Brahmin, Nathuram Godse.

. . .

GANDHI IN LONDON

Gandhi, it has been said, 'alone among the colonial revolutionaries, went to the West and came back unconverted'. He lived for nearly three years in London as a law student, from September 1888 to June 1891, but, while he learned much as a result, 'he chose no more than was needed to vitalise his own beliefs', and returned to India 'to find again, with the help of Western insights, the resources of his own tradition'.[28] But, while some scholars have looked to Gujarat, to Jainism, Hinduism and Indian tradition for the sources of Gandhi's political and social ideas, others have seen his encounters with the West, especially the formative experiences of his London years, as a factor of far greater significance. James D. Hunt, one of those who has made this case most forcefully, argues that Gandhi's two and half years as a student in London represented 'one of the truly shaping events of his career'. This was the place where Gandhi embarked on his political apprenticeship, 'where he began his intellectual awakening, his moral maturation, and the opening of his mind to spiritual questions'. London initiated, for Gandhi, 'a profound encounter with Western civilisation and a deep understanding of the British people'.[29]

For the first time, in leaving Rajkot for London, Gandhi was on his own, free to move away from the conventional expectations of a Modh Bania, growing up in Kathiawar. He was moving from an imperial backwater to the very heart of the British Empire. Not quite nineteen when he arrived in London, Gandhi had seen Bombay and some of the smaller towns and cities of western India, but he could not but have been impressed by the imperial metropolis (although, apart from being 'quite dazzled' by one hotel he visited, his autobiography is singularly reticent on the point). With a population of five and a half million people, London in 1888 was 'the largest city on Earth, capital of the greatest empire, and the centre of the power that was transforming India'.[30] Gandhi later recalled thinking to himself, 'If I go to London, not only shall I become a barrister . . . but I shall be able to see England, the land of philosophers and poets, the very centre of civilisation.'[31]

First-hand experience of London as a student gave Gandhi an opportunity to see more of Britain than the imperial facade. He could witness for himself the divisions within British society, even the existence of a critique of industry and empire, within its own proud citadel. He could meet Englishmen and women in a far more relaxed and open environment than would ever have been possible in India where the lines of racial division were strictly drawn and obsessively guarded. In London, Gandhi had English landladies (including one who had been in India herself), who seemed to show a genuine concern for his welfare, even if they found his dietary needs impossible to meet. He made friends among the English middle classes, including Josiah Oldfield, a fellow vegetarian with whom he shared rooms in Bayswater during his final year in London. Encouraged by her mother, he could even engage in mild flirtation with an English girl over Sunday tea – until he shamefacedly revealed that he was already married. This was far removed from the world of district collectors, political agents and haughty memsahibs. It is striking from a twenty-first-century perspective that Gandhi makes no mention of racism in the autobiographical account of his London years, perhaps because the few Indians in England at the time were viewed more with curiosity than antagonism, or because by the time he wrote the story of his 'experiments with truth', his recollections of London were overlaid by the much bitterer experience of racism in South Africa.

In going to London as a student in 1888 Gandhi was something of a pioneer. Not only was he the first of his Modh Bania caste to visit the imperial metropolis; apart from visiting Indian seamen or lascars, there were very few Indians resident in Britain, only a small number seeking to qualify for the Indian Civil Service or the Bar. In 1890 there were 207 'Indian gentlemen' living in London. Even as late as 1907, just after his second visit, there were barely 700 Indian students in the whole of Britain, roughly half of them in London. But in other respects Gandhi was more conventional. In electing to follow a legal career (albeit under family pressure, since his first inclination had been to become a doctor), Gandhi was following a path already well-trodden by many middle-class Indians aspiring to wealth and professional status. He was not, it should be noted, acquiring a university education, nor was his law training particularly demanding. Apart from passing four examinations, Gandhi had only to meet the residence requirements by attending dinners. His approach to studying law at the Inner Temple, where he qualified in June 1890, seems to have been fairly matter-of-fact and not to have aroused in him any great passion for the law. He was mostly interested in the law as a profession through which to earn a living and recoup his family's ailing fortunes rather than a means to achieve social justice and political rights, though in South Africa and back in India it did give him the skills with which to defend himself in court, most eloquently at his trial in 1922.

After his initial weeks, Gandhi did not apparently have much to do with other Indians, though he did at first attend meetings at the National Indian Association, which since its founding in 1867 had assisted students from India. He also went to hear speeches given by the Parsi Dadabhai Naoroji, a renowned Indian nationalist and, on his election as a Liberal candidate in 1892, the first Indian MP. Gandhi moved mostly in middle-class circles in London, in a sense not unlike the social milieu in which he was brought up in Kathiawar. After a brief stay in Richmond, most of his life in London was spent between lodgings in West Kensington and Bayswater and the Inns of Court in Holborn. For the first few months of his stay he was caught up in the absorbing task of trying to become an 'English gentleman', dressing like a fashionable man-about-town, struggling to discipline his unruly hair each morning in front of a mirror, and signing up for lessons to learn dancing, French, elocution, and even the violin, until he found all these preoccupations expensive and unfulfilling. He could not forget that his family was paying from its scant resources to keep him in London. He had, by contrast, little to do with the poorer parts of the capital, and not until his visit to London (and more especially Lancashire) in 1931 did he see much of the darker side of urban life and social deprivation in Britain. Nor did he see, or at least comment on, the industrial might that had transformed the British economy and ultimately underpinned imperial power in India. Despite the social ferment affecting London in the 1880s, at a time of economic depression and political unrest, Gandhi did not make contact with the emerging left, with the Fabians and leaders of the new trade union movement, though, like most other Indians in London, he did attend the funeral of Charles Bradlaugh, the radical MP, atheist and supporter of Indian rights, in January 1890, and was taken by an Indian friend to meet Cardinal Manning, shortly after he had helped negotiate a peaceful end to a month-long strike by London dock-workers. What Gandhi did see, and was most influenced by, was the other side of empire – the vegetarians and the Theosophists.

Gandhi's interest in the vegetarians began with his personal and increasingly desperate search for a suitable diet in London. Coming from a strictly vegetarian caste in India (despite his high-school flirtation with meat-eating), and having promised his mother to abstain from meat, Gandhi at first experienced great difficulty in finding the right food to eat and enough to sustain him. Finding a vegetarian restaurant just off Farringdon Street, one of the half-dozen or so in London at the time, he picked up and started to read Henry Salt's *A Plea for Vegetarianism*. With its cogent rationale for vegetarianism and its plea for kindness to animals, Salt's book had an immediate impact on Gandhi. Not only did it help him to solve the pressing question of what to eat, but vegetarianism, then a new 'cult' in England, brought him some of his closest friendships with Britons and acquaintance with 'some of London's most eccentric idealists'.[32] Through the Vegetarian Society, of whose executive committee he became a member in September 1890, he began to acquire some familiarity with organisational activity and, despite his acute shyness, initial experience of public speaking. He began to write articles, mostly on Indian vegetarianism, for the Society's weekly paper, *The Vegetarian*, and continued to do so subsequently in South Africa. Vegetarianism gave him entry to a group of middle-class non-conformists and dissidents, whose unconventional and sometimes radical views extended to a range of other controversial social and economic issues, such as vivisection and birth-control. Salt was a friend of another vegetarian, Edward Carpenter, whose book *Civilisation: Its Cause and Cure*, published in 1889, was to be an important influence on Gandhi in writing *Hind Swaraj*, his own account of the sickness and failure of modern civilisation, in 1909, and was duly listed as one of its principal 'authorities'. Others among Gandhi's Vegetarian Society acquaintances were its wealthy patron, the industrialist Arnold Hills, and Dr Thomas Allinson, a dietician and advocate of artificial means of birth-control. Gandhi, whose own views on birth-control were forty years later to land him in controversy, listened to the debate with interest.

But for Gandhi there was more to vegetarianism and the Vegetarian Society than new friends and unfamiliar causes. He was introduced to the ideal of a simple, moral life. He began to acquire a training in polemics and a new language of moral outrage and political dissent, which owed much to non-conformist campaigners and which he was to retain for the rest of his life. It was thus no accident that when he searched for a term sufficiently striking to capture the horror he saw as the Partition of India in the 1940s he described it in terms of 'vivisection', thereby echoing one of the most heated debates in late nineteenth-century Britain. There were also other issues that the vegetarianism cause helped bring to the fore. The question of diet was a vital one, not just to Gandhi's vegetarian friends in London but also in the polemics of nineteenth-century India, for the British identified meat-eating as an underlying reason for their physical and moral power and by contrast attributed the weakness of reputedly non-martial 'races', like the Bengalis and the Gujaratis, to deficient, vegetarian diets. As Gandhi put it in February 1891 in writing for the London vegetarians, 'It must at the outset be admitted that the Hindus as a rule are notoriously weak',[33] and years later in his autobiography he quoted a piece of doggerel current in Gujarat in his youth:

> Behold the mighty Englishman
> He rules the Indian small,
> Because being a meat-eater,
> He is five cubits tall.[34]

To find in London a group of middle-class Britons, members of this same ruling race, who regarded vegetarianism with un-imperial enthusiasm and championed it with such evangelical zeal, greatly impressed Gandhi. He now saw living without meat as a matter of choice, an ideal to be cherished, and not a burdensome part of his cultural inheritance or a matter of blind obedience to his pious mother. He began his own first 'experiments in dietetics' and the spread of vegetarianism now became his 'mission'. He felt, he declared, like 'a convert to a new religion'.[35] In a way he was.

The other major contacts Gandhi established, particularly towards the end of his second year in London, were with the Theosophists. The Theosophical Society had been established in New York in 1875 by Madame Blavatsky, one of the first Westerners to build a cult around Eastern religions, in this case a rather esoteric mixture of Buddhism and Hinduism, combined with a strong whiff of the occult. By the late 1880s Theosophy had begun to establish a small (essentially middle-class) following in London and was starting to shift its focus away from Buddhism to Hinduism. Despite joining the Society's Blavatsky Lodge in March 1891, Gandhi remained on the outskirts of the movement, but, for little better reason than that he was an Indian, he was invited by two 'brothers' (possibly an uncle and nephew) who were Theosophists to help translate the *Bhagavad Gita* from the original Sanskrit and to read it alongside Edwin Arnold's translation, *The Song Celestial*. Arnold's *The Light of Asia* further introduced Gandhi to the life and teachings of Buddha and exposed him to the work of a leading cross-cultural synthesiser, for Arnold – vegetarian, Theosophist, and former Principal of Deccan College in Poona – was endeavouring to combine in his work elements of East and West, of Buddhism, Christianity and Victorian science. Gandhi may thus have gleaned from his Theosophical contacts (rather than from Kathiawar) the idea that religions need not be rigidly compart- mentalised but could speak to each other and share a common truth. But at the time the principal impact of the Theosophists seems to have been in awakening his interest in Hinduism and inducing him 'to study his heritage'.[36] Reading Madame Blavatsky's *Key to Theosophy* (published in 1889, two years before her death) stimulated him 'to read books on Hinduism', and disabused him of the notion 'fostered by the missionaries that Hinduism was rife with superstition'.[37]

Although Gandhi was somewhat exceptional in becoming ac- quainted with Theosophy in London rather than in India, he was certainly not alone in registering its impact on his ideas of the Hindu religion and Indian identity. Jawaharlal Nehru was, in his teens, one of many middle-class Indians who came under the influence of the movement and whose ideas of India's place in world history and civilisation was touched by Theosophy's 'affirmative Orientalism'.[38] However, all was not harmony between Gandhi and the Theosophists. Among those whom Gandhi briefly met in London was the dynamic and redoubtable Annie Besant. Previously a pioneer trade-union leader, an atheist and an advocate of birth-control, Besant, twenty-two years older than Gandhi, converted to Theosophy in May 1889 and rapidly became one of the leading lights of the Theosophical Society in London. At the time Gandhi's relations with Besant were seemingly cordial and, hearing her speak about her new faith, he was captivated by her 'utter sincerity'. But later he came to see Besant as something of a charlatan, representative of the occult side of Theosophy he could never come to terms with. Moreover, she was a white woman (and Gandhi was seldom at ease with powerful white women), appropriating Hinduism for her own ends, turning it into a theatrical and faintly scandalous parody of his own deeply-held, if also decidedly syncretic, beliefs. In 1893 Besant left London for India, eventually moving the headquarters of the Theosophical Society to Adyar, on the southern fringes of Madras city. During the First World War, using the Theosophical Society's many Indian branches as her organisational base, Besant emerged in a new incarnation, as one of the leaders of the Indian nationalist movement. In 1917 she became the first woman (though not the first European) President of the Indian National Congress. Gandhi and Besant thereafter became rivals for political leadership. They fell out over a provocative speech Gandhi made at the opening of the Benares Hindu University in 1916, a meeting over which the increasingly agitated Besant presided. Although her influence waned after 1918, their testy relationship survived until Besant's death in 1933. Any temptation Gandhi might once have had to identify himself more closely with Theosophy had long since evaporated.

His law training complete, Gandhi boarded ship at Tilbury Docks in June 1891 to return to India. He did so with 'regret' for he had become 'attached' to London.[39] But, once back in India, the expectations he and his family had had that he would move easily and prestigiously into the ranks of the professional middle class were soon exploded. Returning to Rajkot, he began rather forlornly to write a 'Guide to London' for other Indian students who might have the good fortune to go there. He disliked the atmosphere of intrigue he found in Rajkot, but found it difficult, given his shyness and lack of confidence, to establish a law practice either there or in Bombay.

Even worse for his personal pride and self-esteem, Gandhi went to see the British political agent, Charles Ollivant, to ask a favour on behalf of his brother, who was caught up in a dispute in the court at Rajkot over some missing state jewels. He knew the political agent slightly, having met him while he was on leave in Britain, but this was India. When Gandhi reminded him of their acquaintance, he was quickly made to realise that Kathiawar was not England and (in an episode that anticipated his humiliating ejection from the train at Pietermaritzburg in South Africa a few months later) he was thrown out of his office. When he protested at this treatment, he was further snubbed by the political agent. When he sought the advice of one of Bombay's leading lawyers, Sir Pherozeshah Mehta, he was told to 'pocket' the insult: it was common enough in India. But Gandhi was deeply upset. 'This shock', he later claimed, 'changed the course of my life.'[40] To a degree to which neither his upbringing as a *diwan*'s son nor his sojourn as an Indian student in London, befriended by white vegetarians and Theosophists, had prepared him, Gandhi found himself a mere colonial subject, without authority, respect, or even recourse against injustice, subject to the whims of another race and another power.

Frustrated, snubbed, caught between the contrasting worlds of Kathiawar and London, Gandhi might then perhaps have vanished into the obscurity of life as a small-town lawyer. But he was rescued from that fate by being invited to go to South Africa to represent the Porbandar-based firm of Dada Abdulla and Co. in a legal dispute. In April 1893, aged 23, he left Bombay once more, bound this time not for London but for Durban in Natal. This was to prove one of the most decisive moments in Gandhi's life, for South Africa, almost from the outset, propelled him into a very different imperial situation from the one he had known either growing up in Kathiawar or during his student days in London.

. . .

NOTES AND REFERENCES

1. Robert A. Jeffrey, *The Indian Mission of the Irish Presbyterian Church: A History of Fifty Years of Work in Kathiawar and Gujarat*, London, 1890.
2. Howard Spodek, 'On the Origins of Gandhi's Political Methodology: The Heritage of Kathiawad and Gujarat', *Journal of Asian Studies*, 23 (1971), p. 362.

3. Romain Rolland, *Mahatma Gandhi*, London, 1924, p. 3.
4. But see Chandran D. S. Devanesan, *The Making of the Mahatma*, Madras, 1969.
5. Ranajit Guha, *Dominance Without Hegemony: History and Power in Colonial India*, Cambridge, Mass., 1997, p. 37.
6. Robert Payne, *The Life and Death of Mahatma Gandhi*, London, 1969, p. 17. 'Juwar roti' is a flat bread made from millet flour; eight annas were half a rupee.
7. Spodek, 'Gandhi's Political Methodology', pp. 363–4; David Hardiman, *Feeding the Baniya: Peasants and Usurers in Western India*, Delhi, 1996, pp. 183–4.
8. *CWMG* VI, p. 432.
9. Louis Fischer, *The Life of Mahatma Gandhi*, New York, 1962, p. 196.
10. Mahadev H. Desai, *Day-to-Day with Gandhi*, III, Benares, 1968, pp. 23–4.
11. Hardiman, *Feeding the Baniya*, p. 88.
12. George Woodcock, *Gandhi*, London, 1972, p. 69.
13. Mirabehn, *The Spirit's Pilgrimage*, London, 1960, p. 106.
14. M. N. Srinivas, *Social Change in Modern India*, Bombay, 1972; cf. David Hardiman, *The Coming of the Devi: Adivasi Assertion in Western India*, Delhi, 1987, pp. 157–63.
15. *The Diary of Mahadev Desai*, I, Ahmedabad, 1953, p. 52.
16. M. K. Gandhi, *An Autobiography, Or the Story of My Experiments with Truth*, Ahmedabad, 1940, p. 1; Susanne Hoeber Rudolph and Lloyd I. Rudolph, *Gandhi: The Traditional Roots of Charisma*, Chicago, 1983, p. 49.
17. Erik H. Erikson, *Gandhi's Truth: On the Origins of Militant Nonviolence*, London, 1970, pp. 113–33.
18. Fischer, *Gandhi*, p. 414.
19. Bhikhu Parekh, *Gandhi's Political Philosophy: A Critical Examination*, Basingstoke, 1989, p. 9; Gandhi, *Autobiography*, p. 49.
20. Jawaharlal Nehru, *An Autobiography*, London, 1936, p. 513.
21. Gandhi, *Autobiography*, pp. 20–2.
22. Martin Green, *Gandhi: Voice of a New Age Revolution*, New York, 1993.
23. Payne, *Gandhi*, p. 20.
24. Stephen N. Hay, 'Jain Influences on Gandhi's Early Thought', in Sibnarayan Ray (ed.), *Gandhi, India and the World*, Philadelphia, 1970, pp. 29–38.
25. J. T. F. Jordens, *Gandhi's Religion: A Homespun Shawl*, Basingstoke, 1998, ch. 2; Gandhi, *Autobiography*, pp. 64, 102.
26. Gandhi, *Autobiography*, pp. 177, 293–4.
27. Ibid., p. 4.
28. Woodcock, *Gandhi*, p. 15.
29. James D. Hunt, *Gandhi in London*, New Delhi, 1993, pp. xvii, 1–2.

30. Ibid., p. 1.
31. *CWMG* I, p. 42.
32. Stephen Hay, 'The Making of a Late-Victorian Hindu: M. K. Gandhi in London, 1888–1891', *Victorian Studies*, 33 (1989), p. 81.
33. Hunt, *Gandhi in London*, p. 26.
34. Gandhi, *Autobiography*, p. 14.
35. Hay, 'Late–Victorian Hindu', p. 81; Gandhi, *Autobiography*, pp. 35, 43.
36. Hunt, *Gandhi in London*, p. 29.
37. Gandhi, *Autobiography*, p. 51.
38. Nehru, *Autobiography*, p. 15. For 'affirmative Orientalism', see Richard G. Fox, *Gandhian Utopia: Experiments with Culture*, Boston, 1989, ch. 6.
39. Hunt, *Gandhi in London*, p. 36.
40. Gandhi, *Autobiography*, pp. 71–3.

Chapter 3

SOUTH AFRICA AND SELF-RULE

Whatever the legacies of his childhood and his London years, there is no doubting that the twenty-one years Gandhi spent in South Africa, from 1893 to 1914, were a decisive phase in his career. It was during this time that Gandhi was able to meld together aspects of his Indian background and tradition with his maturing understanding of the West. It was there that he began his first experiments with political activism and non-violent protest, there that he sought physically as well as mentally to decolonise himself. Although the term was not bestowed on him until after his return to India, these were in effect the years in which Gandhi became a 'Mahatma' and emerged as a figure of both Indian and imperial stature. This part of Gandhi's life has been extensively written about, though too often with the assumption that his emergence was inevitable or relatively unproblematic. Few authors have written critically about why Gandhi followed the path he did and his position in a complicated three-cornered imperial situation – white-dominated South Africa, imperial Britain and India. And yet if we are adequately to explain his subsequent 'rise to power', we need to understand the sources of power and authority that Gandhi was acquiring, or developing, during these years.

. . .

INDIANS IN SOUTH AFRICA

Gandhi arrived in South Africa in May 1893 to find a substantial Indian community already there. Although since the seventeenth century Cape Town had been a port of call for ships sailing between

Europe and India, it was not until 1860 that Indians began to arrive in South Africa in significant numbers. This was largely the result of the extension to southern Africa of a system of Indian indentured labour that had been in operation since the abolition of slavery in the British Empire in 1834. Indians were sent to Mauritius in the Indian Ocean in 1839 and later, with the spread of sugar plantations, to places as far afield as Fiji and Guyana. Sugar production and the demand for labour it generated was the principal reason, too, for the introduction of Indian labourers into the British colony of Natal in southeastern Africa. By 1891, after thirty years of immigration, Natal was home to the great majority of South African Indians. With a population of roughly 41,000, Indians were slightly fewer in number than Europeans (47,000) but considerably fewer than Africans (456,000). The Indian presence continued to grow, until by 1904 they numbered just over 100,000 in Natal. Indians also found their way, as merchants and traders rather than labourers, into what was, until the Anglo-Boer War of 1899–1902, the independent Boer Republic of Transvaal. In 1904 Indians in Transvaal totalled 11,000 compared to 229,000 Europeans and 945,000 Africans. Thus, by the time the Union of South Africa was created in 1910 from the former Boer republics as well as the British colonial territories, Indians, barely 2 per cent of the total population, formed a significant but still relatively small minority.

The indentured labourers in Natal were introduced as 'coolies' on short-term contracts. These were initially for three years, with the option of remaining two further years, after which they were free to live and work as they wished. Many elected to remain in Natal as labourers; some became small-holders, servants and hawkers. By the early twentieth century, Indians were also employed in coal mining in Natal. Among the plantation labourers, the majority were Hindus (some were Christians), and about 60 per cent were from Shudra or untouchable castes. Few of this class came from Gujarat, an insignificant source of indentured labour, but mainly from southeast India, from the Tamil- and Telugu-speaking districts of the Madras Presidency. There were also Parsis from western India who worked as clerks in commercial enterprises, and around the turn of the century some Chinese labourers were also introduced to work on the South African goldfields.[1] It should be borne in mind that the years of Gandhi's involvement in the struggle for Indian rights were a time of rapid economic and political change in South Africa following the momentous discovery of gold on the Rand in 1886, the rapid growth of Johannesburg, the hard-fought Anglo-Boer War, and the attempt through the creation of the Union of South Africa finally to reconcile Boer and Briton.

In addition to the indentured labourers, from the mid-1870s a number of so-called 'Arab' merchants also moved to South Africa and established themselves, especially in Durban, as storekeepers and traders. The name 'Arab' was highly misleading for they were in fact Muslim traders from Gujarat, coming especially from Gandhi's home town of Porbandar. This connection was one reason why one of the most prosperous of these trading firms, Dada Abdulla and Co., looked to Gandhi, a fellow Gujarati as well as a lawyer, to help them in a £40,000 dispute with another Gujarati trading firm based at Pretoria in Transvaal. The 'Arabs' rapidly incurred the wrath of white shopkeepers and traders who saw them as a threat to their own businesses, a factor, among others, that informed their racial opposition to the Indian newcomers. As Indian numbers increased, whites in the towns complained that they were being 'swamped' by these new immigrants. To most whites in South Africa, descended from Dutch, Huguenot and British ancestors, Indians were little better than black Africans. Indeed, in some respects they were deemed to be worse since they were clearly outsiders to the country, and in language, religion and lifestyle differed widely from both the white and African population. They were treated, regardless of their social status and occupation, as if they were all 'coolies' (labourers) or 'samis' (from the word *swami* or 'lord', often incorporated in Tamil personal names, but used by whites in a purely contemptuous fashion). It was partly in order to avoid this crude and abusive stereotyping of all Indians that the Gujarati traders called themselves 'Arabs' and the Parsis 'Persians'. Gandhi's political activism in South Africa needs to be understood against the background of this racist reductionism which treated all Indians alike, as no better than Africans and as an undifferentiated mass of 'coolies'.

Moreover, the urban Indians, while priding themselves on their own sense of civilisation, were accused by many whites of being 'insanitary' and 'dirty'. This racist slur assumed particular malice and potency at a time when cholera, smallpox and other deadly diseases stalked Johannesburg and other burgeoning towns and cities in South Africa. When bubonic plague, spread by rats and their infected fleas but at the time attributed to various factors including a general lack of sanitation and hygiene, reached South Africa from India, Indians were held to blame. On his return to Durban in

January 1897, having collected his wife and children from India, Gandhi found himself in the midst of a hostile demonstration with whites trying to prevent a so-called 'Asiatic invasion' and the landing of Indians from ships that were rumoured to be carrying plague as well as immigrant labourers. In 1898 the *Rhodesia Herald*, reflecting white views in South Africa, alleged that Indians were 'filthy dirty' and warned that their 'uncleanly habits' might 'at any time sow the seeds of deadly epidemics'.[2] Such opinions were echoed by Sir Godfrey Lagden, the Commissioner of Native Affairs in Transvaal, who held that 'the lower castes who form the mass [of the Indian immigrants] are as a rule filthy in habit and a menace to the public health'. He advised that they be excluded entirely from 'the life of civilised thoroughfares' and, if possible, obliged 'to reside for sanitary reasons in places set apart'.[3] It has been argued that the first moves towards urban racial segregation (apartheid) began not with the black African population, who subsequently became its principal victims, but in the 1890s, and even earlier, with measures to separate and sanitise the Indian quarters of Durban and other South African towns.[4] In the late nineteenth and early twentieth centuries, even more than today, disease, medicine and sanitation were powerful social and political metaphors. In imperial situations, like those of India and South Africa, disease, especially epidemic diseases like plague and cholera, were used to represent backwardness and primitivism, while medicine and sanitation were seen as signs of the civilisation Europeans saw themselves as bestowing upon the rest of the world.

For Gandhi, this white attack on Indians' sanitation and lifestyle, this damning identification of race with disease, was especially provoking because it struck at the heart of his growing pride in Indian civilisation. In September 1893, in an angry response to an editorial in the *Natal Advertiser*, which had attacked Indian traders as semi-barbarous and an undesirable element in the colony, the newly arrived Gandhi (sounding as much like an outraged Bania as a London-trained lawyer) launched into a spirited defence of the Indians, concluding:

> It seems . . . that their simplicity, their total abstinence from intox-
> icants, their peaceful and, above all, their business lives and frugal
> habits, which should serve as a recommendation, are really at the
> bottom of all this contempt and hatred of the poor Indian trader. . . .
> Is this Christian-like, is this fair-play, is this justice, is this civilisation?[5]

Health and disease, civilisation and semi-barbarism – these were not the only issues that divided whites and Indians. Gandhi went to South Africa in 1893 believing that the proclamation issued by Queen Victoria in November 1858, which brought the Indian Mutiny and Rebellion to a close and signalled the transfer of power in India from the East India Company to the crown, had provided Indians with a kind of bill of rights. It was the 'Magna Charta of the Indians', promising Indians equality before the law and the right to practise their own religions and follow their own customs without discrimination, and this not only in India itself, but as British subjects throughout the Empire. In South Africa, however, he rapidly discovered that Indians, despite being British subjects, were exposed to all kinds of abuse and discrimination with little prospect of redress, though he long continued to believe that white racism was not intrinsic to the British Empire but (much as he thought of untouchability in relation to the caste system) was 'an excrescence upon a system that was intrinsically and mainly good'.[6]

On his first appearance in court in Durban he wore a turban and was ordered to remove it by the judge. He refused to do so and left the chamber in protest. His first journey, a few days after his arrival, from Durban to Pretoria brought the problem of racism home to him in an even starker way. He was ejected from the train at Pietermaritzburg, despite holding a first-class ticket, because only whites were allowed to travel first class. When he later continued his journey from Charlestown on the Natal-Transvaal border to Johannesburg by stage-coach he was called 'sami' and ordered to sit on the outside, with the driver, and then on the footboard: only whites were allowed to travel in comfort inside. He received further insults and blows before abandoning the coach at Standerton, still well short of his destination. Eventually he reached Pretoria by train, defiantly holding on to the first-class ticket he had bought at Johannesburg. The Indian traders he met en route urged him, as had Pherozeshah Mehta a few months earlier, to 'pocket' such insults to his race and class, but Gandhi, furious at his treatment, resolved not to. Coming on top of the frustrations and uncertainties of the two years since he had left London, Pietermaritzburg was one of the experiences that changed Gandhi's life. During the long night hours on the lonely station, he debated with himself what course to follow. 'Should I fight for my rights or go back to India, or should I go on to Pretoria without minding the insult, and return to India after finishing the case?' Gandhi decided, like Arjuna in the *Bhagavad*

Gita, that it was his duty to fight, and not only for own his rights, but also (switching from military to medical metaphors) to try to eradicate 'the deep disease of colour prejudice'.[7]

Thus it was clear to Gandhi as much from personal experience as from the institutionalised racism of the courts and legislatures, that Indians had no real rights in South Africa, but lived there at the whim of the whites and subject to their prejudices. As he put it in 1922, during his trial for disaffection in India, 'I discovered [in South Africa] that as a man and an Indian I had no rights. More correctly, I discovered that I had no rights as a man, because I was an Indian.'[8] It was this situation that persuaded Gandhi to stay in South Africa and to fight for the rights of Indians.

. . .

A LAWYER IN NATAL

There are broadly two views of Gandhi's role in the struggle of South African Indians. The first draws on Gandhi's own writing on the subject in his autobiography and in *Satyagraha in South Africa* (both written in the mid-1920s, ten years after his departure from South Africa) and reflects the perception of his subsequent mahatmaship. This line of interpretation sees Gandhi as being, almost from the time of his arrival in South Africa, the central figure in organising and mobilising the Indians, leading a previously divided, inert and demoralised community in a heroic struggle with the white authorities (in a manner that parallels accounts of his later leadership of the peasantry in India). It is assumed that from this South African experience Gandhi learned to see all Indians as one, regardless of class and caste, religion and regional origins.

An alternative reading, given by Maureen Swan,[9] sees Gandhi's own account of his entry into Natal politics as 'highly romanticised'. Gandhi was very much a part of the Gujarati merchant elite during the early part of his South African years, but as their representative rather than leader, for, led by Muslims like Haji Ojer Ally and Sheth Haji Habib, they had already begun to agitate against discrimination as early as the mid-1880s. Gandhi, the smartly dressed and relatively affluent Anglophile lawyer, identified himself with the interests of the extremely small community of wealthy merchants, and, like them, showed little interest initially in the 'coolie' underclass. Most writers recognise that there was a significant shift in Gandhi's lifestyle and political outlook between about 1904 and 1910, as an intensified struggle for Indian rights began to unfold, as he undertook his first experiments in communal living and made his vow of celibacy. But when satyagraha began in 1908 Gandhi was still, in Swan's words, 'a politician of the elite groping inexpertly for the means to become the leader of a mass movement'.[10] Not, she suggests, until 1913, the year before his departure from the country, when Indian labourers and mine-workers joined the struggle (impelled more by their own sense of grievance than by Gandhi's leadership) did he begin to command a 'mass movement' of South African Indians. He, moreover, was not the only source of Indian leadership. In addition to the Muslim merchants, the 1890s and 1900s also saw the emergence of a 'new elite' of Natal-born Indians, including Tamil Christians like C. M. Pillay, who were able to provide an alternative leadership of their own, one more directly linked to the concerns of the poorer Indians. Swan thus concludes that Gandhi's leadership role in South Africa has been 'consistently overrated'.[11]

There are certainly grounds to be cautious about Gandhi's role. Despite Pietermaritzburg and despite the entrenched power of white racism in South Africa, Gandhi's transition from elite politics to mass mobilisation was slow and hesitant. His arrival in Natal in 1893 coincided with the granting of responsible government to the colony, thereby diminishing the British government's control over local legislation and allowing a swelling tide of discrimination to be embodied in law. Having earlier welcomed Indian labour, the whites in Natal were now intent on reversing the earlier immigration policy. In an attempt to get them to return to India, a tax of £3 a year (equivalent to six months' wages for a plantation worker) was levied on all 'coolies' who had completed their indenture. Despite protests from India and London, legislation was passed restricting further immigration, limiting the franchise to exclude Indians, and restricting the issue of licences to Indian traders. Gandhi reacted to these developments as best he could. In his early years in South Africa he was a committed believer in constitutional methods, in petitions and the power of the press. He maintained a vigorous correspondence with the newspapers, defending Indians' rights in the face of white sneers and criticism. In June 1894 he helped organise Natal's Indians to petition the legislature for the retention of the Indian franchise and thereafter sent numerous petitions to the Governor, the Legislative Council and the Secretary of State for the Colonies. He also enlisted the support of Dadabhai Naoroji, the 'Grand Old Man of

Indian Politics', whom he had heard speak in London, and used the occasion of his return to India in 1896 to mobilise support there. He published a pamphlet on *The Grievances of the British Indians in South Africa* that detailed the suffering and humiliations of Indians in Natal, where, he reported, they were treated as 'Asian dirt to be heartily cursed'. His political achievements in this period were small and he never succeeded in materially affecting the course of legislation in Natal during the 1890s, though Robert Huttenback has remarked that it would be 'hard to imagine what would have been the lot of Natal's Indians without Gandhi's presence'.[12]

And yet his tactics, even the English in which he wrote to the press and petitioned, underscore the narrowness of his political and social position. In June 1903 he launched *Indian Opinion* in Durban as a vehicle for his views and those of the Natal Indian Congress, but the paper commanded a very limited circulation. At first published in Tamil and Hindi as well as English and Gujarati, it failed to reach even such of the indentured labour class as were literate. In 1904 it had only 900 subscribers and in 1906 the Tamil and Hindi sections were dropped from the paper. The Natal Indian Congress, which Gandhi helped establish in August 1894 and was named after the Indian National Congress, had a high annual membership fee of £3 (equivalent to the entire annual tax on former indentured labourers) and was essentially a platform for the Gujarati elite. Gandhi's dogged opposition to the Natal Licensing Act of 1897 was indicative not only of his determination to contest racially discriminatory legislation, but also to protect, as far as possible, the position of the Gujarati traders. The franchise issue was also one that was far more relevant to the 'Arabs' than to the 'coolies' among Natal's Indian population. Cementing his own class position, Gandhi personally prospered. He had arrived in South Africa an almost penniless barrister on a one-year contract and with the promise of a £300 fee. Having decided to stay, and as one of the few qualified Indian lawyers in South Africa, he was soon earning £5,000 a year and was running a substantial and expensive household in Durban. In February 1903 he opened a new law office in Johannesburg, which employed two clerks and a secretary, and where he remained for the next three years.

In spite of everything, too, his loyalty to the Empire appeared unwavering. As Queen Victoria's Silver Jubilee approached, he sent a memorial expressing the 'loyalty and devotion' of her Indian subjects in Natal, adding, in praise of her 'glorious and beneficent reign', 'we are proud to think that we are your subjects, the more so as we know that the peace we enjoy in India, and the confidence of security of life and prosperity which enables us to venture abroad, are due to that position'.[13] It was never likely that Gandhi, still a 'collaborative nationalist',[14] would urge Indians to side with the Boer rebels against the British in 1899, but he did seek tactically to exploit the situation. He offered to form an ambulance corps 'as an earnest of Indian loyalty', to show that South African Indians shared Britain's 'patriotic zeal' and were worthy subjects of the Queen.[15] Although Gandhi's offer was at first rejected by the authorities in Natal, his thousand-strong corps of stretcher-bearers later served on several fields of battle, before being disbanded in 1900. Gandhi was eventually awarded the Kaiser-i-Hind medal in 1915 by the Government of India for his work in South Africa.

Class was not the only constraint on Gandhi's outlook in South Africa. Although Gandhi moved after 1906 towards closer identification with the Indian underclass in Natal, and briefly collaborated with the leaders of the Chinese community in opposing racist legislation, he showed remarkably little interest in the rights and welfare of the black African population – indeed, his struggle can be seen as part of a collective determination that Indians should not be reduced to the disenfranchised level of Africans but enjoy the same rights as white citizens of the Empire. Gandhi and other members of the Indian community consistently tried to get themselves excluded from classification with Africans over such matters as housing, trading rights, transport and prison conditions. In this respect Gandhi has been bluntly termed a racist. Certainly, he 'accepted and promoted aspects of the segregation doctrine, in so far as he called for a social status for Indians that was different from that of the Whites and Blacks'.[16] Gandhi organised a second Volunteer Ambulance Corps during the Zulu Rebellion in Natal in 1906, as he had in 1900, and showed some compassion for the rebels' hopeless struggle, which pitted the assagai against the machine gun, and disgust at the vicious conduct of the whites. But the creation of the corps can be seen mainly as a gesture directed at the authorities in South Africa (and London), reminding them of Indians' self-sacrificing loyalty to crown and Empire. There is no indication that Gandhi ever thought, as far as Africans were concerned, in terms of a cross-racial alliance against white racism. Swan dubs Gandhi a 'racial purist' and cites him in 1903 as remarking that, 'If there is one thing which the Indian cherishes more than any other, it is the purity of the type.'[17] But Gandhi, while clearly not immune to European racial theories, was not greatly interested in race in a narrowly biological and determinist way. Instead, he saw Africans as 'innocent children of nature' and, though 'not the barbarians we imagine them to be', devoid of civilisation.[18] Indeed, for Gandhi the putative absence of civilisation among the blacks provided a convenient measure by which Indians could advance their superior claim to equality with whites.

. . .

'TRUTH-FORCE'

In a few critical years between 1904 and 1910 Gandhi was transformed by a series of interrelated personal and political developments. One was his growing disillusionment with the politics of constitutional protest. In his efforts to combat racial discrimination in Natal and elsewhere in South Africa, he continued to draw up petitions, protest to newspapers, seek to rally support in India and, as during the Zulu Rebellion, to demonstrate the loyalty of his countrymen to the crown. But these efforts were producing very few results. Gandhi visited London in October 1906 with the Muslim merchant H. O. Ally to lobby Parliament and the Colonial Secretary over a new round of discriminatory legislation in South Africa, spearheaded by the Registration Act in Transvaal (which now, following the Boer War, had passed under British control). The election of a new Liberal Government in December 1905 gave Gandhi and his allies fresh hope, but British unresponsiveness left him frustrated and embittered. Although he visited London on a similar mission in July 1909, partly to appease Indian moderates who thought he was relying too heavily on a strategy of civil disobedience, he did so without much enthusiasm or conviction, and his growing disenchantment with constitutional methods was painfully evident when he wrote *Hind Swaraj* on the ship back to South Africa.[19]

Gandhi seemed at the same time to be reaching a crisis in his personal life. Despite his success as a lawyer, he was growing dissatisfied with his profession (which he abandoned in 1911) and with his relatively comfortable and affluent lifestyle. As so often with Gandhi, his inner anxieties and dilemmas were reflected in his sexual preoccupations. Following the birth of his fourth son, Devadas, in May 1900, he began to think more and more about celibacy, or more exactly about *brahmacharya*, which included not only sexual abstinence but the moderation or elimination of other indulgences and desires.

The experience of the Zulu Rebellion, being away from home and its comforts, witnessing the discipline of soldiers, and living life in the open, further persuaded Gandhi of the need to change, and in July 1906, on his return to Durban (and without apparently consulting Kasturbai) he took his vow of *brahmacharya*. Whatever the personal reasons involved, it signalled a major shift in Gandhi's lifestyle and cleared the way for his increasing commitment to public life and the struggle for Indian rights.

Gandhi was also influenced by the nature of the reading and correspondence he undertook in these years. He had read Leo Tolstoy's *The Kingdom of God is Within You* in London in 1893, but he was now more receptive to its message of Christian pacifism, seeing in it 'the infinite possibilities of universal love'. In October 1909 he began to correspond with the great Russian novelist and thinker, who responded warmly to his non-violence. They shared an opposition to industrialism and militarism, but Tolstoy was less swayed by Gandhi's patriotism which he believed 'spoils everything'. John Ruskin's *Unto This Last* (recommended to him by his young journalist and lawyer friend Henry Polak) in 1904 also made a great impression on Gandhi: 'it captured me and made me transform my life', he later declared. As with the *Gita*, Gandhi brought to Ruskin his own idiosyncratic interpretation.[20] He understood the essential message of *Unto This Last* to be that 'the good of the individual is contained in the good of all', that a lawyer's work has the same value as a barber's, and that the life of labour, i.e. the life of the tiller of the soil and the craftsman, was 'the life worth living'.[21] So impressed was Gandhi by Ruskin that he translated *Unto This Last* into Gujarati in 1908 as *Sarvodaya*, meaning 'the welfare of all'. A further addition to the wide and eclectic range of influences to which Gandhi subjected himself during these years was the essay on 'Civil Disobedience' by the American Henry David Thoreau, which confirmed him in his view that an honest man is duty-bound to resist unjust laws, though Gandhi apparently only read Thoreau after his own ideas on the subject had crystallised. It is curious that at a time of such momentous political change around the world – the Japanese defeat of Russian military and naval forces in East Asia, the abortive Russian Revolution of 1905, the Partition of Bengal and the onset of a new and more militant phase of Indian nationalism – Gandhi should have sought his private revolution in works published several decades earlier (*Unto This Last* first appeared in 1862 and Thoreau's 'Civil Disobedience' in 1849) or even in the ailing Tolstoy (who died in November 1910, shortly after Gandhi published his 'Letter to a Hindu'), though it is true that many of these thinkers and their ideas had a fresh resonance in the uncertain world of the 1890s and 1900s. Gandhi's continuing study of the *Bhagavad Gita* and the Sermon on the Mount, with its message that 'the meek shall inherit the earth', further led him to the conclusion that the life to be aspired to was one of selfless action in the service of one's fellow men, and the best method of righting wrongs was to protest non-violently and to suffer lovingly rather than submit to injustice.[22]

In December 1904, shortly after reading *Unto This Last*, Gandhi embarked on his own experiment in communal living and physical labour. This was the Phoenix Settlement, fourteen miles from Durban and two miles from the railway station after which it was named. The idea of such a settlement may have originated with a visit Gandhi made in April 1895 to a Trappist monastery at Pinetown near Durban, but this was clearly not the only influence. Phoenix has been represented as Gandhi's first ashram, or spiritual community, but he rejected the term at the time as being too Hindu: he wanted it to be an inclusive community and a working one. He gathered around him an eclectic mixture of family, relatives and friends, including several Europeans. The inhabitants built their own living quarters, began to farm (on a modest scale), and here, using an old press, *Indian Opinion* was printed. But, distracted by other causes, the Phoenix Settlement did not become the model centre for agriculture, education and healthy, self-sufficient living Gandhi had originally hoped for. Nor, despite the proximity of a Zulu village, was there much contact with the African population.

In 1906 Gandhi was plunged into a new political struggle, this time not in Natal but in Transvaal, which regained self-government following defeat in the Anglo-Boer War. In August of that year the Boer-dominated government, led by General Louis Botha as Prime Minister and with General Jan Christiaan Smuts as Colonial Secretary and minister in charge of Asian affairs, published a draft Asiatic Law Amendment Ordinance, the underlying objective of which was to restrict Indian immigration and even to expel Indians entirely. The draft ordinance required all Indians in Transvaal, of both sexes and above 8 years of age, to report to the Registrar of Asiatics, provide all their personal details, have a full set of their fingerprints taken, and then carry an identification pass at all times. Failure to register or to produce the documents on demand would result in a fine of £100, three months' imprisonment, or deportation. Fingerprinting was particularly offensive, for it put all Indians on a par with criminals. At a crowded meeting, held at the Empire Theatre in Johannesburg on 11 September 1906, and principally organised by H. O. Ally and his Muslim associates, Gandhi explained the significance of the ordinance and moved a resolution calling for Indians to refuse to obey it, regardless of the severe penalties involved. As other speakers gave their warm support to the resolution, Gandhi spontaneously proposed going a step further, urging Indians to make a solemn pledge to oppose the ordinance, even if it led to fines, imprisonment, the loss of their property or deportation. 'We shall go on till we succeed,' Gandhi declared: 'wisdom lies in pledging ourselves on the understanding that we shall have to suffer things like all that and worse. Provided the entire community manfully stands the test, the end will be near.'[23]

Although the meeting was almost immediately followed by Gandhi's petitioning visit to London in October, the Empire Theatre resolution helped stiffen Gandhi's resolve and launch the 'passive resistance' campaign of 1907–9. This at first enjoyed significant support from the Indian community in Transvaal, and a number of Indians were prepared to face imprisonment for their defiance of the 'Black Act' when it came into force in July 1907. By the end of January 1908, 155 of them were in jail for their refusal to register. Gandhi himself eventually underwent three terms of imprisonment between January 1908 and May 1909, totalling six months in all. But Gandhi continued to entertain other options. At the end of January 1908 Gandhi met Smuts and in the course of their discussion he understood the act would be repealed if a majority of Indians registered voluntarily. In the face of opposition from other Indians, who wanted the act to be repealed in its entirety, Gandhi took the lead in registering. His action was seen as a betrayal and, far from unifying the Indian community in Transvaal, intensified many of its divisions. He was struck by a Pathan, Mir Alam Khan, on 10 February and in an incident that foreshadowed his assassination nearly forty years later, fell badly wounded to the ground, with the name of the god Ram on his lips. He suffered a further humiliation when he discovered that, despite the voluntary registrations, the act remained in force. Gandhi felt he had been cheated by Smuts, and the civil disobedience struggle continued for several months more until it finally petered out in mid-1909. Following a partial agreement with Smuts, now the minister in the Union government responsible for immigration, in April 1911 civil disobedience was formally suspended.

In the course of this struggle Gandhi moved with increasing conviction away from the politics of petitioning to ideas of non-violent confrontation. Dissatisfied with the term 'passive resistance', which appeared to him far too narrow and negative, in January 1908 he adopted the term satyagraha (taken from two Sanskrit words, *satya*, truth, and *agraha*, struggle, and hence meaning 'truth-force' or the 'struggle for truth'), which Gandhi further glossed as 'soul-force' or 'the force which is born of truth and love or non-violence'. Significantly, Gandhi thought it important that the movement, if it were to command the support of Indians in South Africa, should bear an Indian, not a foreign, name. In evoking the principle of ahimsa, or non-violence, Gandhi was looking to Indian, especially Jain, traditions, but he was undoubtedly also influenced by ideas drawn from Tolstoy and the Sermon on the Mount.

The basic principles were these. Satyagraha was to be preceded by a careful study of the situation, the patient gathering of facts, followed by a clear and public statement of objectives, allowing time for the opposing party to negotiate and reach a mutually agreed settlement. Only when this failed was an agitation to be launched, the purpose of which was to convince the opponent of the intensity of the satyagrahi's convictions and the rightness of the cause he (or she, though Gandhi rarely thought in terms of female protagonists) had espoused. Throughout the satyagraha, channels of communication with the opponent were to be kept open, so that attitudes were not allowed to harden: intermediaries between the two sides were to be welcomed. Satyagrahis pledged themselves not to use violence, whatever the provocation, nor to resist arrest or the confiscation of their property. They were to act with calmness and dignity and to enter the campaign in a state of calm introspection. As a prisoner, the satyagrahi was likewise expected to be courteous, to obey prison regulations and not ask for special privileges. Gandhi explained the effectiveness of satyagraha in terms of its spiritual and moral impact. The satyagrahi's love, dignity, self-suffering, and endurance were intended to weaken the opponent's anger and appeal to his higher nature. The satyagrahi's uncomplaining suffering denied the opponent the pleasure of victory and mobilised neutral public opinion in his support.[24]

Love and suffering were to be the essence of satyagraha, but behind them lay Gandhi's concept of non-violent power. 'Power is of two kinds', he remarked two decades after his first satyagraha campaign. 'One is obtained by the fear of punishment and the other by acts of love. Power based on love is a thousand times more effective.'[25] He believed that non-violence was not only morally superior to violence, but also stronger. It was, however, he later recognised open to misunderstanding and even abuse.

> The word *satyagraha* [he explained in 1933] is often most loosely used and is made to cover veiled violence. But as the author of the word I may be allowed to say that it excludes every form of violence, direct or indirect, and whether in thought, word or deed. It is a breach of satyagraha to wish ill to an opponent or to say a harsh word to him with the intention of doing harm. . . . Satyagraha is gentle, it never wounds. It must not be the result of anger or malice. It was conceived as a complete substitute for violence.[26]

It was not, however, until 1913 that Gandhi had a second and more complete opportunity to test the power of satyagraha. With the creation of the Union of South Africa in 1910, the Transvaal Registration Act lapsed, but new legislation in 1913 placed fresh restrictions on Indian immigration and movement within South Africa and the £3 annual tax on ex-indentured labourers in Natal remained a rankling grievance. Then, in March 1913, the South African Supreme Court ruled in a test case that Hindu, Muslim and Parsi marriages were invalid in the eyes of the law, in effect making Indian wives concubines without legal status and liable to deportation and rendering their children illegitimate. Despite the outcry, the government upheld the court's ruling. Gandhi asked Smuts to remove the £3 tax and overturn the ruling on marriages. Otherwise, he warned, in a significant shift towards a more populist idiom of politics, he would advise Indians not to pay the tax and indentured labourers to go on strike.

When no response was forthcoming from the government, in September 1913 satyagraha recommenced. A group of sixteen men and women from the Phoenix Settlement, including Gandhi's wife Kasturbai (increasingly called by the more matronly name 'Kasturba'), were illegally to cross the border from Transvaal into Natal and thereby court arrest. If they were ignored, they would continue to the Newcastle coalfield in Natal and call upon Indian miners there to go on strike. A second group, consisting of 'Natal sisters', were to cross the border in the opposite direction, heading for Johannesburg. Although Gandhi was using the workers and their grievances as a device to widen the struggle for Indian rights, he was surprised by the strength of their response to the strike call, which was supported by several Indian labour leaders.[27] Kasturba was arrested and sentenced to three months' imprisonment; several of the 'Natal sisters' were also imprisoned and the struggle intensified. Seizing the opportunity to put pressure on the government, in mid-October Gandhi called on the strikers and their families to leave their homes and follow him to Charlestown, significantly the place where he had embarked on his humiliating coach ride twenty years earlier. Joined by several hundred supporters, and having got only a dismissive response from Smuts to his renewed demands, on 6 November 1913 Gandhi led a ragged army of 2,000 men, women and children across the border from Natal to Volksrust in Transvaal. The declared aim was to march to Tolstoy Farm, Gandhi's new settlement near Johannesburg, to make it the headquarters of the resistance movement, or to face arrest and imprisonment in the attempt. As the column advanced on Standerton, Gandhi was twice arrested and then released on bail. When a smaller party of protestors advanced towards Greylingstad they too were arrested and sent back by train to Natal to be sentenced.

At the same time as arrests were occurring on the Natal-Transvaal border, conflict on the coalfields intensified and mounted military police, using brute force, were called in to force the miners, now state prisoners, back to work. Within days 50,000 labourers were out on strike and 7,000 other Indians were jailed. Repression on such a scale began to recoil against the Union government, which was under increasing pressure from Lord Hardinge, the Viceroy of India, as well as the British Cabinet to resolve the escalating dispute. To keep up the pressure Gandhi, following his release from jail on 18 December 1913, announced a second protest march, but cancelled it when white railway workers went on strike over grievances of their own. Satyagrahis, he declared, would not take advantage of their opponents' accidental difficulties. This politic abstention gave Gandhi a significant moral advantage and at last in mid-January 1914 Smuts agreed to negotiate with him. The Union government set up a commission to look into Indian grievances and all the main demands – for the abolition of the £3 tax, the recognition of Indian marriages, the easing of immigration and residence controls and the ending of the indentured labour system – were met in May 1914 through the Indians' Relief Bill. Shortly after, in 1916, the Government of India itself resolved to abolish the indentured labour system.

'Truth-force' had apparently triumphed and when Gandhi wrote his account of *Satyagraha in South Africa* in the mid-1920s he presented the Indians' Relief Act as a new Magna Carta and the successful outcome of the struggle that had been waged intensively since 1906.[28] But others have been more sceptical about the outcome. Gandhi had failed to thwart Smuts's primary objective of stopping Indian emigration to South Africa, nor did anti-Indian prejudice abate as a result of the 1914 Act.[29] On the contrary, the struggle for Indian rights in South Africa continued long after Gandhi's departure and white supremacy became even more powerfully entrenched at the expense of Indians and Africans alike.

THE MANTLE OF MAHATMA

Gandhi's evolution during these years of rapid personal and political transformation has been understood as the steady unfolding of his saintliness, or in terms of his gradual progression from elite lawyer to popular leader. But there is a further dimension of Gandhi's evolution to be considered. He arrived in South Africa still painfully shy, introverted and inarticulate in public. But South Africa, and the brutal insult to his race, class and civilisation it presented, especially after the nurturing friendships he had enjoyed in London, and which he continued to foster with white friends and associates in South Africa, required him to become a very different kind of individual. Political conditions called for a leader who could be publicly articulate, courageous and determined in the face of frequent humiliation and brutal adversity. Gandhi perhaps never lost his inner sense of vulnerability and insecurity and from time to time had to retreat from public life, and through his fasting and days of silence strengthen and replenish his inner self. But he learned in South Africa how to take on a more prominent public role by becoming, partly through the expectations of others and partly by drawing upon the idioms of saint and *sadhu* from his Indian background, to take on the mantle of mahatma and to use this outer persona as the means to perform in public life while protecting his vulnerable inner self from closer scrutiny and abuse.

Several significant developments in his South African years propelled him along this path, but arguably among the most important was the decision in 1906–7 to court imprisonment, for Gandhi's 'jail experiences' proved central to his rapid personal and political evolution. His first encounter with a South African jail in January 1908 (though anticipated for several months) threw him back on many of the conventional antipathies of his class, race and religion. To be treated in terms of food, dress and accommodation as no better than Africans (for whom Gandhi uncritically used the white racist term 'Kaffirs'), when one of the prime motives behind the campaign was precisely to distance Indians from Africans and gain equal rights with whites, was deeply galling. This, he reflected in March 1908, was an 'experience for which we were perhaps all unprepared', and yet, being 'classed with Natives' was bitter confirmation of the wider 'degradation' Indians were experiencing in South Africa. He added:

> We could understand not being classed with whites, but to be placed on the same level with the Natives seemed too much to put up with. I then felt that Indians had not launched on passive resistance too soon. Here was further proof that the obnoxious law [the Registration Act] was intended to emasculate the Indians.[30]

While opposing the segregation of Indians from whites, prison soon persuaded Gandhi that the 'separation' of Indians and Africans was 'a physical necessity': Indians had nothing in common with 'Kaffirs' and physically everything to fear from them. He was similarly at first outraged at being denied European or Indian food and being expected to eat 'mealie pap', which he despised as 'Kaffir' food and claimed was 'totally unsuited' to Indians who were 'either in the habit of taking European food or mostly so'.[31]

However, Gandhi, to his credit, rapidly began to regard prison as an educational experience, one that forced him to revise many of his preconceived ideas about his status and identity. Over the next five years, as Gandhi faced three more terms of imprisonment, he came to see jail as a privileged place: it was, as he defiantly called it, 'a palace'. Prison food now came to represent a duty to curb the cravings of the pampered middle classes, a means by which to identify with India's poor and needy, and, from a nutritional perspective, even 'mealie pap' could be regarded as 'a sweet and strength-giving food'.[32] While Gandhi remained vehemently opposed to mixing with 'Kaffirs', prison brought him face to face with divisions in the Indian community and encouraged him to see the shared experiences and intimacy of prison life as a way of countering its many 'false distinctions'. Stung by criticism of Indians as 'filthy' and the bearers of disease,

Gandhi, in a characteristic gesture of inversion, identified the colonial prison as a model regime of health and cleanliness. Prison labour, for all its unremitting hardship, caused Gandhi to reflect positively on Ruskin and the virtues of a 'life of labour'. Even cleaning out latrines, the ultimate symbol of degradation for a caste Hindu, was given moral worth and set Gandhi thinking that no work, even that normally assigned to untouchables, was truly 'humiliating or degrading'. For Gandhi, who had begun his experiments with self-control and celibacy a few years before going to jail, the constraints of prison and control of his 'animal desires' became closely linked. As he wrote in his autobiography: 'I saw that some of the regulations that the prisoners had to observe were such as should be voluntarily observed by a *brahmachari*, that is, one desiring to practise self-restraint'.[33] Prison impressed on Gandhi the need for the warrior fighting for non-violence to possess physical strength and a capacity for endurance as well as mental self-control. The satyagrahi, like the soldier, needed a 'well-disciplined body': 'a physical wreck' would not 'be able to bear jail life'.[34]

Gandhi's prison experiences informed his rapidly evolving ideas and techniques in other ways, too. Some writers have sought the inspiration for Gandhi's experiments in communal living in South Africa, like his later ashrams in India, in a creative reworking of Indian tradition or borrowing from Christian monasticism. Both certainly played a part, but Gandhi personally acknowledged the impact of jail life. The symbiosis between the prison and the ashram was most evident at Tolstoy Farm. Set up in 1910, with the help of a German architect friend, Herman Kallenbach, the settlement was twenty-one miles outside Johannesburg. It had a thousand acres of land and eventually housed about forty residents before it was broken up in 1913. It partly allowed Gandhi to continue his experiments in communal living, but more especially it was designed to provide training and support for satyagrahis and their families, to prepare them physically and mentally for the ordeal of the prison. Gandhi took from the prison a regime of strict discipline and hard labour, a time-ordered working day, common messing and the minimising of personal needs and privacy. Work on the farm, Gandhi recalled, was 'harder than that in jail', and the 'inmates', as he aptly described them, ate, dressed, even shaved their heads, like prisoners.

The change in Gandhi's appearance in these years, recorded in photographs taken of him at the time, is startling. From the smart, Western-dressed lawyer, reminiscent of the dandy of his first London days, Gandhi transformed himself during the years of struggle into the image of a hardened convict, lean, taunt, stripped of all super-fluous clothing or any obvious sign of caste or class identity. This was much more than a satyagrahi's compliance with prison regulations. It represented in outward form Gandhi's inner spiritual and moral reorientation. In October 1912 he gave up European dress entirely. On 21 December 1913, three days after his release from jail and at the height of the struggle over the £3 tax and Indian marriages, he appeared at a meeting in Durban barefoot, in 'coolie' dress and with his moustache shaven off – a sign, he said, of mourning for the strikers who had died during the satyagraha campaign.[35] By thus decolonising his body, Gandhi was symbolically ridding himself physically, as well as mentally, of dependence on the West.

Prison was only one factor in Gandhi's decisive shift away from the outlook and appearance of the successful middle-class lawyer. The years 1904–14 saw other dramatic changes too, for it was during these years of struggle and self-reflection that Gandhi acquired the powerful aura of a Hindu saint. One possible influence in this was the attention of his Christian friends, among them the Reverend Joseph J. Doke, a Baptist minister and Gandhi's biographer of 1906, who seemed to appeal to and strengthen Gandhi's faith in his own saintliness, even while he defied attempts to win him over to Christianity. But just as Gandhi sought an Indian name for his movement (satyagraha) and sought its roots in ahimsa, so was he drawn to the need for an indigenous identity that would associate him positively with India and its distinctive traditions.

The image of the saintly renouncer, or *sannyasi*, was one that was readily available for this purpose, not just from India's ancient past, but from the recent and compelling example of Swami Vivekanada, the Bengali who in his brief life (1863–1902) abandoned his middle-class identity to become a follower of the Hindu ascetic Ramakrishna. In 1893 Vivekananda made a spectacular impact on the World Parliament of Religions at Chicago and in the few remaining years of his life helped propagate a new and dynamic idea of Hinduism in the West and in India. He, too, cultivated the saintly image – with his *brahmacharya* and his *sannyasi* robes, but also in his insistence, that while matters of the body and everyday life were not without import-ance, the spirituality of the East enjoyed undoubted superiority over the material obsessions of the West. Vivekananda was a model of the saint who did not retire into obscure asceticism, but believed passionately in bringing the reforming power of the spiritual to the service of the community (and ultimately to the service of the nation), both through his own example and through the activities of the Ramakrishna Mission which he helped form in 1897.

Gandhi never met Vivekananda (the swami was already ill when he tried to see him in Calcutta in 1901), and apparently read only one of his books. But Vivekananda provided a model of how to contest the hegemony of the West, while yet acknowledging some of its many strengths, and how to restore Indians' pride in their own civilisation and spiritual superiority. His ideals seem to have helped inspire Gandhi in South Africa and to instil in him a growing sense of purpose for his eventual return to India.

.   .   .

'CIVILISATION' AND 'SLAVERY'

The extent of Gandhi's rapid evolution in the early years of the century can be judged from his tract *Hind Swaraj*, the title of which is conventionally but somewhat inadequately translated as 'Indian Home Rule'. Gandhi wrote this in 1909 (in Gujarati: the first English translation appeared in 1910) after the first phase of the satyagraha struggle in South Africa and following a visit to London. It is a clear demonstration that, after sixteen years in South Africa, Gandhi's thoughts were still fixed on India, and that his visits there in 1896 and 1901–2 had confirmed him in his resolution to return there rather than stay on indefinitely in South Africa. But *Hind Swaraj* can also be understood as a bridge, linking ideas and attitudes derived from his student days in London and subsequently derived from his reading of Western thinkers like Ruskin and Thoreau in South Africa, with his understanding of the freedom movement that was gathering increasing momentum in India and to which he wished to apply the lessons of his South African experiences. Thus, while at one level *Hind Swaraj* was a reaffirmation of the non-violent techniques Gandhi had been developing in his campaign for Indian rights in South Africa, it was also a way of arguing for their application to the greater struggle for freedom in India itself.

Hind Swaraj was the nearest Gandhi ever came to writing a political manifesto, but its importance, as a work in its own right and as a key to his political philosophy, remains in question. Some of his closest associates, notably Jawaharlal Nehru, could be ardent supporters of Gandhi without endorsing the 'completely unreal' views presented in his 1909 tract.[36] In similar vein, one recent historian has referred to it as 'unrealistic' and 'obscurantist',[37] but another has called it 'the most imaginative, intense and idiosyncratic' of Gandhi's writing,[38] and many scholars in recent years have returned to *Hind Swaraj* as anticipating many of his later ideas and as a vital source in trying to understand what was radical and original about his political thought.[39]

Hind Swaraj takes the form of a dialogue between the 'Reader' and the 'Editor' (who clearly represents Gandhi). This might be termed a Socratic dialogue, but perhaps Gandhi's more immediate inspiration was the *Bhagavad Gita*, with its debate between Krishna and Arjuna about *dharma* and the right course of action to be followed. It is also typically Gandhian, in as much as one side seeks to persuade the other, and in this verbal combat the Editor clearly emerges as the victor. But *Hind Swaraj* is also in effect a debate between Gandhi, with his strengthening belief in non-violent action, and a small band of Indian intellectuals, students and exiles whom Gandhi had encountered at India House in north London during his recent visits – again, one sees in this encounter the importance to Gandhi's evolution of the imperial metropolis.[40] The group was led by Shyamji Krishnavarma, a former Reader in Indian Languages at Oxford and editor of the *Indian Sociologist*, but included Vinayak Damodar Savarkar, then in his early twenties, whose life and ideology of militant Hindu nationalism were to intersect with Gandhi and his creed of non-violence several times in subsequent decades. The India House group fervently believed that India could only be freed from colonial rule through violence, including terrorism and assassination.

In response to the question, 'What is Swaraj [freedom]?', the Reader looks, as did many militant Indian nationalists of the time, to the example of Japan. India, too, must have its own army and navy: only then will 'India's voice ring through the world'. And it must copy the example of the British themselves, their philosophers and their parliamentary institutions. But the Editor, speaking for Gandhi, retorts that this means 'English rule without the Englishman . . . you would make India English. And when it becomes English, it will be called not Hindustan but Englishstan. This is not the *Swaraj* that I want.'[41] Significantly, Gandhi sees the power of the British as more than a matter of political or military strength. It is their cultural hegemony and the moral authority that needs to be addressed and ultimately undermined. He believes that Indians could only attain genuine freedom by ceasing to want to emulate the British and by overcoming their debilitating fear and weakness in the face of British rule. The central question of *Hind Swaraj* is thus how Indians can free themselves from a position of apparent powerlessness. Although Gandhi does not aspire to a strictly historical interpretation, history provides him with some clues. Contrary to British claims that it would take centuries for India to become a nation, he avers that India had been one nation long before the arrival of the British. It then lost its independence through Indians' own weaknesses and folly: 'The English have not taken India,' the Editor remarks, 'we have given it to them.' Equally the British did not hold India by force alone. 'The sword is entirely useless for holding India. We alone keep them.'[42] Thus, without Indian cooperation, British rule would inevitably collapse.

In seeking to identify and negate the power Britain has acquired over India, Gandhi invokes two contrasting ideas of 'civilisation' and 'slavery', both of which ironically owe a singular debt to Western philosophy and moralising rhetoric. He contrasts the material and divisive nature of 'modern civilisation' with the harmony and spiritual virtue of 'ancient civilisation'. Although these are presented as universal categories, Gandhi clearly means by the former the West, along with those Indians who have been seduced by it, and, essentially, by the latter, India. Gandhi's sweeping condemnation of modern civilisation allows him to identify the ways in which British rule has harmed India and reduced it to a state of abject dependency or what he (echoing both the great anti-slavery campaigns of the nineteenth century and the more recent metaphorical use of the term by Tolstoy and Carpenter) repeatedly calls 'slavery'. Significantly, Gandhi does not equate 'civilisation' with those things that the British most prided themselves on in their 'civilising mission' in India: indeed these, with characteristic inversion, are marked out as the principal objects of Gandhi's scorn. Thus Gandhi attacks doctors at the very time when Western medicine was hailed in imperial rhetoric as an irrefutable boon and an underlying justification for British rule in India. 'To study European medicine', Gandhi remarks dismissively, 'is to deepen our slavery.'[43] Doctors do not solve the problem of sickness, he argues, but merely encouraged people to indulge themselves further. They fall sick and are superficially cured, only to return to their indulgent ways. They grow ever more dependent and addicted to vice: they are not encouraged to take responsibility for their own physical and spiritual well-being. Echoing the title of Edward Carpenter's book,

Civilisation, Its Cause and Cure, Gandhi goes so far as to represent modern civilisation as itself a disease that Indians have to learn to cure or prevent through swaraj. The term thus comes to signify not just 'self-government' in the political sense but also for Gandhi taking control of one's moral and physical being, learning to rule one's self. Conversely, imperialism means not merely the loss of the nation, but also, more intimately, the loss of control over one's physical and spiritual identity or selfhood.

Gandhi then turns to his own profession, the law. Lawyers, too, he considers exploitative, for they prosper by encouraging litigation and dependence. By the time he wrote *Hind Swaraj* Gandhi had largely abandoned his own practice, but even earlier he had begun to urge participants in legal disputes to resolve their differences through mutually agreed, out-of-court, settlements rather than through costly legal proceedings. Gandhi was turning his back on the law as a liberal profession, one that might be a vehicle for human rights and personal justice, and as the career most closely identified with India's nationalist elite and the articulation of their demands. Moving beyond the professions, a further target for Gandhi's condemnation in *Hind Swaraj* is education, especially the English language with which he had himself struggled in his high-school days and which he sees as a further means by which the British deprive Indians of their identity and capacity for self-expression, replacing it with an alien cultural and political hegemony. In Gandhi's view 'It is we, the English-knowing Indians, that have enslaved India', and it would accordingly 'enslave' India's millions if they, too, were to be instructed in English and made to think in ways foreign to their own society and culture. He advocates instead the use of Indian languages as the best medium for instruction and Hindi as the 'universal' language for India.[44]

Finally, Gandhi directs his assault against modern technology and the machinery that forms so central a part of modern civilisation, including the railways and factories that already in Gandhi's lifetime were busily transforming India's urban landscape and rural economy. In keeping with the views advanced by Dadabhai Naoroji in his *Poverty and Un-British Rule* (1901) and R. C. Dutt's two-volume *Economic History of India* (1902–4), Gandhi identified himself with the 'drain theory', i.e. that India, once a land of prosperity and with its own flourishing craft industries, had been reduced to poverty and famine by the importation of British industrial goods, by the heavy burden of land taxes, and by the export of the food needed to feed its own suffering people. Gandhi, combining the West's own internal critique of industrialisation, as espoused by Ruskin and Carpenter, with the exploitation theory of Naoroji and Dutt, represents machinery as intrinsically evil, denying work and ultimately food to those who needed it most and deepening India's economic dependence upon Britain. 'It is machinery that has impoverished India,' he states categorically, and it is due to Manchester that India's handicrafts had 'all but disappeared'. But, more than that, 'It is necessary to realise that machinery is bad. We shall then be able gradually to do away with it.'[45] Implicit here, too, was an emerging preference for the village over the town and city, and for the dignity of human labour as opposed to the dehumanising material-ism of industrial production. Following the work of Sir Henry Maine, former Law Member of the Supreme Council in India and subsequently Professor of Comparative Jurisprudence at Oxford, whose *Village Communities in the East and West* (1871) clearly influ-enced Gandhi, Gandhi believed that before the advent of British rule and the inroads made by modern technology, India's villages were virtually self-sufficient, characterised by interdependence and cooperation rather than the bitter class divisions of modern industrial society.

Gandhi did not equate civilisation with material achievement, and indeed argues in *Hind Swaraj* that it was part of the wisdom of ancient India to have rejected machinery: 'It was not that we did not know how to invent machinery,' he explains, 'but our forefathers knew that if we set our hearts after such things, we should become slaves and lose our moral fibre.'[46] It is, therefore, important to con-sider what Gandhi meant by a term which, as he well understood from his eclectic reading and his London and South African years, carried immense authority and was central to the self-esteem of the West and its empires. Essentially, he viewed civilisation as that which assists the development of moral excellence and advances individuals and society towards the goals of non-violence and truth. True civilisa-tion, for him, was thus an aid to self-realisation and universal brother-hood, not a set of material or technological achievements, like railway trains or factory industries. Significantly, the Gujarati equivalent Gandhi used for 'civilisation' meant simply 'good conduct'. Rather like the concept of *dharma*, civilisation represented 'that mode of conduct which points out to man the path of duty'.[47] The underlying contention of *Hind Swaraj* was that the modern or Western world had lost sight of this ancient objective and that its much vaunted claims to be a true civilisation were in fact a sham.

Given this critique of modern civilisation and Indian servitude, what was to be done? How could lost power be regained? Gandhi's most immediate answer was in the rejection of both constitutionalism and terrorism and the adoption in India of the techniques of satyagraha (or 'passive resistance' as he still termed it in 1909) that he had begun to develop in South Africa. Gandhi's arguments could draw support from the recent example of the Swadeshi movement in India. This had arisen following the partition of the province of Bengal by the Viceroy, Lord Curzon, in May 1905, which unleashed a storm of protest within the province and across India. The idea of swadeshi (meaning that which is made in, or belongs to, one's own country) was to encourage Indians to boycott foreign merchandises and to produce and buy their own goods and services instead, thereby effectively breaking India's economic, and ultimately political, dependence upon Britain. But whereas many of the supporters of the Swadeshi Movement wanted India to compete directly with Britain, as through the manufacture of industrial goods and consumer products, even in the creation of steel mills and steamship lines, Gandhi's version of swadeshi eschewed industrialism in favour of traditional craft technology, including a return to hand-spinning and -weaving.

Gandhi was also opposed to the violence that had sprung up in India in the wake of the Swadeshi Movement, especially in Bengal, but also had ramifications as far away as London. On 1 July 1909, shortly before Gandhi's arrival, an India Office official, Sir William Curzon-Wyllie, had been shot by an Indian student, Madan Lal Dhingra, who had India House connections. As Gandhi reported in October 1909 to Lord Ampthill, a former Governor of Madras and one of his principal contacts in London, 'I have met practically no one who believes that India can ever become free without resort to violence.'[48] But Gandhi argued in *Hind Swaraj* that India would never gain true swaraj by such means: 'the force of arms is powerless', he wrote, 'when matched against the force of love or the soul', in other words, the 'truth-force' of satyagraha. Non-violent resistance was not only a method of 'securing rights by personal suffering' but also a 'specialty of India'.[49] But if Gandhi rejected the violence of the revolutionaries in London and Bengal, he was equally anxious to distinguish himself from the old 'Moderate' wing of the Indian National Congress, even though one of its principal leaders, Gopal Krishna Gokhale, was a committed supporter of his work in South Africa and toured with him there for five weeks in 1912. Gandhi appeared now, in 1909–10, to have decisively turned his back on the constitutional path, on the speech-making and the petitioning, which until 1905 had been the hallmark of the Congress in India and of his own agitation in South Africa. Parliament was dismissed as little more than a prostitute, dependent on the whims and favours of whoever could command it. India's freedom demanded more than speeches: it called for personal self-sacrifice and a willingness to suffer for the cause.

In the final analysis *Hind Swaraj* was about far more than the 'home rule' of its English title. As Gandhi put it, 'It is swaraj when we learn to govern ourselves,'[50] but that meant not just the determination to believe that India could rule itself and was not inferior or beholden to the West in any way, but also the need for Indians to take responsibility for their own lives, for their moral and physical state. Serving the nation thus meant, for Gandhi, giving up doctors and the law, foreign cloth, factories and railway trains. It meant chastity, poverty, fearlessness and strict adherence to truth. *Hind Swaraj* can be seen, as Dennis Dalton has described it, as a 'Proclamation of ideological independence'.[51] It can also be seen, along with the London visit of 1909, as marking the 'intellectual divide between Mr Gandhi, Barrister-at-Law, and Mahatma Gandhi'.[52] In some respects, though, it remains a curious document, too sketchy and one-sided to amount to a satisfactory statement of Gandhi's mature political philosophy. It is an odd (even eccentric) combination of Victorian anti-industrialism and Indian tradition (the latter in turn filtered through Western writers like Maine), which repeatedly castigates the dark side of modern civilisation but sees none of its cultural or material benefits. Nor does it recognise the oppression and inequality, the violence and intolerance, the poverty, ignorance and disease, also to be found in pre-modern societies. Its radicalism arguably lies less in its originality, its factuality or its comprehensiveness than in its defiant refusal to accept either the moral or the material superiority of the modern West and hence British cultural and political hegemony in India. It was arguably less important as the blueprint for a practical programme of political action than as an attempt by Gandhi to reconcile the contending poles, Indian and European, within his own complex personality.

. . .

NOTES AND REFERENCES

1. Robert A. Huttenback, *Gandhi in South Africa: British Imperialism and the Indian Question, 1860–1914*, Ithaca, 1971, chapters 1 and 2.
2. Ibid., p. 377.
3. Ibid., p. 128.
4. Maynard W. Swanson, 'The Sanitation Syndrome: Bubonic Plague and Urban Native Policy in the Cape Colony, 1900–1909', *Journal of African History*, 18 (1977), pp. 387–410.
5. *CWMG* I, pp. 75–6.
6. *CWMG* XXIII, p. 115.
7. M. K. Gandhi, *An Autobiography, Or the Story of My Experiments with Truth*, Ahmedabad, 1940, p. 114.
8. *CWMG* XXIII, p. 115.
9. Maureen Swan, *Gandhi: The South African Experience*, Johannesburg, 1985.
10. Ibid., p. 144.
11. Ibid., p. 270; James D. Hunt, 'Gandhi in South Africa', in John Hick and Lamont C. Hempel, *Gandhi's Significance for Today: The Elusive Legacy*, Basingstoke, 1989, pp. 61–81; Judith M. Brown and Martin Prozesky (eds), *Gandhi and South Africa: Principles and Politics*, Pietermaritzburg, 1996.
12. Robert A. Huttenback, 'Some Fruits of Victorian Imperialism: Gandhi and the Indian Question in Natal, 1893–99', *Victorian Studies*, 11 (1967), p. 180.
13. *CWMG* II, p. 317.
14. Ranajit Guha, *Dominance Without Hegemony: History and Power in Colonial India*, Cambridge, Mass., 1997, p. 43.
15. *CWMG* III, p. 114.
16. Hunt, 'Gandhi in South Africa', p. 78.
17. Swan, *Gandhi*, p. 112.
18. Gandhi, *Satyagraha in South Africa*, in *CWMG* XXIX, pp. 12–13.
19. James D. Hunt, *Gandhi in London*, New Delhi, 1993, chs 3–4.
20. Louis Fischer, *The Life of Mahatma Gandhi*, New York, 1962, p. 76.
21. Gandhi, *Autobiography*, p. 224.
22. 'Editor's Introduction' to Anthony J. Parel (ed.), *Gandhi: Hind Swaraj and Other Writings*, Cambridge, 1997.
23. *CWMG* V, p. 421.
24. Bhikhu Parekh, *Gandhi*, Oxford, 1997, p. 56.
25. *CWMG* XXV, p. 563.
26. *CWMG* LIV, pp. 416–17.
27. Hunt, 'Gandhi in South Africa', pp. 67–70.
28. *CWMG* XXIX, p. 266.

29. Jan H. Hofmeyer, 'Gandhi in South Africa', in S. Radhakrishnan (ed.), *Mahatma Gandhi: Essays and Reflections on His Life and Work*, London, 1939, p. 122.
30. *CWMG* VIII, pp. 120, 135.
31. Ibid., pp. 39, 154.
32. *CWMG* IX, pp. 13, 237.
33. Gandhi, *Autobiography*, p. 245.
34. *CWMG* IX, pp. 225, 236–7.
35. Emma Tarlo, *Clothing Matters: Dress and Identity in India*, London, 1996, pp. 67–9.
36. Jawaharlal Nehru, *A Bunch of Old Letters*, London, 1958, pp. 507–10.
37. Sumit Sarkar, *Modern India, 1885–1947*, Basingstoke, 1989, p. 181.
38. Hunt, *Gandhi in London*, pp. 147–8.
39. Partha Chatterjee, *Nationalist Thought and the Colonial World: A Derivative Discourse?*, London, 1986, ch. 4.
40. Hunt, *Gandhi in London*, 1993, p. 88; Richard G. Fox, *Gandhian Utopia: Experiments with Culture*, Boston, 1989, pp. 216–20.
41. M. K. Gandhi, *Hind Swaraj or Indian Home Rule*, Ahmedabad, 1939, p. 27.
42. Ibid., pp. 35–6.
43. Ibid., p. 54.
44. Ibid., pp. 79–81.
45. Ibid., p. 85.
46. Ibid., p. 55.
47. Ibid.; Raghavan Iyer, 'Gandhi on Civilization and Religion', in Hick and Hempel (eds), *Gandhi's Significance for Today*, pp. 125–6.
48. Hunt, *Gandhi in London*, p. 127.
49. Gandhi, *Hind Swaraj*, pp. 68, 71.
50. Ibid., p. 58.
51. Dennis Dalton, *Mahatma Gandhi: Nonviolent Power in Action*, New York, 1993, p. 16.
52. Hunt, *Gandhi in London*, p. 157.

Chapter 4

PEASANT POWER

'The saint has left our shores,' the South African minister J. C. Smuts famously remarked in 1914, 'I sincerely hope for ever.'[1] Gandhi did not, in fact, return to South Africa, and apart from visiting Britain on his way back to India, did not leave India again until 1931. Having spent more than half his first 45 years abroad, in London and South Africa, Gandhi spent virtually all of his remaining 33 years, from 1915 to 1948, in India. In this respect, if in no other, 1915 marked a significant turning point in Gandhi's life. He returned to India, as the quotation from Smuts ironically reminds us, with the reputation of being a saint. The title of Mahatma was bestowed on him shortly after his return by the Bengali poet and Nobel Laureate, Rabindranath Tagore, and in his dress and demeanour, as in his widening public reputation, Gandhi had gone a long way towards shaking off his earlier identity as an anglicised Indian of the professional middle classes.

And yet South Africa was only a beginning, a long apprenticeship to power in India itself. Despite being banned by governments in India in 1910, *Hind Swaraj* made little impact there and Gandhi was essentially known in political circles not for his opinions on how to win Indian independence but for his work for Indian rights and his views on the indentured labour system in South Africa. When he attended the annual meeting of the Indian National Congress, for the first time, at Calcutta in December 1901, it was to speak in support of a resolution on Indian grievances: his speech was brief and hurried and the resolution passed without debate. A semi-exile in South Africa for nearly twenty-one years, Gandhi appeared in many respects out of touch with political and social conditions in an India that had greatly changed since 1893. While it is tempting to see Gandhi's 'rise to power' in India between 1915 and 1920 as a relatively straightforward progression from his South African years and maturing mahatmaship, in many respects in politics Gandhi was having to start again almost from the beginning. Since it was as a champion of the poor and oppressed, and as a peasant leader in particular, that Gandhi became widely known in India and abroad, this chapter will examine the background to his involvement with the peasantry and the part this played in establishing his leadership in India.

. . .

VILLAGE INDIA

Gandhi did not come from a peasant caste or even from village society, but from the Bania caste and small-town India. While it is obvious that growing up in Kathiawar, even travelling by bullock-cart between Porbandar and Rajkot, Gandhi in his childhood must have caught frequent glimpses of peasant life, in his autobiography he makes no mention of this. In subsequent years, in high-school and college in Rajkot and Bhavnagar, as a law student in London, and as a barrister in South Africa in the 1890s, Gandhi had little opportunity to observe, let alone involve himself in, peasant life. It is striking that, despite the references to India's 'sad condition' and the destruction of its handicrafts, nowhere in *Hind Swaraj* did Gandhi address the 'peasant question' – indeed the word 'peasant' hardly appears. His remarks were directed to members of the educated elite and the urgent need for them to reform their own way of life. Nor should it be assumed that someone of Gandhi's background was automatically well-disposed towards the peasantry. As David Hardiman points out in describing caste perceptions in general, Banias 'were always quick to blame the peasants for their impecuniousness. Peasants were idle and spendthrift by nature. They spent beyond their means . . . [,] bloated themselves with food and drink at the time of a marriage or other festivity, and then starved for the next year.' Many Banias considered peasants 'coarse and ill-mannered. They polluted themselves by eating flesh and other forbidden foods, and by drinking liquor. They had no understanding of the true dharma.'[2] Although Hardiman does not directly identify these attitudes with Gandhi, it would be hard not to see certain similarities here with his propensity for seeing the problems of the peasantry in moral rather than economic terms and with the kind of agenda of uplift and reform he brought to the peasantry and the Indian masses as a whole. As was evident even before his final return to India in January 1915, Gandhi aspired as an educated man to instruct, and not simply to lead, the peasantry. But he went to exceptional lengths in his desire to identify with the poor and the peasants. In 1913 he adopted the dress of an indentured labourer (or 'coolie') and from 1917 embarked on a series of peasant-oriented satyagraha campaigns, culminating in the Salt Satyagraha of 1930. In September 1931, on his final visit to London, he declared that he and the Indian National Congress represented, above all else, 'the dumb, semi-starved millions' scattered over the length and breadth of rural India.[3]

This view of Gandhi as a peasant leader was a critical part, too, of how he was perceived by others in India and abroad and of his authority as a political leader. He was widely understood as being the voice of the peasants, of the 'dumb' masses who could not speak for themselves. For Jawaharlal Nehru, Gandhi seemed to 'emerge' from the masses of India, not from the middle classes or from the old elites. 'He did not descend from the top,' Nehru wrote; 'he seemed to emerge from the millions of India, speaking their language and incessantly drawing attention to them and their appalling condition.' He transformed them 'from a demoralised, timid, and hopeless mass, bullied and crushed by every dominant interest, and incapable of resistance', into 'a people with self-respect and self-reliance, resisting tyranny and capable of united action and sacrifice for a larger cause.' Equally profound, in Nehru's view, was Gandhi's impact on the attitudes of members of the middle classes, like himself. 'He sent us to the villages, and the countryside hummed with the activity of innumerable messengers of the new gospel of action. The peasant was shaken up and he began to emerge from his quiescent shell.' Through Gandhi, men like Nehru saw 'for the first time as it were, the villager in the intimacy of his mud hut and with the stark shadow of hunger always pursuing him.'[4] But, while this tells us much about the personal remoteness of men like Nehru from the peasantry of India, and hence their need to rely upon an intermediary like Gandhi in order to establish a mass base for the nationalist movement, we still need to understand why and how Gandhi gained this remarkable reputation and how it came to be a central constituent of his 'power'.

Gandhi arrived at his 'discovery' of the Indian peasantry by several routes. One lay through his disenchantment with industrial society and Western modernity. South Africa played its part in this. In Johannesburg, with its huge mines and insanitary slums, its ill-fed troops of migrant workers, its cheap drinking-shops, sleazy brothels and criminal underworld, he could see modern city life at its worst – though, to judge from *Hind Swaraj*, he saw Bombay, and the 'slaves' toiling in its mills, in no less unfavourable a light, and, in a telling phrase, dismissed all three of India's principal port cities as 'plague spots'.[5] How pleasing, how morally reassuring, it must have been for Gandhi to retreat from the 'New Babylon' that was Johannesburg to the calm and simple living of his Phoenix Settlement or Tolstoy Farm. In his incipient ashram communities in South Africa Gandhi sought to put into practice the kinds of ideas of 'bread labour' and self-sufficiency he had gleaned from his reading of Ruskin and others. In Gandhi's intellectual and political evolution, these small-scale utopian communities came first. The real villages of India only came later, once the ideal had already been firmly established in his mind.

Following Ruskin, Tolstoy and others, Gandhi could see village society, a society of artisans as well as peasants, as the worthy antithesis of a corrupt and class-divided urban, industrial society. If manual labour were to be understood as dignified rather than, as it tended to be regarded in India, demeaning, then it was natural enough for him to see peasants in particular as fulfilling this role. In his increasingly critical attitude to his own middle class, which he saw as tainted by its adherence to Westernised language, dress and diet, and, as he showed in *Hind Swaraj*, its complicity in colonialism, Gandhi was inevitably drawn by contrast to the peasants as the real people, the very soul of India. They were the uncolonised, the never-colonised, the base from which India's lost swaraj could be salvaged and rebuilt.

Gandhi saw the apparently timeless and unchanging nature of the Indian villages not as evidence of backwardness, but as proof of its enduring value. They were the living link with a time-honoured past. Village India was, in his view rightly, resistant to change because change was not needed: village society had already been tried, tested and found to be good. In their poverty and hardship, the peasants represented for Gandhi people free from the taint of luxury and self-indulgence. While deploring their backwardness and poverty, he could not help but see their absence of material possessions, their lack of contamination by 'modern civilisation' as a positive good, as if it were a consequence of deliberate renunciation rather than imposed by harsh circumstances. Conversely, Gandhi showed singularly little interest in peasant culture. Unlike some of his contemporaries in the West and individuals such as Tagore in India, Gandhi was not anxious to preserve or revive peasant art, music and festivals: he was no collector of folk-songs or preserver of peasant lore and customs. His understanding of the peasantry (like his attitude to sex) was remarkably austere and joyless. He also imagined that village society was based on a kind of self-sufficiency and mutual cooperation that made villages harmonious small-scale societies. He followed colonial administrators and early nationalist thought in seeing village communities as virtual 'village republics', traditionally self-governing and, at least until the coming of the British, largely free from external interference and constraint.[6] It was therefore possible to believe that, if villages naturally enjoyed a high level of autonomy, the role of the state would be correspondingly insignificant. Villages not only made up the bulk of the nation, they also provided a model for how the nation should be constructed – as a collection of largely self-governing 'village republics'.

One can further link Gandhi's growing recognition of, and identification with, India's poor with two developments. One was his increasing acquaintance with India on his two visits there in 1896 and 1901–2. In 1896 plague and famine forced him to think more than he had ever previously done about the plight of India's rural population, and on his return to Natal he organised a Famine Relief Committee to raise funds for those affected. The railway, castigated as one of the evils of 'modern civilisation' in *Hind Swaraj*, in fact provided him with an important vehicle for social observation (for, as the Pietermaritzburg episode showed, railways transformed social distance, throwing together classes and races with unprecedented familiarity or, conversely, legislating to keep them even more strictly apart). Travelling third class on Indian trains during his 1901–2 visit to India aroused in Gandhi indignation at the railway authorities' neglect of travellers' comfort and well-being but also provoked annoyance at the 'dirty and inconsiderate habits' of the passengers themselves. He saw it as the duty of 'educated men' like himself to make a point of travelling third class so as to learn about the masses and so find ways of 'reforming the habits of the people'.[7] Gandhi's middle-class horror at insanitary conditions on the trains (as at places of pilgrimage and worship) in India echoed his sanitary preoccupations in South Africa and the stinging accusation made by whites that Indians were insanitary and hence uncivilised. Gandhi's growing involvement with the poor was thus in part motivated by shame, by the desire of the educated Bania to reform the 'habits' of the poor and make them more 'civilised', whether this was civilisation as defined by the West or by the no less exacting standards of a high-caste Hindu.

The second important development of his South African years was the widening social constituency for Gandhi's campaign for Indian rights. This brought him into contact with the indentured labourers, many of whom came from poor peasant backgrounds, mostly from Tamil-speaking south India rather than his native Gujarat. In his autobiography, Gandhi dates this involvement to his meeting with an illiterate labourer, Balasundaram, who had been ill-treated by his European employer and whom Gandhi successfully had transferred to another master. In taking up this case, Gandhi recalled, his name 'reached the ears of every indentured labourer'. 'I came to be regarded as their friend', and a 'regular stream of indentured labourers began to pour into my office.' He discovered, too, that echoes of the Balasundaram case 'were heard in far off Madras' as well and he was warmly received on his visit to the southern presidency in 1896.[8] It was from about this time that Gandhi began to take an interest in the £3 tax on ex-indentured labourers, which the Natal government introduced in an attempt to curb the number of 'coolies' remaining in the colony. The Natal Indian Congress took up the issue, to limited effect, in the 1890s, but the issue came to a head in 1913–14 and its eventual abolition (along with the indentured labour system itself) has, as we have seen, been regarded as one of the triumphs of Gandhi's second satyagraha campaign.

. . .

THE RAJ AND THE CONGRESS

Apart from his personal experiences in India and South Africa, other circumstances also conspired to push Gandhi further in the peasant direction. One was the attitude of the British themselves. It would be rash to generalise about the attitudes of the Raj – the British administration – in nineteenth-century India as a whole, for they were many and various, but one enduring strand was an identification with the peasantry as fundamentally loyal, hardworking and honest. Not only were peasants the main source of Indian revenues, they also provided the post-Mutiny Indian Army with the bulk of its recruits and from their poorer ranks came the migrant labourers needed to sustain export-oriented plantation economies in India and abroad. To some extent British policy was directed at improving the position of the peasants while regarding the landholding elite, including the substantial hereditary landholders known as *zamindars*, as generally unprogressive and the moneylenders (like those of Gandhi's own Bania caste), who had such a strong hold on rural life, as parasitic and exploitative and from whom the gullible and indebted peasantry deserved, whenever possible, the protection of the law and the courts. Many a district officer looked upon 'his' peasants with a kind of paternalistic affection and was happy to regard himself, in the familiar phrase, as *ma-bap*, as the 'mother and father' of the deferential villagers (so long as they did not rise up in revolt or commit 'heinous' crimes).

As long as the masses of India appeared loyal and contented (or at least inert) the British felt able to dismiss the Indian National Congress, in Lord Curzon's celebrated words, as a 'microscopic minority', unrepresentative of the 'voiceless millions' of India.[9] By contrast, many Europeans in India, not just in the Indian Civil Service, viewed with distaste the rise of an industrial economy and an urban proletariat. India, they argued, was best suited to its old craft traditions and the dignified, self-sufficient ways of rural life. Industrialisation had brought class conflict to the West, had given rise to ugly, sprawling, insanitary cities. Surely, they asked in a manner that anticipated Gandhi's own ideas, should not India be spared the fate of industrial Britain?[10]

Characteristically, Gandhi both absorbed this colonial idealisation of rural life and yet also sought to subvert it. He followed the British, rather than many of his nationalist predecessors, in seeing the peasants, rather than the Western-educated middle classes, as the real India. But one of his unfolding ambitions in the years after his return to India in 1915 was to show that the peasants were not, in fact, loyal and deferential to the British. On the contrary, they were far more likely to mobilise to oppose British rule than the highly compromised Western-educated middle classes: they were the heart and soul of India, the embodiment of many of its ancient traditions. They were not loyal followers of the British and if in their millions they declined to pay the land revenue demand or refused to obey the laws of the colonial state, an empire staffed by a few thousand Europeans and their Indian collaborators was bound to collapse. While Gandhi did not subscribe to the crude arithmetic of electoral politics, he did not fail to see the power of numbers in India, where the British and their allies might be swamped by the sheer weight of the peasantry, if only they could be brought fully into the political process. At a time when 80 per cent of Britons lived in towns and cities, and the percentage of the rural population fell in census after census, 90 per cent of Indians still lived in the countryside. It seemed logical to look to the countryside as the true locus of political power and the engine of swaraj.

A further factor here was, of course, the nature of the nationalist movement itself.[11] From its founding at Bombay in December 1885, the Indian National Congress had been largely composed of the new Westernised middle classes, the heavy predominance of lawyers among its members supported by doctors, journalists, teachers and landlords. Its language had, from the outset, been English. Its politics were essentially those of constitutional debate and occasional protest, via petitions, resolutions and public meetings. Initially it met only once a year, in December, and like the Natal Congress, to which it leant its name, the Indian National Congress was overwhelmingly loyal, wedded to reform, not revolution. It railed against racial discrimination, but four British well-wishers served among its early presidents. An Englishman and an ICS officer, Allan Octavian Hume, was one of its founders and remained for many years its General Secretary. Indeed, the organisation itself is sometimes seen as having been a safety-valve deliberately created by the British in order to pre-empt more extreme forms of opposition. Although it aspired to be an India-wide body, the bulk of its leadership and membership during the early years was drawn from the most Westernised cities of India, Calcutta, Bombay and Madras, themselves the principal centres of British authority in India.

But of late the Congress had itself undergone significant changes and upheavals. The late 1890s saw the growth of a more militant Hindu nationalism in Maharashtra, principally associated with the Poona-based Brahmin Bal Gangadhar Tilak, and to this, in Bombay and subsequently Madras and Punjab, was added the agitational fuel of the Partition of Bengal and the Swadeshi Movement. Acts of terrorism, directed mainly at British officials, erupted in several parts of India, adding to the turmoil and unrest, and establishing the invocation or use of violence as one strategy among the several contending for dominance in India's multi-stranded struggle for freedom. Although Tilak's power-base lay predominantly in Maharashtra, he and others of the so-called 'Extremist' wing of the

Congress seemed poised to seize control of the Congress from 'Moderates' like G. K. Gokhale, also a Brahmin from Poona and an influential member of the Indian Legislative Council, and another of Gandhi's acquaintances, the Parsi lawyer Pherozeshah Mehta in Bombay. But in a fiery meeting at Surat in 1907 the Congress split and the Moderates, led by Gokhale and Mehta, re-established their control. In November that year Tilak was sentenced to six years' imprisonment for inciting violence against the British and was banished to Mandalay in Burma. At its Calcutta session in 1906 Dadabhai Naoroji had declared the objective of the Congress to be swaraj, but it was Tilak who uttered the defiant war cry, 'Swaraj is my birthright, and I will have it.' However, early in 1915, when Gandhi returned to India, the Congress, already thirty years old, seemed to have lapsed into a relatively quiescent phase.

As an outsider to the nationalist establishment and to the debates and controversies of recent years, Gandhi, now dressed in traditional Kathiawari costume, seemed unlikely to make much impact, except as a curiosity from the South African struggle. Gokhale, whom he looked to as his mentor, advised him not to speak on political matters in India for at least a year, until he had familiarised himself with Indian issues and conditions, and Gandhi dutifully set off on a long tour of the country. Gokhale's death on 20 February 1915, shortly followed by that of Pherozeshah Mehta, deprived Gandhi of one possible route into the nationalist political establishment. He was accepted as a probationer for the Servants of India Society Gokhale had set up in 1905, but agreed to withdraw when his lavatory-cleaning caused offence to other members. V. S. Srinivasa Sastri, a Tamil Brahmin and Gokhale's successor as President of the Society, was unimpressed by Gandhi and his 'anarch' views. 'Queer food he eats,' he confided to his brother, 'only fruits and nuts. . . . The odd thing is he was dressed quite like a *bania*.'[12] Gandhi's political isolation – and naivety – seemed even more evident when he made a speech at the opening of the Benares Hindu University on 6 February 1916 in which he railed against the use of English at public meetings, the dirt in temples and places of pilgrimage, the vulgar luxury of India's rich and their unconcern for the poor, as well as appearing to condone terrorist violence.[13] This outburst further alienated him from Annie Besant, who was chairing the meeting, and other nationalist leaders, including the university's founder, Madan Mohan Malaviya. Soon after this incident Besant described Gandhi, not unperceptively, as being of 'the martyr type' and believing 'more in suffering than achievement'.[14] Even more significantly in the longer term, Gandhi quickly fell out with Mohammed Ali Jinnah, one of the leading young lawyers and politicians in Bombay. Jinnah, thirty years later the founder of Pakistan, appeared at the time to be precisely the kind of anglicised, English-speaking lawyer mocked in *Hind Swaraj*, and he was offended by Gandhi's tactless proposal that he should address a group of Gujarati merchants in their own tongue (which Jinnah hardly knew) rather than in English. Years later Gandhi remarked, 'Jinnah has hated me ever since I made him speak Gujarati.'[15]

Gandhi's place on the political sidelines was still more apparent when moves were made to overcome the old Moderate-Extremist split and revive nationalist agitation. The lead was taken in 1916 by Tilak, recently released from imprisonment, and Annie Besant, who set up their own Home Rule Leagues to press Indian demands and intensify pressure on a British administration already reeling from the effects of the First World War. Gandhi attended the Congress annual session at Lucknow in December 1916, which saw a further significant development, a 'pact', which Jinnah helped orchestrate, between the Congress and the Muslim League, an organisation set up ten years earlier as a vehicle for Muslim interests and in opposition to the predominantly Hindu Congress. There seemed little room for Gandhi in these high-level political manoeuvres, but he was already contemplating other possibilities. During his controversial speech at the opening of Benares Hindu University in February 1916 he had contrasted the lives of India's princes with the poverty of its villages and prophesied that its 'salvation' would come only through the peasantry. Even so, the actual initiative came from others. During the Lucknow Congress meeting, Gandhi was approached by an agriculturalist, Raj Kumar Shukla, from Champaran in the north-eastern province of Bihar, who pestered him to come to see for himself the plight of indigo-growing cultivators there. Gandhi at first resisted, but ultimately agreed to visit Champaran. He thereby embarked on his first significant engagement with the hardship and suffering of the Indian peasantry.

But before we turn to Champaran and its significance, it is important to note that Gandhi did not invent the peasantry as a force to be reckoned with in the politics of colonial India, nor was he entirely alone in seeing its potential value to the Indian nationalist movement. As recent scholarship on India has shown, nineteenth- and early twentieth-century India witnessed a series of revolts and uprising in which peasants participated alongside other groups (as in the

Mutiny and Rebellion of 1857–8) or in which they launched their own vigorous protests against state revenue demands, the exactions of oppressive landlords or, as in the case of the 'Deccan riots' in western India in 1875, the crippling rates of interest exacted by moneylenders.[16] Equally, political leaders like Tilak were beginning to grasp the possibility of annexing peasant grievances to the nationalist cause or mobilising them through religious appeals and celebrations. In the provinces, political activity, as reflected for instance through the expanding press, was already moving into the vernacular languages and widening the scope for political communication beyond the Western-educated middle class. Innovative in many ways, Gandhi was to no small degree the beneficiary of the earlier history of peasant movements in colonial India and the increasing interest shown in the peasantry by the nationalist leadership.

. . .

GANDHI IN CHAMPARAN

Champaran, close to India's frontier with Nepal, was a district in which indigo (valued as a source of a rich blue-purple dye) had for several decades been grown by peasants under the direction of European planters. Indigo-growing was arduous and an on-going source of conflict, partly because cultivation was accompanied by a number of illegal levies and exactions made by the planters, but also because the tenant farmers were required under the *tinkathia* system to plant one-seventh of their holdings with indigo in return for a lump sum of money fixed by the planters. The peasants resented the harsh control the planters exercised over their lives and there had been frequent, often violent, local disputes. In 1859–62 a sustained struggle against indigo cultivation took place among peasants in neighbouring Bengal: since this followed close on the heels of the 1857 uprising, it was duly dubbed the 'blue mutiny'. Champaran itself experienced anti-planter agitations in 1866–7, 1894–5 and 1907–9. In this sense at least, then, Gandhi was not creating a new movement among a hitherto supine peasantry, but building on longstanding grievances and a local, if not altogether effective, agitational tradition. The situation had, however, further deteriorated since the late 1890s when a synthetic dye was developed in Germany which depressed the market for Indian indigo, and though the war, in cutting off German exports, had given the planters a respite, they were determined to survive, if necessary by making their grip on the cultivators even tighter. Badgered by Shukla, Gandhi agreed to visit Champaran to try to make 'peace with honour' between the two sides.

On his arrival in Champaran on 10 April 1917 Gandhi discovered that the charges of economic exploitation and oppression were substantially correct. Not only did the planters enjoy the legal and practical support of the provincial administration, to the extent of calling in the police to enforce their exactions, but the peasants were also terrorised by the planters and ground down by the wretched conditions in which they lived and work. There were certain similarities between the plight of the *raiyats* or peasants of Champaran and the indentured labourers he had encountered in South Africa, not least in their shared subordination to a European planter class. But Champaran plunged Gandhi into the politics of a rural society in a region far removed from his native Gujarat and obliged him to involve himself to an unprecedented degree with the lives of the cultivators themselves. It provided him with the kind of entrée into peasant life that neither his early life in Kathiawar nor his years in . London and South Africa had equipped him for. And yet the very things that made Gandhi appear crude and crankish in the eyes of India's English-speaking elite here made him appear attractive and accessible to the people. He travelled third class and spoke in basic Hindustani. His manner was modest and unpretentious. He made a deliberate effort to live among the peasants, shared their meagre food and heard their complaints. He also employed simple religious imagery to convey his ideas, imagery that could appeal directly to the popular religious beliefs of the villagers. It is true that through Shukla, a Brahmin and a relatively prosperous cultivator by Champaran standards, Gandhi was partly aligned with a local elite of wealthier cultivators and moneylenders who had grievances of their own to pursue and whose economic interests were in conflict with the European planters (who also gave advances to the peasants or lent them money at usurious rates). Gandhi also derived support for his work in Champaran from Banias and Marwaris (merchants and moneylenders, originally from Marwar in Rajasthan). But few nationalist politicians at the time, neither Tilak nor Gokhale, would ever have ventured to investigate the grievances of the peasants first-hand, and certainly not with such determination and empathy.

Gandhi and his assistants set about their task with brisk efficiency, systematically collecting and recording the complaints of more than 8,000 *raiyats* from over 800 villages, and ensuring, as far as possible, that their testimony was accurate and free from wild accusations. Gandhi acted in his own name, rather than invoking the authority of the Congress, which (even if it would endorse his actions) he knew would arouse the planters' ire. Moreover, he made it clear that his aim, in accordance with the principles of satyagraha, was not to provoke a confrontation with the planters but to reach a mutually acceptable agreement. He even wrote to, and offered to meet, those planters against whom there were particularly serious charges. He sought to emphasise, too, that this was a search for social justice and not a political crusade: he therefore asked that the government remain neutral.

Predictably, though, events took a different turn. Within days of his arrival at Champaran, and even before the collection of evidence had begun, the British District Collector issued a notice to Gandhi to quit the area or else face trial for disobeying an official order. With the benefit of his South African experience, Gandhi elected to face arrest and trial rather than be hustled out of Champaran, but before he could be sentenced the Lieutenant-Governor of Bihar and Orissa overturned the Collector's decision and ordered the case to be withdrawn. This left Gandhi free to pursue his enquiry and for the *raiyats* to present their testimony without fear of intervention from the police or magistracy. It was a remarkable victory, and one which added greatly to Gandhi's personal prestige in the area. Subsequently, the Lieutenant-Governor invited Gandhi to sit on an official committee of enquiry to look into the peasants' grievances. The unanimous recommendation of the committee was that the *tinkathia* system should be abolished and that there should be reductions of 20 to 25 per cent in the revenue paid to the planters. An agreement along these lines was signed by Gandhi and the planters on 29 September 1917 and the main points were embodied in legislation.[17]

On the face of it this was a 'spectacular victory', but Gandhi did not fail to recognise that the agreement had not fundamentally changed the balance of power in Champaran. As in his negotiations with Smuts in South Africa in 1914, this was a compromise, not an out-and-out triumph for victorious peasants over vanquished planters. Gandhi believed that the planters had been made to suffer enough and that, as part of the technique and philosophy of satyagraha, an agreed compromise was to be preferred to the humiliating defeat and lasting rancour of one's opponents. Moreover, Gandhi was quick to see how in Champaran economic exploitation and social conditions were closely linked. Hitherto largely unacquainted with the realities of Indian peasant life, Champaran came as a grim revelation for Gandhi. The *raiyats*, he wrote in his autobiography, were illiterate, their ignorance 'pathetic'. 'The villages were insanitary, the lanes full of filth, the wells surrounded by mud and stink and the courtyards unbearably untidy. The elderly people badly needed education in cleanliness. They were all suffering from various skin diseases.' In order to make the *raiyats* more self-reliant and less vulnerable to intimidation, it was necessary to educate them, do sanitary work in the villages and 'penetrate every department of their lives'[18] – in short, to use the language to which Gandhi had become habituated in South Africa, to civilise them. Champaran marked, in effect, the birth of what came to be known as the Constructive Programme, designed to achieve 'village uplift' and social reform, principally through the revival of hand-spinning and other cottage industries, Hindu–Muslim cooperation, the removal of untouchability, improving the condition of women, prohibition, basic education, and village sanitation.

For Gandhi the political and the social could never be entirely separate domains of thought and action. Indeed, he saw in Champaran proof that 'disinterested service of the people in any sphere ultimately helps the country politically'.[19] Nevertheless, his 1917 campaign in Bihar marked the beginning of a divergence between his political programme and the search for swaraj to be attained through the Congress organisation and mass-based agitational campaigns, and his social programme which called, less spectacularly, for local-level activism and a separate body of dedicated volunteers. Gandhi left behind in Champaran fifteen village workers, though by May 1918 only three remained. Nonetheless for Gandhi Champaran, with its acute poverty and social misery was what village India had become under colonial rule and represented the plight from which educated, dedicated social workers had to rescue it. When an American journalist, William Shirer, was travelling by car with Gandhi through the villages of Kheda and Bardoli districts in central Gujarat in 1931, he commented that he could not see much evidence of the grinding poverty and starving peasantry to which Gandhi had drawn attention. Gandhi admitted that these were 'rather prosperous' districts but they were not, he said, typical of the Indian countryside in which most people lived such wretched lives.[20] Champaran fourteen years earlier had helped to imprint that image of rural India so vividly on Gandhi's mind.

What is significant, too, about Champaran is the extent to which Gandhi was revered by the *raiyats* as a semi-divine or messianic figure. Perhaps stimulated by stories and rumours spread by his local allies, he was compared to a Hindu god fighting against the demon planters. One eyewitness commented on the extraordinary spectacle of hundreds of peasants coming before Gandhi to present their grievances and looking at him 'as a god who had come to save them. They would sit gazing and gazing and gazing, hour after hour.' This was their *darshan*, their viewing of the auspicious person or divine image that would in turn confer on them blessings. The British Sub-Divisional Magistrate also noted Gandhi's messianic impact on the peasants of Champaran: 'to the *raiyats* he is their liberator, and they credit him with extraordinary powers . . . he is daily transfiguring the imaginations of masses of ignorant men with visions of an early millennium.'[21] It was even rumoured that Gandhi had been sent by the Viceroy or the King-Emperor to redress the peasants' grievances, and confidently expected that Gandhi would abolish all oppressive ties to the planters, who would no longer have to be obeyed. The practical result was that the peasants were prepared to present their grievances openly and, despite some minor outbreaks of arson and violence, stood fairly united behind his campaign. However uncomfortable Gandhi might be with his growing 'messianic appeal', he was beginning to learn the usefulness of having a saintly image and a god-like reputation.

Champaran brought further benefits for Gandhi. Credited with successful defiance of the planters and the provincial government, he was now seen as a peasant leader of all-India stature, whose advice and leadership began to be sought elsewhere. There was clearly a market for his skills: he did not have to embark on the labourious process of trying to create one. This confirmed for him the possibility, clearly not apparent to him when he wrote *Hind Swaraj* eight years earlier but evidently in his mind when he spoke at Benares in 1916, of invoking the peasants and their grievances as an ideological weapon and using them as the basis for building up a nation-wide satyagraha campaign. Previously on the margins of Indian politics, known mainly for his work in South Africa, and without any organisational support of his own, Gandhi through his campaign in Bihar had begun to exercise a new charisma and to attract a number of young supporters to his cause. These were principally members of the local intelligentsia, often high-caste lawyers with educational and professional backgrounds not dissimilar to his own. Some had been inactive in the old schools of politics or grown disenchanted with their inability to secure significant results; few had previously had an active interest in the conditions of the peasantry. One was J. P. Kripalani, then a teacher, later a leading Gandhian activist. Another was Rajendra Prasad, a High Court lawyer in Patna, but subsequently one of Gandhi's closest associates and eventually President of India. By the end of 1917 Gandhi was no more just a provincial figure or a single-issue politician. He was beginning to be seen as the only leader who had his finger on the pulse of peasant India.

. . .

THE KHEDA SATYAGRAHA

Gandhi's second 'peasant satyagraha' seemed to confirm the lessons of the first at Champaran. This time the campaign was in Gandhi's home region, but in Kheda (or Kaira) in the generally more prosperous central districts of Gujarat rather than in his native Kathiawar. It occupied Gandhi's attention for a shorter time than Champaran, barely three months from late March to the end of June 1918, and for part of that period he was also involved in an industrial dispute in Ahmedabad. There were other significant differences from Champaran. There were no European planters in Kheda: this was more transparently a campaign for peasant rights and against colonial authority, with the state held directly responsible for the high level of land revenue payments demanded from peasants.

Kheda, lying to the southeast of Ahmedabad, in a fertile tract of land between the Sabarmati and Mahi rivers, had formerly been a thriving agricultural region. One of the richest and most productive in the entire Bombay Presidency, it had been badly affected by plague since 1898, by a series of deficient harvests following the famine of 1899, and finally by severe floods. The loss of cattle as well as commercial crops that normally found a ready market in nearby Ahmedabad, left the once prosperous peasant elite, the Patidars, and especially the poorer sections of the community, facing severe hardship. The bad harvest of 1917–18, combined with high prices for salt, cloth and fuel (kerosene), added to their already difficult plight. But the Patidars had a reputation for being a tough, independent and enterprising class of peasant proprietors, virtual rulers of their own villages. In Kheda, too, primary education was relatively widespread among the Patidars, and from a base at

Ahmedabad, set up in October 1916, the Home Rule League reached Nadiad, the principal town of the district, where a branch of the League was established in July 1917. Kheda was, therefore, less of a political backwater than Champaran but here, too, the incentive for a no-revenue campaign (in one of the most heavily assessed districts in India) came from village leaders: Gandhi agreed with some reluctance in March 1918 to take up their cause.

In an attempt to gain concessions for the peasants, the first phase of Gandhi's agitation consisted of appeals to the government to suspend the revenue demand on the grounds of hardship and, as at Champaran, to appoint an enquiry committee to investigate peasant grievances. When this failed to secure results, there followed a satyagraha, in which more than 2,000 peasants, mainly Patidars, signed a 'sacred pledge', vowing to hold out for their demands, despite the threat that they would face fines and have their property confiscated for not paying the land revenue. The satyagraha was in some respects a rather patchy affair, with only a minority of villages directly involved, and with serious tensions developing between wealthier and poorer Patidars. Gandhi appealed to the more well-to-do peasant proprietors in terms of Hindu *dharma*: it was their duty to make sacrifices and to use their wealth to support the poorer peasants. He also used the opportunity, as in Champaran, to instruct his educated supporters to live simply and fit into the village environment, to promote education, sanitation and the ideals of satyagraha. But Gandhi himself found the campaign unsatisfactory. Within a few weeks the peasants were becoming frightened and exhausted, and he was 'casting around for some graceful way of terminating the struggle which would be acceptable to a Satyagrahi'.[22] On 6 June he called the campaign off after the District Collector decided to suspend revenue payments for the poorer cultivators. Nonetheless, his supporters could claim a kind of victory and Gandhi saw in the campaign evidence that India was awakening from 'its long sleep'. The *raiyats* 'do not need to be literate to appreciate their rights and their duties', he declared. 'They have but to realise their invulnerable power and no Government, however strong, can stand against their will.'[23]

Tactically, Kheda was important as providing Gandhi with his first opportunity in India to target the land revenue assessment, a cause not only dear to the peasants but one which struck directly at the authority and resources of the colonial state. But part of the significance of the Kheda Satyagraha also lies in what it indicates about the nature of the peasant support Gandhi was beginning to command. At issue here is what is meant by 'peasant' in the Indian context. Although the term (or Indian equivalents like *raiyat* and *kisan*) is widely used in association with Gandhi and in a wide variety of other contexts, it is remarkably difficult to generalise across India as a whole, and scholars have often invoked a three-fold division of the Indian peasantry to try to explain its wide regional differences and its most prominent internal distinctions. At the top of the peasant hierarchy were 'rich peasants', proprietors of their own land and often sufficiently wealthy to employ subordinate labourers to perform such basic manual tasks as helping with the harvest. These rich peasants, *kulaks* in the Russian terminology, might often be in transition to being enterprising small capitalist farmers with interests in money-lending, trade and transport. Rich peasants, including some (albeit a minority) among the Patidars in Kheda, enjoyed relatively high caste status and lorded it over low-caste or tribal farm labourers, such as the lowly Koli and Bhil tribals.[24] Below them on the second tier were the middle peasants. In many ways these formed the archetypal peasant category – having little but their own family labour to draw upon and living by subsistence farming on plots of land barely equal to their needs. Below them in turn were the poor peasants and landless labourers. In the Indian case, these were usually low-castes, untouchables or tribals. Many held no land at all or too little to be self-sufficient: some were tied labourers, virtual serfs; others were migrant labourers moving with the harvest, often as whole families, from one district to another. They lived by selling their labour to others or by receiving a share of the grain harvest, supplemented by occasional 'presents' of cloth, salt and other necessities.

This tripartite division is critical in trying to assess the extent of Gandhi's support among the peasants and his appeal to them. In Champaran Gandhi's initial contacts were with the richer peasants (like Raj Kumar Shukla) but he rapidly established a rapport with the poor indigo-growing peasants. In Kheda the leading role was played by the relatively prosperous and high-status Patidars, consisting of rich and more especially middle peasants. Particularly important was the support Gandhi enjoyed from Vallabhbhai Patel, a London-trained barrister, six years younger than himself, from a Patidar family in Kheda district, who had also worked for the mill-owners of Ahmedabad. Patel provided Gandhi with some vital contacts and support among the peasants of central Gujarat and brought with him an astute awareness of peasant attitudes and concerns. Through the

Kheda campaign Patel became one of Gandhi's leading lieutenants and principal peasant adviser, though over the years he also became an increasingly conservative and pro-business figure in the national Congress leadership.

Gandhi's appeal to the socially conservative Patidars was based on several things, which helps to explain his attraction for the upper sections of the peasantry but also his limitations as a peasant leader.[25] One part of this was Gandhi's emphatic non-violence. As property-holders, albeit on a relatively modest scale, and as a relatively high-status group with a stake in the social status quo, the Patidars were drawn to a movement which promised to free them from the vexatious exactions of colonial rule without threatening violent revolution and a revolutionary social upheaval by subordinate peasants and landless labourers. When the law-and-order situation threatened to break down, the wealthier Patidars began to waver in their support. A second factor was Gandhi's religious appeal. For all his religious eclecticism, Gandhi was seen as exemplifying the Gujarati *bhakti* tradition, which was particularly strong in Kheda. The religious language and imagery Gandhi employed and his appeal to *dharma* helped to reinforce this identification between devotional Hinduism and nationalist politics, and Gandhi was sometimes seen, as in Champaran, as an incarnation, an avatar, of the god Vishnu. He was also a local hero in whom the Patidars could feel a patriotic pride, especially as until Gandhi Gujarat had not enjoyed a prominent place in national politics, overshadowed by leaders like Gokhale and Tilak from Maharashtra and by the Parsis of Bombay city. The Patidars thus represented the entry into the nationalist movement, in part through Gandhi's own intervention and appeal, of India's rich and middle peasant classes. By contrast, many of the very poorest peasant strata remained, for the time being at least, unmoved by Gandhi or were left on the margins of Gandhian politics.

· · ·

THE AHMEDABAD STRIKE OF 1918

Gandhi's concerns in 1917–18 were not focused upon the peasants alone and in these years he experimented with various groups and issues. In the early months of 1918, at the same time as the Kheda Satyagraha, Gandhi was caught up in a mill-workers' dispute in the city of Ahmedabad. By 1918 Ahmedabad, once a flourishing centre for handmade cotton textiles, had followed Bombay along the route to rapid urban growth and industrialisation. With the arrival of the railway in 1864 and the establishment of its first modern textile mills, Ahmedabad rapidly ceased to be the medieval city it had appeared to be even in the 1850s. By 1900 it had 27 mills, employing nearly 16,000 workers; by 1918, the year of Gandhi's involvement, there were 51 mills, employing 39,440 mill-hands. By 1921, with a population of 270,000 people, Ahmedabad was the sixth largest city in India.[26]

It was here that Gandhi made his home shortly after his return from South Africa. On 20 May 1915 he established the 'Satyagraha Ashram' on the outskirts of the city, close to the Sabarmati river. This was his base for the next fifteen years and provided him with the environment within which to continue his experiments in communal living, education, health and spinning begun in South Africa. Although rural Gujarat was not far away, this was a somewhat curious location for anyone interested in establishing closer contact with India's peasantry. Mirabehn, who joined the ashram from England in November 1925, recalled that despite being situated on the banks of the Sabarmati and having some fields near by, it did not have a 'country atmosphere'. 'One looked across the river at a forest of factory chimneys, whose smoke often polluted the air.' Walks consisted in 'trudging along an uninteresting road' from the ashram to the gates of the local prison and back.[27] Why did Gandhi choose Ahmedabad? He clearly wanted to return to Gujarat, but not to the personal associations and endless intrigues of princely Rajkot (and, anyway, by 1915 both his brothers were dead). Ahmedabad and its wealthy Bania community provided him with the financial backing he needed for the ashram and for his other schemes, social as well as political. In choosing Ahmedabad as his headquarters, Gandhi rejected the backwaters of Kathiawar while still remaining essentially on his home ground and opted instead for a dynamic urban centre.[28]

Ahmedabad's textile mills were owned and run by Indian entrepreneurs, who over the course of the following decades gave Gandhi millions of rupees to help finance his nationalist campaigns and constructive programme. Although Gandhi used very little of this money for his personal needs, one cannot but be struck by the extent to which India's saintly Mahatma and foremost peasant leader was bankrolled by the capitalist class. The contradictions of this position were not slow in manifesting themselves. One of his earliest donors and supporters was Ambalal Sarabhai, a young mill-owner and philanthropist, who presented Gandhi with Rs 13,000 to save the Sabarmati Ashram when it was threatened with collapse because of Gandhi's insistence that it should be open to untouchables as well as caste Hindus. But the Ahmedabad strike in 1918 affected a mill run by Ambalal Sarabhai, a situation further complicated by the fact that his sister, Anasuya, had sided with the workers. The mill-workers' dispute was over the loss of a bonus (worth up to 70 per cent of their wages) paid since 1916 to retain their labour at a period of high output but also of plague. The mill-owners were now replacing the bonus with a wage increase of only 20 per cent, which the workers wanted increased to at least 50 per cent. Although for the mill-owners of Ahmedabad, like many elsewhere in India, the war had brought unprecedented profits, for the poor 1917–18 was a time of deficient harvests, food shortages and economic unrest, and India's industrial proletariat, now a million strong, was hard hit by the widening gap between wages and prices. The years 1918–20 saw the first steps taken towards the establishment of trade unions for urban workers, with mill-hands among the first to be unionised. In this movement various local politicians were involved, among the most influential being Annie Besant in Madras. It is not perhaps surprising that Gandhi did not want to be left out and was keen to demonstrate the versatility of his techniques of conflict resolution, even in the kind of urban, industrial setting which seemed such anathema to him in *Hind Swaraj*. He may possibly have seen the mill-hands of Ahmedabad as peasants in another guise since many of them originated from the surrounding agricultural districts. Or perhaps he remembered Cardinal Manning and his role in resolving the dock-workers' strike during his student years in London. More likely, his personal acquaintance with two of the leading participants in the dispute, Ambalal and Anasuya Sarabhai, may have convinced him that this was precisely the kind of face-to-face situation in which his intervention might bring about a speedy, non-violent resolution.

The dispute over the wartime bonus led to a lock-out at the mills on 22 February 1918, with both the mill-owners and the government fearful that violence would shortly follow. Gandhi employed his now familiar satyagraha technique, using pledges of solidarity (like the peasants' vows in Kheda) to try to create solidarity and commitment among the workers.[29] Characteristically, Gandhi laid down certain conditions for his leadership – there was to be no violence; the strikers were forbidden from molesting any strike-breakers brought in by the owners; they were not to beg or seek alms but only to earn a living by honest labour; and they were to remain firm however long the strike lasted. As a compromise between what the owners were prepared to offer and what the workers wanted, Gandhi pressed for an increase of 35 per cent, but this failed to produce any immediate results and the resolve of the strikers began to waver when on 12 March the owners offered to take back any workers who accepted the 20 per cent increase. He was stung by the accusation that while the locked-out mill-hands were starving he was well-fed and associating with the families of mill-owners. In one of those sudden inspired moves that startled Gandhi's supporters and caught his opponents off-guard, on 15 March he decided to fast in support of the strikers' demands. Although Gandhi had fasted in South Africa for short periods in response to breaches in ashram discipline, this was the first time he had done so over a public issue and in pursuit of solidarity rather than as a form of atonement. This was an important new departure for Gandhi, and one that was to have important ramifications later in his career, but it was perhaps also indicative of his anxiety over how the strike was progressing. Gandhi was arguably out of his depth in an industrial dispute – apart from his brief involvement with mine-workers in South Africa in 1914 (when he was not centrally concerned with their work conditions or demands), he had no experience of industrial workers and only a limited under-standing of the issues involved. From having urged arbitration and negotiation, he was now, in desperation, using his own authority and his health to try to force a resolution.

This fast tipped the balance. The mill-owners capitulated three days later, on 18 March, and agreed to the 35 per cent increase rather than face the possibility of Gandhi's death and the vengeance of the striking mill-hands. Despite the rise of modern industrial capitalism, there remained in Ahmedabad a tradition of ahimsa and a desire for social harmony and the peaceful settlement of disputes. Aided by the fast, which Gandhi conceded placed the mill-owners under duress and left them no freedom in the matter, he succeeded in reminding them of the material as well as social benefits of con-ciliation and compromise. As part of the settlement the mill-owners agreed to a permanent Board of Arbitration, of which Gandhi was a member, and recognised the Ahmedabad Textile Labour Association. It is sometimes suggested that as a result of Gandhi's intervention and his encouragement of worker–employer cooperation, Ahmedabad had a less troubled history of labour relations than other major industrial centres in India, but in fact the Ahmedabad mills were hit by a series of strikes between 1919 and 1923 and again in 1935–7, though they were relatively strike-free in the late 1920s and early 1930s at a time when Bombay city experienced a number of major strikes.[30]

The Ahmedabad strike of 1918 was as important in its way as the peasant campaigns in Champaran and Kheda, though in a more negative fashion. Gandhi emerged from the dispute with the reputation for being a defender of workers' rights (much as he was seen as a champion of peasant interests) and for a decade or more thereafter groups of striking workers and trade union activists appealed to him for help and advice. But, outside Ahmedabad, Gandhi showed no further interest in industrial workers. Perhaps the antipathy he expressed to industrialisation in *Hind Swaraj* had been strengthened as a result of the strike. Certainly Gandhi gave unhelpful advice (as in the case of the Madras textile workers in March 1919, who, when they pressed Gandhi for help, were urged to give up drink and gambling, and abandon mill-work in favour of hand-spinning), or they were warned against employing what they saw as Gandhian techniques (as when strikers on the South Indian Railway in 1926 planned to lie down in front of trains in support of their demands and were curtly told by telegram 'Satyagraha unlawful in this case'). The net effect of the Ahmedabad strike was thus to confirm Gandhi in looking to the peasantry rather than to India's emerging industrial proletariat as the basis for the nationalist struggle and his determination to restrict the use of satyagraha to what he personally believed to be suitable causes and situations. In general, Gandhi seems after 1918 to have found peasants more congenial than proletarians, more compatible with his ideals and more responsive to his strategies.

. . .

A PEASANT CONGRESS?

The Non-Cooperation and Civil Disobedience Movement of 1920–2, discussed more fully in the following chapter, was not fought primarily over peasant issues, for Gandhi's aim was to bring all classes together in a united struggle against colonial rule, but their mass support was sought as the ideological and organisational bedrock for the nationalist campaign. In reality, though, as was evident in *Hind Swaraj* a dozen years earlier, Gandhi looked first to his own kind, to the middle classes, to make the necessary personal sacrifices that would bring to an end the Indian collaboration which upheld British rule and whose withdrawal would, he believed, precipitate its collapse. Holders of titles and other honours were to relinquish these marks of favour from the British, government servants were to resign from their posts, the electorate (still a small and privileged class) was to abstain from voting in elections to the provincial and central legislatures, and schools, colleges and law courts were to be boycotted, to be replaced by national educational institutions and arbitration committees. If these measures, primarily affecting the middle classes, failed to move the British to concede swaraj within a year, as promised by Gandhi in September 1920, only then would the peasants be asked (as at Kheda in 1918) to lend their support to the cause by refusing to pay their land revenue assessments. This, Gandhi believed, would bring about the virtual end of British rule and self-government for India would swiftly follow.

In fact, from the peasant perspective, the campaign followed a more erratic path. The middle classes were no more than lukewarm in their response to the Gandhian campaign – some titles and honours were returned and a not insignificant number of students boycotted schools and colleges, but, conversely, candidates were found to fill virtually all the seats in the legislatures in 1920–1 and there were few desertions from the police and army. It could be argued that such support as Gandhi's campaigns enjoyed was largely the result of the machinations of local politicians – that there was no emotionally inspired or ideologically driven nationalist movement as such but a series of local power struggles in which disaffected individuals and groups seized the opportunity to make life difficult for the British authorities or to displace Indian rivals for control of legislatures, municipalities, caste associations and other positions of profit, prestige and authority.[31] But what is most striking about the political movements of the period 1917–22 was the breadth and strength of Gandhi's appeal, especially to the peasantry, and it was this, more than any other factor, which seemed to endow his campaigns with a vitality and popularity unprecedented in the history of Indian nationalism.

As already indicated in discussing the Champaran and Kheda campaigns, a significant part of Gandhi's appeal had less to do with his own carefully reasoned and constructed programme of non-cooperation and civil disobedience, or even the ideas of freedom laid down in *Hind Swaraj*, than with perceptions of Gandhi that arose from the popular imagination. There were two dimensions to this.

The first was that Gandhi had rapidly acquired the reputation of being a holy man, a semi-divine figure, even an avatar. His career in South Africa may initially have contributed to this in places like Champaran, but of greater importance was his appearance and manner, the 'saintly idiom' evident in his simplicity of language, dress and lifestyle, his willingness to mingle with the common people and to face real hardship for the causes he espoused. This belief in Gandhi the demi-god drew many thousands of peasants to his meetings or caused them to gather in huge crowds at railway stations to catch a glimpse of him, to have his *darshan*. Gandhi's own response to the restless, milling crowds, pushing and shoving around him, or awakening him with their curiosity and clamour in the middle of the night as he passed through some remote railway station in a striking reversal of the Pietermaritzburg episode, was often one of indignation and annoyance. Unlike most of the nationalist politicians who preceded him, Gandhi had a use for the peasants, but he wanted them on his own terms, harnessed to the nationalist campaign, disciplined, orderly and obedient.[32]

This first dimension of Gandhi's appeal – the quest for *darshan* – was supplemented by a second that was even further from Gandhi's ideals and ambitions. In a largely illiterate society where rumour played a vital role in communication, reports spread rapidly in rural and small-town society that Gandhi was a saviour who would liberate the people from their misery and oppression. He became the vehicle for a host of millennarian expectations and from their own sense of powerlessness, the peasants looked to someone who seemed to promise them deliverance. 'From out of their misery and hope', Sumit Sarkar has remarked, 'varied sections of the Indian people seem to have fashioned their own images of Gandhi, particularly in the early days when he was still to most people a distant, vaguely glimpsed or heard-of tale of a holy-man with miracle-working powers.'[33] The peasants could imagine Gandhi as using his exceptional powers to end the exploitation of the *zamindars*, to stop illegal evictions, distribute free land, remove the land revenue burden, or even replace British rule with Gandhi Raj. All manner of things might be said or done in Gandhi's name, as when tea estate workers in Assam left their work en masse in May 1921, saying that they were simply obeying Gandhi's orders. As one CID report on the *kisan* (peasant) movement in the United Provinces in northern India commented in January 1921, 'The currency which Mr Gandhi's name has acquired even in the remotest villages is astonishing. No one seems to know quite who or what he is, but it is an accepted fact that what he says is so, and what he orders must be done.'[34]

Gandhi's name and presence inspired a host of rumours about his magical powers that had little to do with nationalist aspirations and ideals. This popular 'idea' of Gandhi has been discussed in fascinating detail by Shahid Amin with respect to Gorakhpur district, but his local case study can be taken as broadly representative of the kind of support Gandhi acquired across large parts especially of northern India. It is indicative of the way in which rather than Gandhi mobilising the peasants, the peasants were summoning up their own mahatma, one far removed from the real Gandhi. He visited Gorakhpur in the eastern half of the United Provinces only briefly on 8 February 1921, but, as Amin shows, his impact on the district was far greater than that fleeting encounter would suggest. Even before his arrival, stories about Gandhi's powers had begun to circulate in the countryside and to appear in the local press. Amin groups these reports together into four categories – testing the power of the Mahatma, opposing the Mahatma, opposing the Gandhian creed especially with respect to dietary, drinking and smoking taboos, and finally boons granted and/or miracles performed by the Mahatma in the form of objects lost and the magical regeneration of trees and wells.

A few examples will suffice to give the general flavour of these reports. Under the first category – testing the power of the Mahatma – was a story that a domestic servant had said that he would only believe in the authenticity of the Mahatma if the thatched roof of his house was raised. The roof rose ten cubits into the air and only returned to its original position when the servant folded his hands in submission to Gandhi. Among stories in the second category – opposing the Mahatma – were those of an individual who had called Gandhi names, as a result of which his eyelids became stuck together, and another whose ghee turned bad as a result of slandering the Mahatma. Under the third group, relating to dietary and other prohibitions (and here perhaps Gandhi's reformist views were not entirely irrelevant), Amin quotes the story about the sons of a betel-leaf seller who killed and ate a goat. Some people tried to dissuade them but they paid no heed. Later all of them started vomiting and they became very worried. 'In the end when they vowed in the name of Mahatmaji never to eat meat again their condition improved.' Finally, as an example of the fourth (or regenerative) type of story, it was reported that the well in a certain village sank so low on

27 April that not even a small drinking vessel could draw water from it. 'Seeing this, one Misrji offered to distribute Rs 5 in the name of Gandhiji. Subsequently, water began to rise slowly. By the afternoon of 28 April the well had filled up to five cubits, [and] the next day it was eleven cubits deep.'[35] While some of these stories represent an invocation of Gandhi's reputation to humble individuals seen to be arrogant, greedy or boastful, others relate to familiar aspects of rural life or to specific ideas, already widely in circulation in areas like Gorakhpur before Gandhi's visit, of the desirability of adopting or upholding caste or religious prohibitions on alcohol, meat-eating and drug-taking. Taken together, Amin concludes, 'these stories indicate how ideas about Gandhi's *pratap* [power] and the appreciation of his message derived from popular Hindu beliefs and practices and the material culture of the peasantry.'[36]

Stories of this kind, by no means unique to Gorakhpur, go a long way towards dispelling the idea that Gandhi had a unique capacity to speak for and represent the Indian peasantry. Instead they indicate the extent to which Gandhi in his early years of national leadership in India became a magnet, attracting to himself a wide, often bizarre, range of popular ideas and expectations. The converse of this was that Gandhi and his supporters were not prepared to accept the peasants on their own terms, nor did they seek to utilise and validate the peasants' own traditions of resistance and defiance. Rather they sought in their quest for Indian freedom to educate and discipline the peasants, requiring them to follow a strict path of non-violent action and class conciliation. Sacrifice, discipline and self-control were constantly urged upon them.

A striking illustration of this occurred during the *kisan* movement in the United Provinces in 1921–2. Faced with a movement largely directed against the *zamindars*, the Indian landlord class, Gandhi found it necessary to issue to the peasants a series of 'instructions' telling them how to behave. Attainment of swaraj, he told them, would be 'impossible' unless they complied. His list included the following:

We may not hurt anybody . . .
We may not loot shops.
We should influence our opponents by kindness, not by using physical force . . .
We may not withhold taxes from the government or rent from the landlord.

The peasants were further instructed:

> It should be borne in mind that we want to turn *zamindars* into friends.
> We may not stop railway trains nor forcibly enter them without tickets.
> We must abolish intoxicating drinks, drugs and other evil habits.
> We may not indulge in gambling.
> We may not tell an untruth on any account whatsoever.
> We should introduce the spinning-wheel in every home . . .

And finally, Gandhi reminded the peasants, the 'most important thing to remember is to curb anger, never to do violence and even to suffer violence done to us.'[37]

For much of 1920–1 Gandhi strove to control and direct the peasant agitations in the United Provinces and elsewhere that were threatening to pitch the Congress either into an anti-*zamindar* class war or into violent conflict with the government. In Malabar, in the southwest of India, in August 1921 poor Muslim peasants, known as Moplahs or Mappilas, rose in revolt against their high-caste Hindu landlords. There had been a long tradition of risings or 'outrages' of this kind, but this occurred on an unprecedented scale, with many thousands killed and with widespread reports of the rape and forced conversion of hundreds of Hindus. Despite the government's imposition of martial law, it took several months of bitter fighting before the conflict was finally suppressed, leaving a legacy of communal unrest and anxiety across south India.[38] Gandhi was not directly involved in the uprising, but it began to shake his faith, and that of others, in the possibility of a peaceful mobilisation of the Indian peasantry.

His attempts to bring the peasants in a more direct and controlled manner into the Non-Cooperation and Civil Disobedience Movement also proved hazardous. On 5 November 1921 the Congress Working Committee, the party's executive, gave its approval to a major escalation of the conflict by authorising the start of mass civil disobedience through a refusal to pay taxes. Gandhi agreed to initiate this move towards open defiance, but, in recognising the danger inherent in what amounted to a 'civil revolution' and 'an end of Government authority',[39] he approved such a campaign only in the Bardoli *taluk*, or sub-division, of Surat district, an area similar in its social structure and agrarian conditions to Kheda, the site of his

1918 satyagraha. Only there did he believe that peasants were suitably prepared for a non-violent, no-tax campaign, though Congressmen in the Guntur district far away in Andhra also clamoured to join them. Outbreaks of violence elsewhere in India caused Gandhi to delay the start of the Bardoli campaign until February 1922, but before it could begin in earnest on 4 February 1922 a police station at Chauri Chaura in the United Provinces was attacked by peasants, set on fire, and in the resulting conflagration twenty-three policemen were killed.

Gandhi responded to this, and a worrying number of episodes of urban violence in Bombay, Madras and elsewhere, by suspending the entire civil disobedience campaign. On 10 March 1922, he was arrested for sedition and shortly after sentenced to six years' imprisonment. The first phase of Gandhi's engagement with the peasantry, which had lasted barely five years, from 1917 to 1922, was over, even before the peasants of Bardoli had had the opportunity of putting Gandhi's faith in peasant power to the test.

. . .

NOTES AND REFERENCES

1. W. K. Hancock, *Smuts: The Sanguine Years, 1870–1919*, Cambridge, 1962, p. 345.
2. David Hardiman, *Feeding the Baniya: Peasants and Usurers in Western India*, Delhi, 1996, p. 88.
3. *CWMG* XLVIII, p. 116.
4. Martin Deming Lewis (ed.), *Gandhi: Maker of Modern India?*, Boston, 1965, pp. 5–8.
5. Charles van Onselen, *Studies in the Social and Economic History of the Witwatersrand, 1886–1914*, 2 vols, Harlow, 1982; M. K. Gandhi, *Hind Swaraj or Indian Home Rule*, Ahmedabad, 1939, p. 83.
6. Louis Dumont, *Homo Hierarchicus*, Chicago, 1979, p. 58; M. N. Srinivas and A. M. Shah, 'The Myth of Self-Sufficiency of the Indian Village', *Economic and Political Weekly*, 10 September 1960, pp. 1375–8.
7. M. K. Gandhi, *An Autobiography, Or the Story of My Experiments with Truth*, Ahmedabad, 1940, pp. 180–1.
8. Ibid., pp. 114–15, 134.
9. Judith M. Brown, *Modern India: The Origins of an Asian Democracy*, Oxford, 1985, p. 139.
10. David Arnold, *Science, Technology and Medicine in Colonial India*, Cambridge, 2000, pp. 124–8.
11. Brown, *Modern India*, pp. 160–86.

12. T. N. Jagadisan (ed.), *Letters of the Right Honourable V. S. Srinivasa Sastri*, Bombay, 1963, p. 41.
13. *CWMG* XIII, pp. 210–16.
14. Martin Green, *Gandhi: Voice of a New Age Revolution*, New York, 1993, p. 259.
15. Ibid., p. 251.
16. Sumit Sarkar, *Modern India, 1885–1947*, Basingstoke, 1989, pp. 43–60.
17. Jacques Pouchepadass, *Champaran and Gandhi: Planters, Peasants and Gandhian Politics*, New Delhi, 1999.
18. Gandhi, *Autobiography*, pp. 316–17.
19. Francis Watson, *The Trial of Mr Gandhi*, London, 1969, p. 70.
20. William L. Shirer, *Gandhi: A Memoir*, New York, 1979, p. 101.
21. Judith Brown, 'Gandhi and India's Peasants, 1917–22', *Journal of Peasant Studies*, 1 (1974), p. 469.
22. Gandhi, *Autobiography*, p. 332.
23. Judith M. Brown, *Gandhi's Rise to Power: Indian Politics, 1915–1922*, Cambridge, 1972, p. 103.
24. David Hardiman, *Peasant Nationalists of Gujarat: Kheda District, 1917–1934*, Delhi, 1981, pp. 31–45.
25. David Hardiman, 'The Crisis of the Lesser Patidars: Peasant Agitation in Kheda District, Gujarat, 1917–34', in D. A. Low (ed.), *Congress and the Raj: Facets of the Indian Struggle, 1917–47*, London, 1977, pp. 58–61.
26. Kenneth L. Gillion, *Ahmedabad: A Study in Indian Urban History*, Berkeley, 1968.
27. Mirabehn, *The Spirit's Pilgrimage*, London, 1960, pp. 90–1.
28. Howard Spodek, 'On the Origins of Gandhi's Political Methodology: The Heritage of Kathiawad and Gujarat', *Journal of Asian Studies*, 30 (1971), pp. 365–7. For other possible reasons for choosing Ahmedabad, see Green, *Gandhi*, pp. 252, 260.
29. Erik H. Erikson, *Gandhi's Truth: On the Origins of Militant Nonviolence*, London, 1970, pp. 322–63.
30. Sujata Patel, *The Making of Industrial Relations: The Ahmedabad Textile Industry, 1918–1939*, Delhi, 1987, especially Appendix I.
31. This view was particularly associated with the 'Cambridge School' in the 1970s: see especially J. Gallagher, Gordon Johnson and Anil Seal (eds), *Locality, Province and Nation: Essays on Indian Politics, 1870–1940*, Cambridge, 1973.
32. Ranajit Guha, *Dominance without Hegemony: History and Power in Colonial India*, Cambridge, Mass., 1997, pp. 135–43.
33. Sarkar, *Modern India*, p. 181.
34. Ibid., p. 182.
35. Shahid Amin, 'Gandhi as Mahatma: Gorakhpur District, Eastern U. P., 1921–2', in Ranajit Guha (ed.), *Subaltern Studies III*, Delhi, 1984, pp. 27–44.

36. Ibid., p. 48.
37. *CWMG* XIX, pp. 419–20; Gyan Pandey, 'Peasant Revolt and Indian Nationalism: The Peasant Movement in Awadh, 1919–22', in Ranajit Guha (ed.), *Subaltern Studies I*, Delhi, 1982, pp. 143–97.
38. Sarkar, *Modern India*, pp. 216–17.
39. *CWMG* XXI, p. 396.

Chapter 5

POWER TO THE NATION

Gandhi was not an Indian nationalist – or at least not conventionally or exclusively so, and one of the problems with many interpretations of his life and ideas has been precisely the attempt to force him into a narrowly nationalist mould. Informed by his experiences in London and South Africa, as well as in India itself, Gandhi took on a more complex and multi-faceted identity. At one level he was a Gujarati patriot, believing in the importance of self-expression through his mother tongue, and it is significant that both *Hind Swaraj* and the *Autobiography* were first written in Gujarati, and that during the 1920s Gandhi ran a Gujarati weekly, *Navajivan*, in addition to his English-language *Young India*. The years 1915–30, starting with establishment of the Sabarmati Ashram and culminating in his Salt March through southern Gujarat, cemented his identification with the region, its language and people. But this period, especially the years 1918–22, centring on the Rowlatt Satyagraha and Non-Cooperation and Civil Disobedience Movement, also saw Gandhi establish his credentials as a nationalist leader, striving to mobilise India-wide support for opposition to British rule. With this objective in mind, Gandhi campaigned for national solidarity, seeking to unite all classes and communities, the peasants and the middle classes, Hindus and Muslims, in the quest for swaraj, and he sought to reform the Congress as an organisation capable of achieving that goal. These years saw Gandhi at his most resolutely nationalist.

But for Gandhi nationalism was more a vehicle than an end in itself. His emphasis upon civilisation – ancient and modern – in *Hind Swaraj* and his repeated use of terms like swaraj and Ram Rajya are indicative of the extent to which Gandhi was uninterested in creating a nation state, which, while free of the British, would still retain the coercive power, the administrative structure, the divisive practices and the gross inequalities which had characterised the colonial regime. To Gandhi, utilising a theme widely articulated in Western as well as Indian writing about India in the nineteenth century and also in the West's reflections on its own achievements and identity, India was not merely a nation, but a civilisation, equal to, different from, in some ways superior to, modern Europe's. Defined by its antiquity, its rich spiritual heritage and diverse cultural identity (but within a broadly Hindu matrix), India was able through its unique message of *dharma*, ahimsa and social harmony to make a distinctive contribution to world civilisation. In seeking to transcend the insults and the oppression of the imperial order, Gandhi eschewed the narrowness of chauvinistic nationalism. He aspired to a kind of universalism that left the pettiness of political agents in Rajkot or racist bullies in Durban and Johannesburg far behind, that lifted Indian aspirations to a more dignified and honourable plane, and made even the Empire in which he had once placed such loyalty and faith appear mean and trivial by comparison. But, while Gandhi brought the uniqueness of his own personality and experiences to this aspiring universalism, he was not in this a solitary figure. Indeed, goaded by colonial denial on the one hand and sustained by a sense of India's uniqueness and world mission on the other, India in the half-century from 1890 to 1940 produced an extraordinary constellation of thinkers who, while acknowledging the achievements of the West, sought to restore India to its rightful place on the world stage – among them Swami Vivekanada, the poet Rabindranath Tagore, the scientist Jagdish Chandra Bose, and the politician-historian Jawaharlal Nehru.

But as the First World War drew to a weary close, Gandhi had still to prove his nationalist credentials. He needed to show that he could engage with politics on a national, all-India scale and that his style of leadership and his agitational techniques were of direct and practical relevance to the issues then facing India. The years 1918–22 gave him a unique opportunity to do this.

* · ·

GANDHI AND THE FIRST WORLD WAR

The First World War created unprecedented momentum for political change in India. Its human and material contribution to the British war effort was enormous, even though South Asia itself was scarcely touched by the fighting. India supplied more than a million soldiers and thousands more non-combatants: Indian troops fought (and died) in prodigious numbers in France, East Africa and the Middle East. Princes raised funds for hospital ships; industry stepped up a gear to supply ammunition, clothing and equipment for Indian and British troops; and Indian revenues contributed nearly £150 million to the imperial war effort. The Indian economy felt the strain of a severely disrupted internal transport system and steeply rising prices.[1]

It was not surprising that in these circumstances India's politicians should demand for their country a greater share in running its own internal affairs and a status comparable to that given to the white Dominions – Canada, Australia, New Zealand and, since 1910, the Union of South Africa. Although India had been granted its own legislative councils – at first at the centre in 1861 and then in the provinces from 1892 – their powers were very restricted, and this remained so even after the constitutional reforms, called the Morley-Minto reforms after the Secretary of State for India and the Viceroy of the time, in 1909. In December 1911 the Government of India partly reversed the controversial Partition of Bengal of six years earlier: Bengal was reunited but with Assam and Bihar detached to form separate provinces. It was further announced that the capital of British India was to be moved from Calcutta, seen as a hotbed of sedition, to Delhi, one-time seat of the Mughals. By the end of the war, New Delhi was beginning to rise from the dusty plain to the south of the old walled city. It was there, against a backdrop of broad avenues and gleaming buildings of pink and brown sandstone, that many of the final episodes of British rule – and Gandhi's life – were enacted.

Constitutional reform and the reunification of Bengal brought the British little respite. Demands for a greater degree of representation and self-government were voiced through the Indian National Congress, by 1915–16 with its Moderate and Extremist wings temporarily reunited, but also supported by the Muslim League, founded in December 1906 to represent Muslim interests and until the First World War even more loyalist and elitist than the Congress. After several years in which the Balkan Wars and the decline of Ottoman power had brought mounting concern, in 1914 India's Muslims were further unsettled to find their country at war with Turkey, whose Sultan, as Caliph, remained the spiritual head of Islam. In December 1916 (at the meeting where Gandhi was waylaid by Raj

Kumar Shukla and invited to Champaran) the Congress and League gathered in joint session and in the so-called 'Lucknow Pact' pressed their mutual demand for India's constitutional advance to Dominion Status. About the same time, in August-September 1916, Tilak and Besant formed their Home Rule Leagues to press for greater autonomy for India. By the end of 1917 the Leagues had 60,000 members and were making their influence felt through the press as well as on public platforms.

As the fighting dragged on inconclusively in Europe, the British government grew alarmed at the erosion of its support in India. On 20 August 1917, at a critical stage in the war on the Western Front, the Secretary of State for India, Edwin Montagu, made a seemingly momentous declaration to Parliament in which he offered India, once the war was over, a greater degree of responsibility for its own affairs and came close to promising the coveted prize of Dominion Status. His statement referred to the 'increasing association of Indians in every branch of the administration, and the gradual development of self-governing institutions, with a view to the progressive realisation of responsible government in India as an integral part of the British Empire.'[2] This did little to pacify increasingly vocal nationalist sentiment, and Annie Besant, white-haired and at 67 one of the flamboyant figures in the Home Rule movement, was briefly interned for her outspoken criticism of British rule. Constitutional reform proceeded, nevertheless, at a slow and grudging pace. In 1918 Montagu and the Viceroy, Lord Chelmsford, produced a report, which while recommending enhanced powers for the provincial legislative councils, withheld responsible government both in the provinces and at the centre. What was proposed instead, and came into force with the Government of India Act of 1919, was a system of divided government, or 'dyarchy', by which administration in the provinces was split between a 'transferred' half with Indian ministers responsible for local government, education and public health, while the key portfolios – law, the police, and revenue – remained with British or Indian members of the governor's executive council who were not directly accountable to the legislature. The governors also retained considerable powers of their own, including a right to veto legislation and restore cuts in budget grants. The hopes of rapid and substantial constitutional change, awakened by the war and the August 1917 declaration, had by 1919 largely been scuppered.

Gandhi's role in the developments was somewhat anomalous. Just as in South Africa he had organised stretcher brigades during the

Boer War and the Natal Rebellion in order to demonstrate Indian loyalty to the crown, so during his brief stay in London from August to December 1914, he planned to recruit an ambulance corps from Indians in Britain.[3] Back in India, Gandhi continued to believe that some form of collaboration with the imperial war effort was desirable. In April 1918, after attending the Viceroy's War Conference in Delhi, he undertook to assist the British in their drive to recruit more soldiers for the Indian Army. This, moreover, was at a time when recruitment had become intensely unpopular and when nationalist criticism of the British had reached unprecedented levels. He did not, in fact, have much success as a recruiter – even in Kheda, where peasants had recently feted and garlanded Gandhi, they now turned their backs on him. But this was one of several episodes in his life when his bizarre conduct is not easily explained. For a dedicated believer in non-violence to assist in sending Indian soldiers to fight, and quite likely die, far from home in the service of the imperial power, must seem inconsistent, if not hypocritical. But Gandhi did not regard himself as a pacifist in the conventional sense. He could rationalise his recruitment activities as being a demonstration, despite his own strongly held non-violent convictions, that if the British were in danger it was the duty of Indian subjects to show their loyalty by assisting the Empire in whatever way was necessary. Gandhi even presented his recent satyagrahas in Champaran and Kheda in a similar light, informing the Viceroy that, by removing any source of 'bitterness' among Indians, they made a 'direct, definite and special contribution to the war'.[4] As a gesture of love and loyalty, recruiting might not in itself expect reward, but it would surely persuade the British to view more favourably Indian demands for Home Rule. As Gandhi put it to a friend in July 1918, if he succeeded in his recruiting activities, 'genuine swaraj' was 'assured'.[5] But his stance on recruitment seems more convincingly to show how out of touch Gandhi was with India's increasingly militant mood on the one hand and British intransigence on the other. Gandhi himself appears to have become increasingly uneasy about the quixotic position he had assumed and the effects began to tell on his health, with Gandhi always a sign that he was struggling with an insoluble dilemma. In October-November 1918 Gandhi lay seriously ill, exhausted and close to a nervous breakdown.

For their part, the British and Indian governments were still unsure what to make of Gandhi. When he met him in Delhi in November 1917, Montagu, the Secretary of State for India, recorded

in his diary that Gandhi was 'a social reformer' with a 'real desire
to find grievances and to cure them, not for any reasons of self-
advertisement, but to improve the conditions of his fellow-men'.
With as much bemusement as many Indians felt, Montagu added
that Gandhi 'dresses like a coolie, forswears all personal advancement,
lives practically on air, and is a pure visionary. He does not understand details of schemes; all he wants is that we should get India
on our side.'[6] Even as late as 1919 an official publication described
Gandhi as 'a Tolstoyian of high ideals and pure selflessness. Since
his stand on behalf of the Indians in South Africa, he has commanded
among his countrymen all the traditional reverence with which the
East envelops a religious leader of acknowledged asceticism.'[7] But,
for the British, much of that ambiguity was about to end.

. . .

THE ROWLATT SATYAGRAHA

Gandhi was rescued from his dilemma – was he destined to be a
loyalist or a rebel? – by a new and bitter twist to British policy in
India. In December 1917 Justice S. A. T. Rowlatt had been appointed
by the Government of India to head a committee of enquiry into
'sedition' and 'revolutionary conspiracies' in wartime India. In its
report in April 1918 the Rowlatt Committee recommended the
continuation of existing measures to curb unrest and the introduction
of new legislation to strengthen government control after the war.
Instead of the diet of responsible government it craved, India was to
be served another helping of repression. When two bills based on
the Rowlatt report were presented to the Imperial (i.e. all-India)
Legislative Council in January-February 1919 there was bitter
opposition from Indian members led by the Moderates (or Liberals
as they had now begun to call themselves). V. S. Srinivasa Sastri
declared that if the bills were passed 'all talk of responsible government' would become 'a mockery'.[8] Only one of the bills in fact
became law, on 18 March 1919. It is ironic, in view of the intense
opposition it aroused, that even this was never used and was repealed
less than three years later.

It is perhaps no less ironic that Gandhi, the opponent of India
House terrorism, should ride to all-India prominence on the back of
a law that sought to suppress 'revolutionary conspiracies'. However,
like the 'Black Act' for Indian registration in South Africa a decade

earlier, the Rowlatt bills provided Gandhi with a specific issue around which to construct a coordinated nationwide satyagraha campaign. While other politicians hesitated, or clung to largely discredited forms of constitutional protest, Gandhi seized the opportunity to act boldly. Freeing himself from his embarrassing role as a recruiting sergeant, he announced his opposition to the Rowlatt legislation and informed the Viceroy on 24 February 1919 of his intention to resist this and other unjust laws. His first plan of action was a modest one, with volunteers courting arrest through the sale of *Hind Swaraj* and other prohibited publications. Through the Bombay-based Satyagraha Sabha Gandhi organised a 'satyagraha pledge' and attracted a substantial number of signatures, mostly in Bombay city and western India. He then decided on 23 March to extend the protest to include an all-India *hartal*, or day of protest, on 30 March. The date of action, already cautiously scheduled for a Sunday, was later postponed by a week to 6 April 1919.

Gandhi threw himself tirelessly into the campaign and though afterwards he could ask 'Who knows how it all came about?', as if it were the unprompted expression of national will, he used all his organisational and agitational skills to launch the kind of movement he had been dreaming about since he wrote *Hind Swaraj* ten years earlier.[9] The response to the Rowlatt Satyagraha was in fact patchy, but in many towns and cities the *hartal* resulted in the closure of shops, and there were processions, demonstrations and mass meetings. The countryside, to which Gandhi had given much of his attention over the previous two years, was little enthused, and although industrial workers took part in Bombay and Madras, the protest remained a largely middle-class affair. But it also, contrary to Gandhi's hopes and wishes, involved some violent clashes between demonstrators (or those members of the urban underclass the British called 'hooligans' and 'rowdies') and the police. Urban hardship resulting from high prices and shortages of food-grains, cloth and other essential commodities helped fuel the intensity of discontent and the pressures, welling up from below, on middle-class political leadership.[10]

The agitation took its most momentous form in the northern province of Punjab. Since its annexation by the British in 1849, Punjab had been a major recruiting ground for the Indian Army. By the close of the nineteenth century when the 'martial races' theory was at its height, a large percentage of the army was drawn from this one province, from the Sikhs in particular but also from Muslims and Hindus. The First World War resulted in unprecedented pressure on the province to supply yet more recruits for the army, and this along with widespread economic hardship had caused a strong undercurrent of resentment against British rule, including signs of violent opposition. The Lieutenant-Governor of the province, Sir Michael O'Dwyer, responded by imposing severe repressive measures on the province, culminating in martial law. On 13 April 1919 around 10,000 Indians gathered in Punjab's second largest city, Amritsar, in a square known as Jallianwala Bagh. Without prior warning or allowing those trapped in the enclosed square time to disperse, the commanding officer, Brigadier-General Reginald Dyer, ordered his Gurkha and Baluchi troops to open fire on the unarmed crowd, believing that this would have a suitably 'moral effect' on the city and restive Punjab. Firing continued for ten to fifteen minutes. In the resulting massacre at least 379 civilians were killed and a further 1,200 wounded: some estimates of the dead and wounded ranged far higher. The massacre sent shock waves throughout India, aroused intense anger and deep antagonism to British rule. If a single event were to be chosen as the critical turning point in the entire history of India's nationalist movement, the Jallianwala Bagh massacre would surely be it, for it revealed the intrinsic violence of British rule, a savage indifference to Indian life, and an utter contempt for nationalist feeling and peaceful protest. The situation was made even worse by other acts of humiliation and repression inflicted on Amritsar in the wake of the massacre, including a notorious 'crawling order', imposed on all Indians walking along a street where a British school mistress had earlier been attacked.[11] No less offensively, even though Dyer was forced to retire from the army for his conduct, praise was showered on him in some quarters in Britain, for having saved the empire in India, and a public gift of £26,000 was raised in a single month through the *Morning Post*. Many Indians recoiled in horror from these events. Not a few were sufficiently incensed by what had happened to abandon their education and careers and throw themselves wholeheartedly and selflessly into the nationalist cause. Caught between repression and anger, the politics of moderation no longer seemed to have a viable place.

This was not a development Gandhi could have anticipated. His initial response was to declare remorsefully that he had made a 'Himalayan miscalculation' in launching the anti-Rowlatt agitation. The violence at Amritsar and elsewhere (including Ahmedabad on 11 April) made Gandhi thereafter more wary about starting movements without having previously established adequate organ-isational support and firm ideological control. He held a three-day fast in penitence and called off the satyagraha on 18 April 1919.[12] But like police atrocities in South Africa in 1914 and on many sub-sequent occasions in India, the violent end to the Rowlatt Satyagraha also demonstrated the extraordinary upsurge of public feeling, and the accompanying moral advantage that resulted when non-violent protest met with such a blunt and brutal response. One of the pro-found ironies of Gandhi's non-violent tactics was this essential and symbiotic relationship with violence. Non-violence in a non-violent world might achieve little, but in a society ruled through sporadic violence (which yet stopped short of total repression) its impact could be immense. Whether Gandhi ever fully recognised the satyagrahi's paradoxical reliance upon violence is hard to say, but it was surely the lesson to be learned from his first all-India campaign.

The Government of India was itself greatly discomfited by the Amritsar massacre, censoring Dyer's conduct and vowing to be far more selective in future about the use of armed might and martial law in response to civil unrest. The massacre was as much a turning point for the British as it was for their nationalist adversaries, and for the next twenty years the colonial authorities tried to find ways of moderating and refining the use of force during civil disobedience movements, though without surrendering the practical necessity (as they saw it) for some degree of controlled violence by the state and the propaganda value of attributing violence, or its incitement, to the nationalist camp. The burden of responsibility for controlling nationalist agitation after April 1919 rested with the police, the courts and the jails. Apart from exceptional moments, as during the Quit India Movement of August 1942, the army was kept cautiously in reserve. In the immediate aftermath of the massacre, the Government of India set up a committee of enquiry (the Hunter Committee) to investigate the circumstances surrounding Jallianwala Bagh and related events, while the Congress dispatched its own inquiry committee, including Gandhi, Motilal Nehru and C. R. Das, to Punjab in June 1919 to investigate and present the nationalist side of the story. The Congress report, published at the end of March 1920, placed responsibility for violence in Amritsar firmly on the British. It showed, Gandhi later observed, what 'inhumanities and barbarities' the British government in India was capable of perpetrat-ing in order to maintain its power.[13] When the Hunter Committee produced its own report two months later, in May 1920, it further

fuelled nationalist anger, for it appeared to be a 'whitewash', con-
doning much of what had happened as being justified in order to
suppress 'sedition' and unrest.

To this 'Punjab wrong', which Gandhi saw mainly as a concern of
the Hindus (though many of those killed at Jallianwala Bagh had
actually been Sikhs), was added a second 'Muslim' grievance, the
Khilafat.[14] This concerned the fate of the Sultan and the holy places
of Islam following the defeat of Turkey in the First World War
and the decision of the British and French, confirmed by the Treaty
of Sèvres on 14 May 1920, to dismember what remained of the
Ottoman Empire. This was seen in India (though not elsewhere
in the Muslim world) as a threat to the position of the Caliph and
a move that was likely to put Mecca and Medina in the hands of
non-believers. A Central Khilafat Committee was formed with the
brothers Muhammad and Shaukat Ali among its leading figures. It
held its first all-India conference at Delhi in November 1919, at
which Gandhi, keen to show support for the cause, spoke in Urdu,
the language of many north Indian Muslims. Once it became clear
what the Allies' objectives were, the Khilafat leadership demanded the
restoration of the Caliph and guarantees that the status of Mecca and
Medina would be fully protected, and it called on the Government
of India to implement these demands. Already from his South African
days an advocate for Hindu-Muslim cooperation, Gandhi saw the
opportunity to drive this essentially Muslim agitation in tandem with
the outcry over the Jallianwala Bagh massacre and Hunter Report,
as the dual basis for a new nationwide movement. His aim was to
seek redress for these 'wrongs', but, if no redress were forthcoming,
to use Indian discontent to wrest swaraj from the British, though not
until September 1920 was this wider objective made entirely clear.

Gandhi's decision to align himself with the Khilafat movement
remains one of the most controversial of his career. It can be seen as
a 'clever manoeuvre',[15] for it gave Gandhi an organisational base
and a much-publicised cause at a time when his standing within the
Congress was still weak. It might also be seen as Gandhi's attempt,
in the wake of Jallianwala Bagh, to curb the violent impulses of some
Khilafat leaders, who saw the movement as a kind of *jihad* or religious
war, and to steer it, through the adoption of his non-violent non-
cooperation programme by the Central Khilafat Committee in May
1920, towards calmer, more controllable waters. As Gandhi remarked
earlier that year, he would 'co-operate wholeheartedly with the
Muslim friends in the prosecution of their just demands', so long as

he felt sure that 'they do not wish to resort to or countenance violence'.[16] But Gandhi's espousal of the Khilafat cause has also been seen as 'bizarre',[17] a 'unity born of expediency',[18] a 'cynical' transaction and an 'opportunist' move designed purely to capture support and ultimately win the Congress leadership for himself. The Khilafat was not an issue that caused concern to most non-Muslims and, by emphasising the primary loyalty of Muslims in South Asia to the world of Islam, it implicitly challenged their identification with Indian nationalism and gave legitimacy to their 'separatist' interests. It was at best a high-risk strategy, and in retrospect can be seen as a moment when Gandhi gave a prominence to distinctively Muslim demands that he might later, in the light of the demand for India's partition and the creation of a separate Muslim state of Pakistan, have deeply regretted.

But at the time it was a stunningly successful move, one which captured the restless, uncertain mood of India and the widespread disenchantment not only with the British but also with the timid responses of moderate nationalists. Gandhi was helped in this by Besant's waning popularity and the more cautious stance of 'responsive cooperation' proposed by Tilak. The latter's death in July 1920, along with that of Gokhale in 1915, created new opportunities for Gandhi to push himself into the national limelight and to devise a militant middle way in Indian politics between the old Extremist and Moderate camps. Recovering with remarkable resilience from his near-collapse in November 1918 and the 'Himalayan miscalculation' of April 1919, Gandhi in 1920 became 'a whirlwind of energy'. In mid-1919 he had taken up editorship of two weekly journals, *Young India* and *Navajivan*, and used them to great effect to advance his views. In April 1920 he was elected President of the All-India Home Rule League, and in early September that year, at a special session of the Congress at Calcutta, aided by his Congress and Khilafatist supporters, he overcame staunch opposition to carry a decisive vote in favour of his programme of non-cooperation. This success was confirmed by resolutions passed at the annual Congress session at Nagpur in central India in late December. Significantly, Gandhi owed his victory not just to his own allies and followers but also to the endorsement of a more moderate group of Congressmen, led by C. R. Das of Bengal and Motilal Nehru of Allahabad, who recognised the impatient mood of the time, the wide popularity Gandhi had acquired, and the lack of any viable alternative strategy. Gandhi had a programme for action and a proven capacity for leadership. Others did not. The more moderate Congressmen were prepared, for the present at least, to give Gandhi his head.[19]

. . .

CONGRESS REORGANISATION

The two sessions at Calcutta and Nagpur gave Gandhi strategic control of the Indian National Congress for the first time, though he himself did not become president (a post he only held once, in 1925). This is a significant indication of how for Gandhi power lay not in holding high office, whether in the party or in government, but in the exercise of effective influence and policy-making. One of the keys to Gandhi's power was his ability to work from behind the scenes or to use his moral authority in a personal capacity, free from the trammels of formal party and state structures. Gandhi's was never a conventional 'profile in power' even in the years when his authority was at its height.

At the Nagpur Congress in December 1920 Gandhi set about re-organising the Congress which, despite many changes over the years, had retained some of the characteristics of the elite organisation set up in 1885. Leadership of the party was strengthened through the creation of a fifteen-member executive, the Congress Working Committee, elected annually (like the President), and intended to give day-to-day direction to the party, bring discipline to the organisation, and 'watch and guide public opinion'. The CWC supplemented the role of the All-India Congress Committee (AICC), founded several years earlier, but expanded as part of the Gandhian reforms from 181 to 350 members. This served as a parliament of regionally elected representatives, debating key issues, representing the views of the local Congress constituencies, and assisting in the overall direction of party affairs. Beneath this the party was reorganised into twenty-one Provincial Congress Committees (PCCs) along the lines of India's linguistic areas rather than the British provinces, which for historical and administrative reasons cut arbitrarily across linguistic boundaries. Thus within the Madras Presidency, where a separate Telugu or Andhra PCC had already been created in response to linguistic pressures, the old Madras PCC was scrapped and replaced by new PCCs for the Tamil, Kannada and Malayalam districts. The Bombay Presidency was similarly divided up between the provincial committees for Gujarat, Maharashtra and Karnataka, though the status of Bombay city, divided between Gujarati and Marathi speakers, remained a source of contention (as did Madras city between Tamil and Telugu Congressmen).

Despite his belief in the use of India's vernacular languages, Gandhi's support for linguistic provinces was by no means automatic, and might rather be taken as another example of his pragmatism. His overriding concern was the adoption of Hindi (or Hindustani) as the national language of India, which became approved Congress policy at this time. The argument for running the PCCs on a linguistic basis was that this would give greater cohesion to regional party organisations, allowing them to conduct their business in the vernacular and thereby facilitating mass involvement. In a country where barely 1 per cent of the population spoke English, this carried the Congress further away from the old political elites, especially the Moderates and Liberals, with their Gladstonian philosophy and English eloquence, who were left increasingly marooned by the rising tide of the Gandhian Congress.

Beneath the PCCs was a hierarchy of committees, for the districts (DCCs) and, below them, for the *taluks* or sub-districts, and below these in turn at the level of individual towns and even villages. This ensured that the Congress became a kind of parallel government, reaching like the British Raj itself in one unbroken line of command from the all-India level down to the towns and districts, though it was also intended to provide, unlike the Raj, a democratic system through the election of Congress members from the villages upward to the PCC and from there to the President and AICC. A further gesture toward the democratisation of the party was Gandhi's introduction of an annual membership fee of only four annas (a quarter of a rupee) on the grounds that this was within the reach of even the poorest: Gandhi had come a long way from the £3 annual fee for members of the Natal Indian Congress twenty years earlier. In a further departure from the earlier politics of petitions and deputations, the London-based British Committee of the Congress, formed in 1889 to generate interest and woo public opinion there, was abolished in 1920, thus making India appear even more emphatically the court in which its own future would be decided.

The extent to which these reforms and the accompanying shifts in the Congress programme actually transformed the Congress from an elite organisation to a mass, or peasant, party remains a matter of controversy. Gandhi himself believed that a radical change had come about, if not in 1920, then over the course of the years that followed, referring in 1931 to the Congress as 'essentially a peasant organisation'. Gopal Krishna has argued that there was a significant shift in the character and composition of the Congress under Gandhi. In 1918 the Congress had some kind of organisation in roughly half the districts of British India, but by 1921 there were 213 DCCs, covering almost the entire country. The number of delegates attending Congress sessions sharply increased, with hitherto-backward 'provinces' like Gujarat and Bihar gaining representation at the expense of the old Presidency elites. There was, too, some widening of the social composition of Congress, though the bulk of its membership continued, Krishna notes, to be recruited 'from the upper strata of Indian society'.[20] In April 1921 the AICC set the party the ambitious goal of recruiting 10 million members by the end of June, at a time when the total population of British India stood at 330 million. Figures suggest that close to 2 million party members were enrolled by the end of 1921, though this does not reflect the full extent of popular involvement at the height of the Non-Cooperation Movement. The rapid increase in party membership was matched by a greatly improved financial situation. In April 1921 the AICC also resolved to collect Rs 10 million for the Tilak Swarajya Fund. As Krishna observes, Gandhi was 'something of a genius in collecting money',[21] and he helped lift the Congress from near penury (the AICC had only Rs 43,000 at its disposal in 1920) to an estimated income between 1921 and 1923 of Rs 13 million, nearly half of which came from Bombay city and Gujarat alone. Although this high level of income could not be sustained in subsequent years, it made it possible for the Congress under Gandhi to expand its activities on an unprecedented scale. Overall, Gandhi can be seen as laying the foundations for the Congress as a mass party, endowing it, through its nationwide organisation, its financial resources and its popular membership, with sufficient strength and authority to challenge the power of India's colonial regime.

And yet it would seem that Gandhi's reorganisation and reorientation of the Congress in 1920–2 provided the blueprint for a mass organisation rather than its actual realisation. Not until the 1930s, especially the late 1930s, did the framework of district and *taluk* organisations become anything like complete across British India or acquire effective, year-on-year continuity. It remained even then largely absent or ineffective in the princely states that covered a third of India. Although many of the old Congress leaders disappeared, through death or retirement, from active politics, or shuffled across into the Liberal Party (formed by T. B. Sapru and M. R. Jayakar in 1918), leadership within the Congress, whether at national, provincial, or even district level, tended to remain with the higher castes, and often, as formerly, with members of the professional and commercial middle classes. Among Gandhi's immediate entourage in the interwar years there were few men of peasant origin: even Vallabhbhai Patel, for all his Patidar origins and rather rustic manner, had (until he fell under Gandhi's sway in 1918) been a lawyer and an associate of Ahmedabad's mill-owners and businessmen. Not until the late 1930s was a significant peasant presence apparent in the composition of Congress committees and leadership at district and provincial level. Even then it tended to be from middle and rich peasants of the Patidar type.

. . .

NON-COOPERATION AND CIVIL DISOBEDIENCE

The programme advanced by Gandhi in 1920 and adopted by the Congress at Calcutta and Nagpur involved an ascending scale of measures that were intended to put increasing pressure on the government and, ultimately, paralyse British rule in India. The initial stage was one of boycotts. Indians were called on to withdraw from all aspects of their cooperation with the British – to renounce any titles or honours they held from the British, to boycott and destroy foreign cloth, leave government schools and colleges and set up 'national' educational institutions instead, abandon the law courts in favour of arbitration councils, and to boycott the elections to the new legislatures created under the 1919 Government of India Act. A further stage was to ask government servants to resign from their posts, and, from October 1921, to ask Indians to leave the police and the army. Finally, if these measures failed to secure redress for the Punjab and Khilafat 'wrongs', there would be mass civil disobedience, with open defiance of the law and a refusal to pay government revenue or taxes. At this point, it was anticipated, the British would either have to concede Indian demands or swaraj would already, in effect, have come into being.

For Gandhi non-cooperation was not only a practical political programme but a moral crusade, a means by which Indians could purify themselves from the corrupting taint of a foreign rule he now decried as 'Satanic'. For the middle classes it meant giving up those sources of profit and status acquired under the Raj, as well as many of those privileges and indulgences which had helped foster inequality and selfishness among Indians. In a symbolic rejection of his own loyalist past, in August 1920 he returned the Kaiser-i-Hind medal he had received five years earlier for his humanitarian work in South Africa. But even though the initial burden of non-cooperation fell most heavily on the middle classes, Gandhi's message was intended to reach out to other classes as well: they, too, were to exercise self-denial and self-restraint – by giving up alcohol and intoxicating drugs, by spinning and wearing khadi, by striving for Hindu-Muslim unity and the removal of untouchability. For Gandhi non-cooperation was about having the courage to defy the British and recognising the power that defiance could bring. 'How is it', Gandhi asked in October 1920, 'that a mere lakh [100,000] of whitemen are able to lord it over thirty-three crore [330 million] of Indians?' The answer, echoing *Hind Swaraj*, was that 'we have become slaves, even mentally'. If Indians were to tell them 'we are not going to remain your slaves any longer', the British 'would either leave the country or stay on as its servants'. Gandhi's rhetoric in these years constantly highlighted two themes – the 'slavery' of foreign rule on the one hand and, to a degree startling in an apostle of ahimsa, a language of armies, campaigns, and fighting on the other.[22] In order to free themselves from 'slavery', Gandhi reasoned, Indians needed to summon up their physical bravery as well as moral courage. While strictly adhering to non-violence, they must show, like Arjuna in the *Gita*, the true spirit of the Kshatriya.[23]

Gandhi threw himself into the movement with extraordinary energy, touring India by train and car from Assam to Tamilnadu, making countless speeches (sometimes several a day), writing and revising articles for *Young India* and *Navajivan*, collecting money for the Tilak Swarajya Fund, participating in Congress and Khilafat committee meetings at dozens of towns and cities across India, making occasional visits to Sabarmati Ashram, and all the while maintaining a voluminous correspondence and trading ideas and information with a large number of friends, colleagues and sceptics, in India and abroad. His charismatic energy and zeal were infectious and drew to him a coterie of dedicated followers, many of whom remained close companions and co-workers for years thereafter. His tours demonstrated wide support, even adulation, for Gandhi himself. His secretary, Krishnadas, was amazed to discover in August 1921 during

Gandhi's journey through Assam, one of the most politically backward of India's provinces, how 'Mahatmaji's name' had penetrated into the remotest parts. 'Even in the depth of the night, we could hear cries of *Mahatma Gandhi ki jai* (Victory to Mahatma Gandhi) at every station where the train had to stop.' At many small stations 'we saw people assembled from distant villages, and waiting with lighted torches for Mahatmaji's darshan.'[24]

Nonetheless, despite the nationalist fervour he helped arouse and the unprecedented scale of the movement he presided over, the impact of Gandhi's programme was mixed and momentum slow to build. Although the all-India nature of the movement was one of its most striking features, some regions, especially those that had pioneered the nationalist movement before Gandhi, notably Bengal, Maharashtra and Madras, resented the loss of their former pre-eminence or joined with no more than lukewarm enthusiasm in some of Gandhi's most idiosyncratic causes, such as hand-spinning. By March 1921 only 24 title-holders (out of more than 5,000) had surrendered their honours and 180 lawyers had given up their practices. Candidates stood for all but six of the 637 seats in the legislative council and assembly elections in November 1920, and though polling was low in many places, such as Bombay city and Lahore in Punjab, this could not prevent the new legislatures coming into being or Indian minsters taking office under the new constitution. Non-cooperation thus failed in one of its primary objectives – to prevent the provincial governments from working and claiming a measure of popular support. One of Gandhi's continuing difficulties over the next twenty years was to find a way to undermine the appeal of constitutional politics and in this he was never more than partly successful. Likewise, attempts to seduce Indian policemen and soldiers from the service of the British almost entirely failed, and this was one of the most important reasons why the movement ultimately collapsed and the British position remained, for the present, relatively strong. It would take a further twenty years of nationalist pressure, and the very different circumstances of the Second World War, for this 'loyalty' to be seriously eroded.

Arbitration courts proved popular in some areas – 866 were set up in Bengal alone between February 1921 and April 1922. The educational boycott, too, attracted support, in part because of the strength of Gandhi's personal appeal to students and teachers alike. By early 1922 an estimated 100,000 students had left government colleges and enrolled in national colleges, though many of these did not long survive the collapse of the Non-Cooperation Movement later that year. The economic boycott, backed by the picketing of foreign-cloth shops and controversial bonfires of non-swadeshi clothing, had even greater effect, as the value of imports of foreign cloth nearly halved between 1920–1 and 1921–2. Prohibition and the picketing of drink-shops, not part of the original non-cooperation programme, also commanded widespread support, partly because they appealed to the desire of some religious and caste leaders to improve their community's social status by abstaining from drink. The anti-liquor campaign had an adverse effect on revenues in several provinces and both the loss of income and the friction caused by aggressive picketing were among the provincial governments' main causes for concern. On the other hand, despite continuing labour unrest during 1921, Gandhi ruled that industrial strikes did not fall within his programme, and, as we saw previously, he, along with other Congress leaders such as Jawaharlal Nehru, sought to harness the peasant movement, especially in the United Provinces, to the nationalist cause and to prevent it from becoming more militant and anti-landlord. Gandhi was also unwilling to support the informal 'forest satyagrahas' that sprang up among peasants in parts of Andhra and Bengal, aggrieved by restrictions on the use of government-owned forests for the collection of fuel and the grazing of animals.[25]

As the campaign grew in intensity in the second half of 1921, many thousands of Indians were prepared to court imprisonment for the nationalist cause, making 'jail-going' one of the principal and most publicised weapons of the nationalist struggle. In the course of 1921 and the early months of 1922, there were some 17,000 convictions for offences relating to the Non-Cooperation and Khilafat movements. Given Gandhi's own ordeal in South African jails, repeated by many thousands of mainly middle-class protestors in 1920–2, this was a remarkable demonstration of public commitment. It was also a source of alarm to the government, which found its jails filled to overflowing, but it remained mindful after the debacle of Jallianwala Bagh of the need to avoid using armed force and 'excessive' violence against peaceful protestors. While Gandhi commanded a significant degree of support among the middle classes – the professionals, intellectuals and students, as well as sections of the commercial and business classes – too few of them were prepared to make the degree of sacrifice he demanded from them if the campaign of non-cooperation and civil disobedience were really to bear fruit. Gandhi's promise made in September 1920 of swaraj in one year, however inspiring a battle-cry, was utterly unrealistic, even allowing for a loose interpretation of what the term actually meant. It was all very well to look to the middle classes for support, and in many ways they were the natural home for his kind of nationalism, but the sacrifices demanded from them – to give up livelihood and career, to face repeated fines and imprisonment – in the uncertain hope of freedom were increasingly difficult to satisfy or sustain.

Many of these mounting anxieties were expressed in the middle months of 1921 by Rabindranath Tagore, the man who had first hailed Gandhi as a 'Mahatma', with whom he shared a number of English friends (notably C. F. Andrews), and whose national educational establishment at Shantiniketan had given shelter to some of Gandhi's followers on their arrival from South Africa in 1915. In some respects conflict between the two appeared inevitable. 'No two persons could probably differ so much as Gandhi and Tagore,' Jawaharlal Nehru once remarked. Tagore, Bengali Brahmin, poet and novelist, artist and thinker, with his long beard and flowing robes, stood in evident contrast to Gandhi, the Gujarati Bania, the ascetic and man of action, clothed only in a loin cloth.[26] And yet, they were not so dissimilar – in their adherence to Indian nationalism and their search for a wider universalism that would unite the best in the civilisations of East and West. Tagore had nationalist credentials of his own and in May 1919, in the wake of the Jallianwala Bagh massacre, had repudiated his knighthood. But Tagore had also seen from the experience of the Swadeshi Movement of 1905–8 in Bengal how nationalist activism, inspired by a millennial dream of revolution, could demand great sacrifice but yield no result apart from incipient anarchy and the wasteful destruction of individual lives and livelihoods.

In an article published in May 1921, Tagore accused Gandhi of educational nihilism in calling for a boycott of government schools and colleges before there were enough national institutions to replace them, and he expressed alarm that Gandhi's apparent rejection of the West would lead to a narrowly chauvinistic nationalism, whereas he was striving for better understanding between East and West. In reasserting his claim to the high moral ground of civilisation, and not merely the politics of nationalism, Gandhi replied that he and his movement had been misunderstood: non-cooperation would not erect a barrier between East and West but create genuine respect and trust. 'The present struggle', he wrote, returning to a now familiar theme, was being waged against 'compulsory co-operation' and 'the armed imposition of modern methods of exploitation, masquerading under the name of civilisation.' The British had made Indians into clerks and interpreters and built their prestige upon 'the apparently voluntary association of the governed'. 'And if we were wrong to cooperate with the Government in keeping us slaves, we were bound to begin with those institutions in which associations appeared to be most voluntary.'[27]

In his reply Tagore again honoured Gandhi as the 'Mahatma' who 'stood at the cottage door of the destitute millions, clad as one of themselves, and talking to them in their own language.' And yet, while recognising Gandhi's honesty and integrity ('Here was the truth at last, not a mere quotation out of a book'), Tagore, reflecting patrician unease at Gandhi's unruly populist following, deplored the new spirit of compulsion and persecution non-cooperation had set in train, unleashing a new despotism of its own. Those who doubted or disagreed with it were harshly dealt with by Gandhi's followers, while the vagueness of the promised swaraj added further 'mischief'. It would take time and patience, study and thought to build India's freedom, not 'magical formulas' like burning foreign cloth or spinning. 'Mind', Tagore declared, 'is no less valuable than cotton thread,' and India, rather than closing in on itself, must respond to encouraging signs of what he hailed as a new 'universal humanity'. Gandhi would not accept this. Calling Tagore 'the Great Sentinel', he stressed in his reply in October 1921 the paramount needs of India's poor, the starving masses who cried out for food, not poetry. Besides, he argued, non-cooperation, non-violence and swadeshi were not for India alone, but 'a message to the world', a rallying-cry against greed and exploitation around the globe. 'A drowning man cannot save others. In order to be fit to save others, we must try to save ourselves. . . . India must learn to live before she can aspire to die for humanity.'[28]

The debate between the two men, interrupted by Gandhi's imprisonment in 1922, rumbled on for many years, almost until Tagore's death in 1941. In the short term Gandhi held the advantage, seizing the opportunity to parade his credentials as a man of the people, while making Tagore appear elitist, a dreamy poet and privileged intellectual out of touch with the desperate needs of the starving poor and the urgent mood of nationalist fervour. But Tagore was arguably the best critic Gandhi ever had, and his fears about the direction in which the Non-Cooperation Movement was going were increasingly echoed by others across the political spectrum as Gandhi's campaign became more desperate for results and as the threat of violence grew. The Malabar Rebellion broke out in late August 1921 and involved a protracted guerilla war against Indian and British troops. Armed gangs of Mappilas, estimated to number 10,000, held control of the southern *taluks* of Ernad and Walluvanad for several months. With the reported slaying of 600 Hindus and the forced conversion of 2,500 others, the rebellion stoked fears throughout south India that the Khilafat and Non-Cooperation movements were getting out of hand and would end in a communal bloodbath.[29] Added to this in November 1921 there were several outbreaks of urban violence and rioting, sparked by *hartals* and demonstrations against the visit to India of the Prince of Wales. Disturbances in Bombay city on 17–18 November, involving Hindus, Muslims and Parsis, left 58 people dead and 381 wounded. In more than one hundred and thirty separate incidents, individuals were attacked, policemen injured, liquor shops destroyed and cars and trams damaged. Gandhi did what he could to quell these outbreaks, touring the riot-torn areas of the city, talking to community leaders, issuing appeals and, in one of his first uses of this technique for political purposes, fasting for five days to try to restore calm. But he chose, for the present, to regard these disturbances as an insufficient reason to call off the movement.[30] By late 1921 it was perched at its most critical phase: would Gandhi authorise the move to mass civil disobedience that might either undermine British rule or, as his critics feared, pitch India into anarchy?

The pressure of non-cooperation and the threat of civil disobedience was also starting to tell on the Government of India. It had long been uncertain how to proceed against Gandhi, preferring to deflect attention away from him by showing support for the fledging ministries and legislatures in the provinces, or to focus on the violence that Gandhi, for all his peaceful intentions, had aroused in the cities and in the countryside. It was anxious not to deport or intern him and so make a martyr of the Mahatma. But in October 1921, fearing the further loss of its authority and prestige, the government embarked on a more aggressive policy, with mass arrests, the banning of Congress and Khilafat meetings and the outlawing of their 'volunteer' organisations. This, however, merely intensified the conflict and alienated the government's Liberal supporters, alarmed at the rising tide of state repression. By the end of the year India seemed to be 'on the brink of immensely variegated, disorganised, but formidable revolt'.[31] In mid-December the Viceroy, Lord Reading, discussed with the Secretary of State, Montagu, a series of possible measures – the release of political prisoners, an early revision of the 1919 constitution, or the calling of a round table conference involving Indian politicians of all parties – to defuse the crisis, but the British Government in London was as loath to compromise as Gandhi was to forgo his experiment with mass civil disobedience. (He and his viceregal adversary were to manage matters very differently ten years later at the time of the Gandhi-Irwin Pact.) The moment for compromise and negotiation passed and the Government of India pressed on with its policy of repression. This helped turn the tide against Gandhi, and his rather desperate bid to launch the peasant no-tax campaign in Bardoli, coupled with the violence at the north Indian market town of Chauri Chaura on 4 February, in which the local police station was set on fire and twenty-three policemen were killed,[32] finally precipitated the collapse of the movement. Only now did the government feel safe to act against Gandhi personally. His arrest and imprisonment quickly followed.

What did emerge from the Non-Cooperation and Civil Disobedience Movement of 1920–2 was a recognition that swaraj, however defined, could not be won in a single year. In 1920 Gandhi had promised 'a fight to the finish', but British rule had not collapsed, the police and army remained intact, the legislatures still functioned, and though support for the government among the middle classes and the peasantry had undoubtedly wavered, it had not disintegrated as Gandhi had anticipated. Instead, it became clear over the following years that the value of his agitation campaigns was that they cumulatively eroded support for the British and their legitimacy as rulers in the eyes of many Indians, and this year by year steadily reduced the British capacity for negotiation and manoeuvre. In the end, British rule suffered a slow but debilitating haemorrhage, as moral authority leaked away from the British to the increasing benefit of Indian nationalists and politicians of other persuasions. There was no sudden death, and Gandhi's tactics proved, in the end, an effective way of applying pressure, of winning some concessions and political advantages, and then, as the momentum of protest waned, it was necessary to suspend the agitation and wait five years or so for agitational pressures to build again.

Swaraj could not be won, against so formidable an adversary and by non-violent means, in a single campaign, but only through several episodes of sporadic struggle. The other outcome was the tacit recognition that, despite Gandhi's basic antipathy to ballot boxes, council chambers and constitutions, the trough between each wave of agitation had to be filled by experiments in more moderate political activity, building on the concessions won by the Gandhians or, by showing their hollowness, helping to fuel the next wave of agitational warfare. This symbiotic relationship between satyagraha and constitutionalism (and even, at the opposite end of the political spectrum, terrorism) may not have been to Gandhi's liking and did not fit well with the dogmatic ideology of *Hind Swaraj*, but it was the manner in which India's advance to freedom in fact proceeded and in which nationalist leaders eventually made the transition from prison to political power.

. . .

KHADI AND THE
CONSTRUCTIVE PROGRAMME

Civil disobedience was not, however, Gandhi's only weapon. Shortly before his arrest and imprisonment, the Congress Working Committee met at Bardoli on 12 February 1922 and agreed to suspend the civil disobedience campaign, replacing it with the 'Constructive Programme'. This drew together various items of the social and economic reform programme Gandhi had developed since his later years in South Africa, and especially since the Champaran campaign of 1917. It included Hindu-Muslim unity, the spread of 'national' schools and colleges, spinning and the making of homespun cloth (khadi), the promotion of temperance, the removal of untouchability, and sanitary reform. In part this was intended as a practical reform programme – to uplift, educate and promote the self-sufficiency of India's rural population, and thus to move the often miserable reality of India's villages closer to Gandhi's ideals of self-reliance, dignified toil and social harmony. But it was also a programme rich in national symbolism and the assertion of cultural independence from colonial rule.

Particularly emblematic was Gandhi's belief in spinning and khadi. Gandhi saw the decline of the indigenous textile industry, one of the ancient glories of India, as a symptom of the nation's tragic decline under British rule and a clear illustration of the evils of the machine age. At the time of his trial in February 1922, Gandhi claimed that before the British, 'India spun and wove in her millions of cottages', and that this provided 'just the supplement for adding to her meagre resources'. But this cottage industry, 'so vital for India's existence', had been ruined by 'incredibly heartless and inhuman processes', leaving the 'semi-starved masses of India' to sink 'slowly . . . into lifelessness'.[33] It was poverty and hunger, Gandhi told Tagore in October 1921, that was 'driving India to the spinning-wheel'. This was not faddism. The spinning-wheel 'was the reviving draught for the millions of our dying countrymen and country-women'.[34] Even though he had not even seen a spinning-wheel when he wrote *Hind Swaraj*, Gandhi believed that rural India could only be revital-ised by re-establishing spinning and weaving in its villages. Khadi would restore villagers' pride and rescue them from their 'enforced idleness'; it would recreate the self-sufficiency of rural India. Khadi and the spinning wheel, or *charkha*, were powerful symbols of India's capacity to regain control of its own economy and sever the imperial connection. If the principal reason for British involvement in India was economic, then the loss of Lancashire's textile trade through the spread of khadi and the boycott of foreign cloth would surely convince Britain that India was no longer worth keeping. Further-more, plying the *charkha* was noble toil – by contrast with the dehumanising effects of mill production. 'A plea for the spinning wheel', he wrote, echoing Ruskin, 'is a plea for recognising the dignity of labour.'[35]

In theory, the spinning-wheel and khadi were intended to be of practical benefit to India's villagers. In reality, their impact on the villages and the lives of most peasants was negligible, an indication of how Gandhi sometimes made a fetish of symbols at the expense of measures that might promote real change. Of greater significance than any material impact was the political importance of khadi and the spinning-wheel. They symbolised identification not just with the poor of India but with Gandhi himself. Following his victories at the Calcutta and Nagpur Congress sessions of 1920, Gandhi stepped up the party's commitment to the *charkha* and khadi. At the AICC meting at Vijayawada (Bezwada) on 31 March and 1 April 1921, it was resolved that, alongside recruiting 10 million party members and raising 10 million rupees for the Tilak Swarajya Fund, 2 million spinning-wheels should be in operation by 30 June. And each time the decision to launch civil disobedience was postponed by the AICC and CWC, the appeal to spin, boycott foreign cloth and adopt khadi was augmented and repeated. The party's commitment to this programme was indicative of the extraordinary personal authority Gandhi now enjoyed over the Congress, but it was something of Pyrrhic victory, for many Congressmen spun only out of loyalty to Gandhi and not from any conviction that it would either aid the peasants or hasten swaraj. And, if spinning and khadi-wearing became the criteria by which loyalty to the Gandhian cause came to be judged, so denunciation of the 'cult of the *charkha*' equally became, as for Tagore in 1921, one of the principal criticisms of Gandhi's leadership and ideology.

For his part, Gandhi grew impatient at the slow pace at which khadi was taken up. In a moment of apparent desperation, in September 1921, in the southern city of Madurai, he took the final step in his personal journey towards bodily decolonisation, begun a decade and a half earlier in South Africa. To the dismay of some of his followers (especially some Muslims who regarded such semi-nakedness as an affront to their religion), he adopted the loin cloth that thereafter became a familiar and integral part of his public – and saintly – image. He did so in part as a symbol of his commitment to the poor, but more especially as a personal penance to atone for the slow progress khadi was making among the Indian people.[36]

Despite the intense boycott of foreign cloth in 1920–2, khadi was never able to compete economically with mill-cloth (increasingly the product of Indian, not British, factories). It was often crudely made, heavy and awkward to wear, and harder to keep clean than machine-made cloth. But to Gandhi the economic argument was never the sole reason for the adoption of khadi. In his eyes, it taught the middle classes the virtues of humility, the dignity of labour and the value of limiting one's material needs; it likewise instructed the masses in discipline and self-restraint and, by devotion to the wheel, weaned them away from violence.

The *charkha*, he believed, was a means of promoting national solidarity and building a society free of class and caste divisions. The high caste and the untouchable could alike spin and wear khadi. Hand-made cloth could be spun, woven and worn by Muslims, Christians, Hindus and Sikhs without affront to their religion; it could clothe women as well as men. In actuality, though, spinning was traditionally women's work and one of its virtues for Gandhi was that it kept women busy and in the home rather than allowing them to seek work in the satanic mills. It was, as we will see in Chapter 7, part of his philosophy to encourage identification with what were conventionally thought of as female roles and virtues, and thereby to counter and subvert the aggressive masculinity of colonial rule. The quiet patience and nimbleness of finger spinning required were precisely the kinds of feminine attributes that Gandhi wanted Indian men to learn from their womenfolk.

Khadi was of symbolic value in other ways, too. It was indigenous, in contrast to the fashion for foreign cloth, and it was cheap (though not as cheap as some varieties of mass produced mill-cloth). It was plain to the point of austerity; its whiteness and simplicity were symbols of purity and honour. For Gandhi, it was a 'sin to wear foreign cloth', which should be consigned to the purifying flames of the bonfire. 'In burning my foreign clothes', he told Tagore, 'I burn my shame.'[37]

Khadi thus represented a further stage in the rejection of Westernised, middle-class luxury, pride and indulgence. It was simultaneously a badge of defiance, 'the livery of our freedom' as Nehru dubbed it, a visible and open means of identifying with the nationalist cause which the British would find hard to suppress (though they did try intermittently to quash the wearing of the 'Gandhi caps', the cheap, classless khadi forage caps devised by Gandhi and worn by nationalist youths and politicians).[38] Once the civil disobedience movement had collapsed, khadi assumed additional importance, for it could be used as a source of income and means of employment for party activists who had given up school, college and profession to follow Gandhi. It allowed one wing of the nationalist movement to remain openly active at times when the Congress party itself was outlawed and its property confiscated. After his release from prison, in September 1925, Gandhi established the All-India Spinners' Association as a branch of the Congress. By the end of 1926, it claimed more than 40,000 spinners and 3,400 weavers based in 150 centres across the country.

But the Constructive Programme was partly devised in recognition that the Congress was not in itself an adequate vehicle for Gandhi's wide-ranging anti-colonial ambitions. The Congress duly represented the political arm of the nationalist movement, but not the broader 'civilising' objectives Gandhi had in mind. While he strove to overhaul the party organisation and give it a mass base, he looked to other means by which to implement his plans for social reform and the revitalisation of the Indian peasantry. In some ways, the Congress was too like the Raj itself, a vehicle for the vain, the ambitious, the power-seekers. Gandhi obligingly served a term as Congress President in 1925 after his release from prison, but holding high party office was not central to the kind of power he sought to exercise. 'Whatever special qualities I may possess', he observed in August

1929 in declining the Congress presidency in favour of Jawaharlal Nehru, 'I shall be able to exercise more effectively by remaining detached from and untrammelled by, than by holding, office.' So long as he retained 'the affection and confidence of our people', he went on, there was 'not the slightest danger of my not being able without holding office to make the fullest use of such powers as I may possess.'[39]

Gandhi declined to see political life as the only, or even the principal, means of challenging foreign hegemony and effecting social change. As he remarked in November 1921, 'political power is not an end but one of the means of enabling people to better their condition in every department of life.'[40] Part of his power thus lay in his ability to devise different programmes and organisations through which to pursue his multiple objectives and to recruit and train different cadres of committed activists. The All-India Spinners' Association was one of the most important of these Gandhian agencies, but another was the Sabarmati Ashram itself. Although much of the day-to-day running of the ashram was left to others, especially his nephew Maganlal Gandhi, it was there, between 1915 and 1930, that Gandhi continued his experiments with spinning and weaving, diet and self-healing, but also with education.[41] In 1920 he launched the Gujarati Vidyapith as a college of national education, and eight years later established the Khadi Seva Sangh as the vanguard of the rural khadi movement and to work, in association with the Vidyapith, for the creation of rural schools in Gujarat. He experimented, too, with dairying and agricultural improvement, and the Go Seva Sangh (Cow Service Society) set up at the ashram in 1928 combined a Hindu attachment to cow protection with a practical desire to improve animal husbandry and peasant agriculture.[42]

To some extent this was Gandhi, who imaginatively described himself at the time of his arrest in 1922 as 'a weaver and a farmer', playing at being the artisan and peasant, a kind of Ruskinian rustic, from within the relative comfort and security of his ashram, rather than engaging with the real lives of the industrial worker and the impoverished villager, and being able to do so by virtue of the substantial sums of money he received from friends and philanthropists (mill-owning magnates among them). On the grand scale of India's national politics, these activities might appear marginal, delusory, at times derisory. But to Gandhi they were part of the proof that he was not a mere utopian, part of the means by which he sought to put ideas into practice and pursue his wider vision of swaraj.

. . .
TRIAL AND IMPRISONMENT

Gandhi was arrested at Sabarmati Ashram on 10 March 1922. To the relief of the British the arrest provoked no mass demonstrations, though rumours were rife that no prison bars could hold the Mahatma, whose semi-divine or magical powers were such that he would simply walk free. Eight days after his arrest (and, coincidentally, on the third anniversary of the passing of the Rowlatt Act, so rapidly had events moved since 1919), Gandhi was put on trial for sedition before a British judge, Justice Robert Bloomfield. He was accused of having, through articles published in *Young India* since September 1921, attempted to seduce members of the armed forces from their duty, and bringing into hatred or contempt, or attempting to excite disaffection against, 'His Majesty's Government established by law in India'. He pleaded guilty to the charge, but the trial provided him with one of the few occasions, and indeed the last, when he was able to use his legal training and the theatre of the courtroom to defend his political actions and elaborate his philosophy of non-violent non-cooperation.

Gandhi recounted his career in South Africa and those events in India since 1915 – the Rowlatt Act, the Punjab and Khilafat 'wrongs' – that had converted him from 'a staunch loyalist' into 'an uncompromising disaffectionist and non-cooperator'. More generally, he argued, non-cooperation was justified by India's poverty and by the British connection which 'had made India more helpless than she ever was before, politically and economically'. 'No sophistry, no jugglery in figures', he declared in a written statement to the court, 'can explain away the evidence that the skeletons in many villages present to the naked eye.' This was 'a crime against humanity ... perhaps unequalled in history', for which both England and India's own city-dwellers would ultimately have to answer. While many British and Indian officials honestly believed that they were administering one of the best systems of government in the world, Gandhi could see only a 'subtle but effective system of terrorism' and an 'organised display of force', which combined with 'the deprivation of all powers of retaliation or self-defence', had 'emasculated the people' and induced in them the 'awful habit' of 'simulation'. Gandhi claimed to have no ill-will against any single administrator, but it was his duty to Britain, as much as to India, to oppose this system of government. 'Non-cooperation with evil is as much a duty as is cooperation with good,' he declared. The judge had, therefore, no choice in Gandhi's view but either to resign his post and dissociate himself from this 'evil', or to inflict on Gandhi the severest penalty the law allowed.[43]

A more crudely repressive regime might simply have shot Gandhi, and so, at the price of his martyrdom, brought his political career to a premature end. It might have imprisoned him indefinitely, or exiled him to some remote and distant island (as happened to many other nationalists and revolutionaries who fell foul of imperial authorities). But there was no Gulag Archipelago for Gandhi, no Robben Island. He met a milder fate, sentenced to six years' imprisonment. This was the same length of time as Tilak had spent in prison at Mandalay, but Gandhi was sent to Yeravda Central Jail near Poona to serve his term. It needs to be born in mind, though, that six years was far longer than Gandhi's total imprisonment in South Africa (which, spread over his four terms of imprisonment there, amounted to eight months in all). Moreover, the British were determined to starve him as much as possible of the 'oxygen of publicity' by restricting his access to visitors and his contacts with the outside world. He was allowed only selected newspapers and other printed materials, and was denied, as much as possible, knowledge even of other nationalist prisoners in Yeravda. Gandhi found these conditions extremely irksome.

He was, however, aware of the collapse of the Non-Cooperation Movement and the recapture of the Congress by more moderate elements led by C. R. Das and Motilal Nehru, whom he had out-manoeuvred in 1920 and who had acquiesced in his leadership over the following two years without sharing his defiant radicalism. He was, therefore, forced in jail to rethink his career and political position, and from this self-examination and search for self-vindication emerged two of Gandhi's most important works, *Satyagraha in South Africa*, begun in November 1923, and *The Story of My Experiments with Truth* (to which only later was added the title *An Autobiography*). The latter, though first mooted in 1921 and planned in prison, was only begun in November 1925 after his release. It appeared serially in *Young India* before being published in book form in two parts in 1927 and 1929. Written largely from memory, these works tell us much about Gandhi's inner travails. *Satyagraha in South Africa* is a confident statement of how his techniques had worked successfully in their first extended trial and, despite hardship, brought the struggle for Indians' rights to a triumphal conclusion. Its dominant message is that, given a similar degree of commitment, the satyagraha struggle could be won in India as well.[44] However, if his South African narrative presents satyagraha as an all-conquering hero, Gandhi's autobiography is a more 'erratic and disturbing work', at times presenting readers with scenes of remarkable frankness and revealing intimacy (as with his father's death), but at others passing over his actions and decisions without pausing for explanation or reflection. Often read as a conventional autobiography and a reliable source of factual information (even though Gandhi often declared that 'Truth transcends history'), his life-history more closely resembles a series of moral parables, extracted from his early life, the London and South African years. It is also an account of the 'experiments' that brought him to *brahmacharya* as much as to nationalist leadership in India. Even for an autobiography, it is a remarkably self-centred work. Gandhi occupies centre-stage throughout: he has 'no gift for bringing any other characters to life'.[45] The autobiography ends abruptly in 1921, with the remark that from that point onwards his life has been 'so public that there is hardly anything about it that people do not know',[46] but perhaps it ends in this way too because when Gandhi wrote it he was deeply uncertain where his personal and political life was heading.

Within a few months Gandhi's prison ordeal was beginning to tell on his health – as in 1918 a sure sign of mental as well as physical unease. He tried to push his body and stamina harder and harder, restricting his diet more and more, until he became very ill with an acute appendicitis in January 1924. He was operated on by a British surgeon, Colonel Maddock, and released from prison on 4 February by a government anxious he should not die while still in their hands. He had served only two years of his six-year sentence. Gandhi had partly craved his release, to escape the misery and frustration of prison life, but he also resented being given his freedom on grounds of ill-health (as if his feeble body had failed his iron will) and when he had not completed the prison term with which the British had rewarded his self-confessed sedition. There was something of a presumption on the part of the British that Gandhi was now a broken man. Non-cooperation and civil disobedience had collapsed, the Congress had fallen into more moderate hands, and the Khilafat cause lost its rationale when Turkey's modernising reformer, Kamal Ataturk, abolished the Caliphate in 1923. Gandhi was too weak and ill to take any active part in nationalist politics in the immediate future. It might have seemed that Gandhi, already well into middle age by the time of his release, was finished. History, however, tells a very different story. His greatest triumph still lay ahead of him.

. . .

NOTES AND REFERENCES

1. Judith M. Brown, *Modern India: The Origins of an Asian Democracy*, Oxford, 1985, pp. 188–9.
2. Ibid., p. 197.
3. James D. Hunt, *Gandhi in London*, New Delhi, 1993, pp. 165–71.
4. Francis Watson, *The Trial of Mr Gandhi*, London, 1969, p. 73.
5. Martin Green, *Gandhi: Voice of a New Age Revolution*, New York, 1993, p. 267.
6. Edwin S. Montagu, *An Indian Diary*, London, 1930, p. 58.
7. Watson, *Gandhi*, p. 84.
8. Ibid., p. 91.
9. H. F. Owen, 'Organizing for the Rowlatt Satyagraha of 1919', in R. Kumar (ed.), *Essays on Gandhian Politics: The Rowlatt Satyagraha of 1919*, Oxford, 1971, pp. 64–92.
10. As in Lahore: R. Kumar, 'The Rowlatt Satyagraha in Lahore', in ibid., pp. 272–5.
11. Louis Fischer, *The Life of Mahatma Gandhi*, New York, 1962, p. 189.
12. M. K. Gandhi, *An Autobiography, Or the Story of My Experiments with Truth*, Ahmedabad, 1940, pp. 356–8.
13. Ibid., p. 362.
14. See Gail Minault, *The Khilafat Movement: Religious Symbolism and Political Mobilization in India*, New York, 1982.
15. George Woodcock, *Gandhi*, London, 1972, p. 61.
16. Watson, *Gandhi*, p. 124.
17. Ibid., p. 132.
18. A. B. Shah, 'Gandhi and the Hindu-Muslim Question', in Sibnarayan Ray (ed.), *Gandhi, India and the World*, Philadelphia, 1970, p. 191.
19. Brown, *Modern India*, pp. 214–17.
20. Gopal Krishna, 'The Development of the Indian National Congress as a Mass Organization, 1918–1923', *Journal of Asian Studies*, 25 (1966), p. 425.
21. Ibid., p. 426.
22. On Gandhi's 'rhetoric of rage', see Green, *Gandhi*, p. 214.
23. Mahadev H. Desai, *Day-to-Day with Gandhi: Secretary's Diary, III*, Benares, 1968, p. 24.
24. Krishnadas, *Seven Months with Mahatma Gandhi*, Ahmedabad, 1951, p. 30.

1. Mohandas Gandhi, aged 17 (right), with his brother Laxmidas
Source: Camera Press

2. Gandhi in South Africa, c. 1906
Source: Popperfoto

3. Gandhi in South Africa, 1914, dressed as a satyagrahi
Source: Popperfoto

4. Gandhi with his wife Kasturba, on his return to India from South Africa
Source: Popperfoto

5. Gandhi and Sarojini Naidu at Dandi, 5 April 1930
Source: Hulton Getty

6. Gandhi at the Second Round Table Conference, London, 14 September 1931.
On Gandhi's right are Lord Sankey, Chairman of the Conference, Sir Samuel
Hoare, Secretary of State for India, and the Prime Minister, Ramsay MacDonald.
On his left are Pandit Madan Mohan Malaviya and V. S. Srinivasa Sastri
Source: Popperfoto

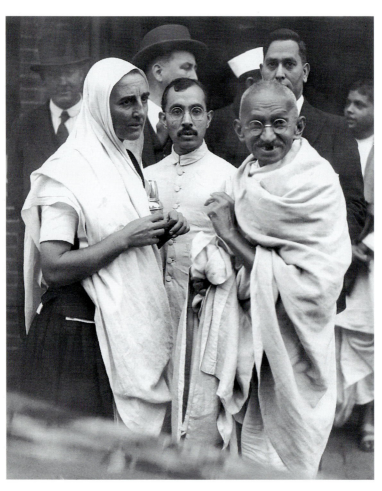

7. Gandhi (right) with Mirabehn at Kingsley Hall, London, 16 September 1931
Source: Associated Press

9. Gandhi with Muhammad Ali Jinnah, September 1944
Source: Popperfoto

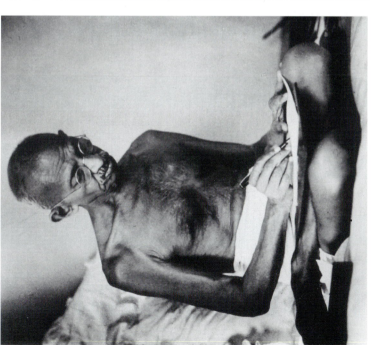

8. Gandhi in Bombay, 1942, on the eve of the Quit India Movement
Source: Images of India/Dinodia

10. David Low cartoon 'Unrest in India', *Evening Standard*, 26 September 1945
Source: Centre for the Study of Cartoons and Caricature, University of Kent, Canterbury/Trevor York

11. Gandhi with Jawaharlal Nehru at a meeting of the All-India Congress Committee, Bombay, 6 July 1946
Source: Hulton Getty

25. For an overview, see Judith M. Brown, *Gandhi's Rise to Power: Indian Politics, 1915–1922*, Cambridge, 1972, ch. 9; Sumit Sarkar, *Modern India, 1885–1947*, Basingstoke, 1989, pp. 204–26.

26. Krishna Dutta and Andrew Robinson, *Rabindranath Tagore: The Myriad-Minded Man*, New York, 1996, p. 237.

27. Sabyasachi Bhattacharya (ed.), *The Mahatma and the Poet: Letters and Debates between Gandhi and Tagore, 1915–1941*, New Delhi, 1997, pp. 54–68.

28. Ibid., pp. 68–92.

29. David Arnold, *The Congress in Tamilnad: Nationalist Politics in South India, 1919–37*, New Delhi, 1977, pp. 71–6.

30. Krishnadas, *Seven Months*, pp. 122–51.

31. Sarkar, *Modern India*, p. 205.

32. For this incident and popular recollections of it, see Shahid Amin, *Event, Metaphor, Memory: Chauri Chaura, 1922–1992*, Berkeley, 1995.

33. *CWMG* XXIII, p. 117.

34. Bhattacharya (ed.), *The Mahatma and the Poet*, p. 89.

35. Ibid.

36. Emma Tarlo, *Clothing Matters: Dress and Identity in India*, London, 1996, pp. 71–82.

37. Bhattacharya (ed.), *The Mahatma and the Poet*, p. 90.

38. Tarlo, *Clothing Matters*, pp. 83–6.

39. *CWMG* XLI, pp. 240–1.

40. Mark Thomson, *Gandhi and His Ashrams*, London, 1993, p. 174.

41. Krishnadas, *Seven Months*, pp. 55–9.

42. Thomson, *Gandhi*, ch. 3.

43. *CWMG* XXIII, pp. 115–19.

44. Gandhi, 'Satyagraha in South Africa', *CWMG* XXIX, pp. 5–6.

45. Robert Payne, *The Life and Death of Mahatma Gandhi*, London, 1969, pp. 376–7; Woodcock, *Gandhi*, p. 67.

46. Gandhi, *Autobiography*, p. 382.

Chapter 6

'HALF-NAKED FAKIR'

After the heady days of non-cooperation and civil disobedience, the mid-1920s were for Gandhi something of an anti-climax. The high expectations of swaraj in one year had brought few apparent gains and Gandhi left Yeravda prison in 1924 weak and demoralised. He was still 'the Mahatma', but the upsurge of millennial hope that had underpinned his 'rise to power' had all but vanished. Romain Rolland's biography of 'The Man Who Became One With The Universal Being', published in 1924, helped establish his international reputation as a saintly figure and long remained the definitive account of Gandhi in the West, but it closed, somewhat ominously, with 'the great apostle' still in prison, 'his body walled in as in a tomb'.[1] On his release, Gandhi seemed to have returned to the margins of Indian politics. Although chosen as Congress President for the first and only time in December 1924, his slow recuperation from illness and the greatly changed nature of Indian politics, prevented him from resuming a more active role.

. . .

THE SWARAJISTS AND THE BARDOLI SATYAGRAHA

The mood within the Congress had shifted away from Gandhian non-cooperation and civil disobedience, and back to participation in the provincial and central legislatures. This was done initially under the auspices of the Swarajya Party set up in March 1923 by C. R. Das and Motilal Nehru. Their declared aim was to carry non-cooperation into the legislatures through a systematic programme of obstruction, thereby creating a constitutional deadlock and making British rule through the councils inoperative. Those loyal to the still imprisoned Gandhi, led by C. Rajagopalachari and dubbed the 'No-Changers', tried at the Gaya Congress in Bihar in December 1922 to resist the return to a pre-Gandhian style of constitutional politics, even if it claimed to act in the name of non-cooperation, and to maintain the Constructive Programme as the main focus of Congress activity. But, with Gandhi in jail and the momentum for civil disobedience already lost, control of the party shifted steadily towards the Swarajists. Gandhi's release in February 1924 revived the No-Changers' hopes of holding on to the party organisation, but when at the AICC session at Ahmedabad in June 1924 Gandhi pressed, unsuccessfully, for a minimum spinning quota for Congress membership, he was forced to recognise that he had been 'defeated and humbled'. A compromise agreement between Gandhi, Das and Nehru followed in November 1924, allowing the Swarajists to work within the legislatures 'as an integral part of the Congress organisation'. In 1925 Gandhi, as Congress President, placed control of the entire Congress organisation in the hands of the Swarajists, preferring the newly formed All-India Spinners' Association as the vehicle for his own activities. In 1923, in the first elections held under the dyarchy constitution since the partial boycott of November 1920, the Swarajists won a significant number of council seats, including nearly half (48 out of 105) of those for the central Legislative Assembly in Delhi. They had further successes in the third round of elections in 1926, especially in the Madras Presidency, but by then they had lost C. R. Das, one of their ablest and most widely respected leaders, who died in June 1925.[2]

While Gandhi was in jail, the Khilafat Movement, which had helped carry him to nationwide leadership in 1920, had also collapsed and finally ended in 1923 when Kemal Ataturk abolished the Caliphate. After several years of closer collaboration, from the Lucknow Pact of 1916 onwards, mounting communal conflict was pushing the leaders of the Hindu and Muslim communities further apart. Muhammad Ali was elected Congress President in December 1923, but in September 1924 communal rioting broke out at Kohat in the North-West Frontier Province and 155 people were killed. In an attempt to restore Hindu–Muslim harmony, Gandhi undertook a twenty-one day fast (his longest fast thus far), but thereafter, and for most of the next fifteen years, the promotion of Hindu-Muslim unity assumed secondary importance to his many other interests. Indeed, in the course of the 1920s, as the Khilafat cause waned and the Christian influences of his South African years became more fully absorbed into his saintly persona, Gandhi appeared more and more to be a Hindu leader. Having completed his term as Congress President in December 1925, he announced that 1926 was to be his 'year of silence'. There was speculation that this meant his effective retirement from Indian politics altogether.

But Gandhi, and his gospel of satyagraha and swaraj, had not entirely disappeared from view. Although he returned to live at the Sabarmati Ashram and devoted himself to Constructive Programme work there, he kept his political presence alive by frequent tours of India – in 1925 alone he visited Kathiawar, Central India, Bengal, Travancore and Malabar – making speeches, fund-raising for the Congress, and tirelessly advocating hand-spinning and khadi. As well as the autobiography, he wrote prolifically for *Young India* and *Navajivan*, and, as his *Collected Works* attest, engaged in seemingly endless correspondence on matters as varied as prison life, health, diet, education, South Africa, and swaraj, writing to individuals both in India and abroad. Even in ill-health, Gandhi was never idle. He continued to experiment with his techniques, including fasting: in addition to his fast for Hindu–Muslim unity in September–October 1924 (barely six months after his release from prison on health grounds), there was a seven-day fast in 1925 over the 'misdeeds' of young inmates at Sabarmati Ashram, and a further three-day fast for a similar 'lapse' in mid-1928.

Satyagraha, Gandhi's trade-mark form of direct action, had by the early 1920s become an established part of India's political culture, and though the Non-cooperation and Civil Disobedience Movement had collapsed, there were several sporadic attempts to deploy the technique for specific purposes. A 'flag satyagraha' was organised at Nagpur in Central India in 1923: Congress volunteers paraded the 'national flag' in defiance of the magistrate's order and thereby courted arrest and imprisonment. In the Akali Movement in Punjab from 1921 to 1925 Sikh militants employed largely non-violent methods to wrest control of their temples or *gurdwaras* away from the government. Satyagraha was also beginning to be used in the India of the princely states. In March 1924 a campaign was launched at Vaikam (or Vykom) in the state of Travancore in the extreme southwest of India over the right of untouchables and low-caste Hindus to walk along a road that passed in front of a temple used exclusively by high-caste Hindus. Gandhi did not initiate this struggle, but visited the town of Vaikam in March 1925, declaring, to the annoyance of local Christians who saw this as part of a wider struggle for social change, that the satyagraha should be confined to Hindus. The campaign, which ended in November 1925, secured some concessions from the government but diversionary roads were built for the untouchables to ensure that they did not pass too close to the temple itself. The movement had considerable local impact and showed how techniques of satyagraha could affect daily lives, but in the short term it did little to resolve the underlying problems of caste discrimination, which in Kerala were particularly acute.[3] There were attempts, too, as with the bitter and protracted South Indian Railway strike of 1928, to invoke Gandhi and satyagraha in industrial action, but these failed to draw his approval or support.[4]

The most effective use of satyagraha in the 1920s was, however, in the already tried and tested context of local, peasant-based campaigns, though after Champaran and Kheda Gandhi left these largely to others to run on his behalf. In 1923–4 Vallabhbhai Patel conducted a highly efficient satyagraha in Borsad *taluk* in Kheda district against the imposition of a new tax (levied to meet the costs of suppressing local dacoits or criminal gangs) and successfully forced its cancellation by early January 1924. In 1928 Patel, increasingly dubbed 'the Sardar' for his doughty leadership, directed a second struggle, this time in Bardoli, the *taluk* of Surat district in Gujarat that had been selected to lead the non-tax campaign in 1922. Significantly, this was a *raiyatwari* area, where peasants paid revenue directly to the government and without the complication of substantial Indian landlords or *zamindars*. This was an area, too, where support from the Patidars was strong and where years of Congress activity and the Constructive Programme had built up a loyal and disciplined peasant base. The issue here was the government's periodic revision of the land revenue assessment, which in this case resulted in an increase of 22 per cent, even though prices for cotton, one of the main cash crops produced by peasant cultivators in the *taluk*, had been falling.

The Bardoli campaign began in February 1928. Despite arrests and brutal distraints of property, the campaign was largely successful in securing peasant solidarity across class and caste lines. Skilful use was made of religious idioms and devotional songs, caste associations were mobilised and the identity of each caste and community, including the tribal landless labourers, was effectively invoked. Social boycotts were used against those failing to support the no-tax campaign. The great majority of the 87,000 peasants in the *taluk* refused to pay the land revenue demand, despite the attachment of their cattle and land. Even when property confiscated from peasant defaulters was offered for sale it failed to find any buyers. At a time of mounting political unrest across India, Bardoli attracted nationwide attention. After six months, in August 1928, the government, alarmed that the Bardoli Satyagraha would spark similar protests elsewhere in India where revenue assessments were also being revised, gave in. All prisoners were released, and a commission of enquiry was appointed which accepted that the revenue enhancements had been excessive and should be reduced. Peasants were further compensated for goods that had been seized from them. Plans by the Bombay government to raise land revenue assessments elsewhere in the province were shelved and, indeed, after Bardoli all provincial administrations began to regard land revenue, once the mainstay of government revenue and authority in the countryside, as a dwindling asset.

Bardoli represented the kind of local, single-issue campaign in which Gandhi's satyagraha techniques were most effective. Where Champaran and Kheda had ended in compromise, and the Rowlatt Satyagraha and the Non-Cooperation Movement had resulted in violence and disarray, Bardoli was a 'textbook' satyagraha, the 'first fully successful civil disobedience campaign' undertaken on behalf of the peasants and against the British government in India.[5] This was a major victory, not just for the peasants of Gujarat and elsewhere, but also for Gandhi's techniques. Although satyagraha had been effectively employed in Bardoli without much direct involvement from Gandhi himself, his name was repeatedly invoked in the campaign and Vallabhbhai Patel repeatedly sought his guidance during the campaign. It was widely recognised that Gandhi remained the supreme master of this form of agitational politics. Enhanced by the experience of Bardoli, his reputation for having devised satyagraha and shown how it could be successfully implemented remained one of Gandhi's principal assets in the fast-moving politics of the late 1920s and early 1930s. After the set-backs of recent years, Bardoli reaffirmed his own faith in satyagraha and created the possibility of a new nationwide campaign. 'Bardoli has shown the way and cleared it,' he observed. 'Swaraj lies on that route.'[6]

. . .

'SIMON GO BACK'

The gradual revival of Gandhi's fortunes was timely, for by 1928 the Swarajists were beginning to run into serious difficulties. While they had secured a significant number of seats in the legislatures, sufficient to constitute the main opposition party in several provinces, their campaign of obstruction (delaying government business, moving special resolutions to publicise or protest at political events, or making cuts in budget expenditure) had yielded only modest results. On the Swarajists' initiative, in February 1924 members of the central Legislative Assembly passed a resolution calling for a conference to discuss constitutional progress to responsible government, but their plea went unheeded. Government business continued largely unaffected (as through the action of provincial governors in restoring budget cuts) and enough ministers could always be found to maintain the Indian half of the dyarchy system of government. The Swarajists could neither bring the provincial governments to a complete stand-still, nor were they permitted by their own rules of engagement from taking up power for themselves, though they sometimes, as in Madras in the late 1920s, provided tacit support for pro-nationalist ministers. Life in the legislatures, with all their conventions and rules of procedure, tended to make the members more and more remote from the rest of the Congress party and from their supporters in the country at large. Divisions, factions and splinter parties began to emerge as the Swarajists disagreed among themselves over object-ives and tactics. Like the Moderates and Liberals ten years earlier, the situation of the Swarajists in the late 1920s demonstrated the limitations of constitutional politics under colonial rule and the need to supplant, or at least supplement, it with a more active, agitational strategy.

Paradoxically, growing disillusionment with the constitutional process was accelerated by the policy of the British government itself. On 8 November 1927 Lord Birkenhead, the Secretary of State for India in Stanley Baldwin's Conservative government, sought to pre-empt the return to power of a Labour government, and what was presumed to be its more sympathetic attitude to Indian demands, by appointing a Statutory Commission to investigate the progress made since the Government of India Act of 1919 and hence India's wor-thiness for a further round of constitutional reform. The seven-man Commission, headed by the Liberal politician Sir John Simon (and generally known as the 'Simon Commission') consisted entirely of British members, drawn from the two Houses of Parliament and, incidentally, including the future Labour Prime Minister, Clement Attlee. Its composition and terms of reference were decided upon without any prior consultation with politicians and parties in India. This was immediately seen as a grievous affront to Indian political leaders and a further retreat from the kind of 'responsible government' promised by Edwin Montagu in 1917. Indians of all parties, from the Congress to the Liberals and a section of the Muslim League led by M. A. Jinnah, responded by resolving to boycott the Commission. In what can be seen as the first Indian attempt to frame a viable constitution, the members of this cross-party alliance joined together under Motilal Nehru and the Liberal Tej Bahadur Sapru to draft their own report. Intense discussion failed, however, to resolve the conflicting demands of Hindu and Muslim leaders, and Jinnah withdrew, believing that too much weight was being given to Hindu interests. The Nehru Report of August 1928 clearly stated the demand for responsible government both at the centre and in the provinces, but in pressing for Dominion Status rather than complete independence it reflected moderate nationalist opinion and took a substantial step back from the swaraj Gandhi had set his sights on in 1920–2.

The response to the Simon Commission was not confined to constitution-making. As the Simon Commission toured India twice – in February 1928 for a preliminary two-month reconnaissance and again for a more extended visit in October 1928 – it met with boycotts and demonstrations, *hartals*, the waving of black flags, and cries of 'Simon Go Back'. Heavy-handed police action in breaking up demonstrations (including an incident in Lahore in October 1928 in which the veteran Punjabi leader Lala Lajpat Rai was fatally injured, and another, the following month, in which Jawaharlal Nehru was beaten with police *lathis*, or metal-tipped staves, while leading a protest on the streets of Lucknow), further inflamed the mood of anger and impatience. While the Liberals prevaricated, the Congress leaders, impelled by frustration over both the Simon Commission and the Swarajist impasse, edged gingerly towards a more openly confrontational position. At the annual Congress session in Madras in December 1927 Jawaharlal Nehru had moved a resolution calling for Indian independence, but the main Congress leadership, including his father Motilal, proceeded with greater caution. Meeting a year later at Calcutta in December 1928 the Congress agreed to a compromise formula by which it accepted the demand for Dominion Status outlined in the Nehru Report, provided the British granted it by the end of 1929. If they failed to do so, then the Congress would be free to opt for *purna swaraj* (complete independence) and use civil disobedience as the means to achieve it. A further factor in increasing the political temperature and impelling the Congress leadership towards a more assertive stance was a new phase of labour unrest and revolutionary terrorism.[7]

Despite Bardoli, and perhaps still conscious of the failure to win swaraj in 1920–2, Gandhi was not in the forefront of these moves. Pressure for a more radical shift in Congress policy came mainly from younger Congressmen like Jawaharlal Nehru and Subhas Chandra Bose, who with the death of C. R. Das had assumed leadership of one faction of the Congress in Bengal. Gandhi disapproved of Nehru's independence resolution at Madras in December 1927 and favoured compromise rather than confrontation at the Calcutta Congress a year later. Promoting the Constructive Programme, rather than embarking on a new phase of mass satyagraha, seemed to be his principal concern, and as late as July 1929 he declared that he saw no prospect of his kind of civil disobedience on the horizon. For those who still had faith in constitutional progress, the advent of the new Labour government in Britain in June 1929 held out a faint possibility of progress.

On 31 October 1929, in an attempt to forestall the deepening crisis, the new Viceroy, Lord Irwin, claimed that Dominion Status had all along been 'implicit' in the Montagu declaration of 1917 and was the 'natural issue' of India's constitutional progress. He proposed that once the Simon Commission's report had been published, a round table conference should be held to review the constitutional situation. On 2 November Gandhi, along with Motilal Nehru, the Hindu nationalist Madan Mohan Malaviya and the Liberals, welcomed the principle of the 'Irwin Offer', but held out for greater concessions, including immediate progress to discussing the implementation of Dominion Status for India rather than merely debating the principle of it. Gandhi met Irwin on 23 December, but the Viceroy rejected the nationalist demands. At the end of that month the Congress met at its annual session, this time at Lahore and with the younger Nehru as President. Jawaharlal made an impassioned address in which he frankly professed himself 'a socialist and a republican', and 'no believer in kings and princes, or in the order which produces the modern kings of industry'.[8] Bose, too, injected a note of radicalism into the proceedings, proposing immediate non-payment of taxes, a nationwide general strike and the creation of a parallel government, but this was rejected. The Congress passed a resolution declaring its objective to be *purna swaraj*, but without entirely closing the door to further negotiations. With no significant concessions or constitutional progress in the offing, on 26 January 1930 the Congress celebrated its first 'Independence Day'.

The AICC, authorised to launch civil disobedience, passed the responsibility over to Gandhi. No real alternative leadership had emerged. Eight years after the collapse of his previous all-India campaign, and six difficult years after his release from prison, Gandhi was again the focal point of the nationalist struggle. Indeed, he now commanded more genuine support, more personal respect and political authority than in the heady years 1918–22. At the relatively advanced age of 60, Gandhi had reached the zenith of his political power.

. . .

THE SALT SATYAGRAHA

In the early months of 1930, Gandhi appeared uncertain how to proceed with his civil disobedience mandate. On 31 January he sent Lord Irwin a letter in which he stressed the plight of India's peasantry under British rule and listed eleven grievances which, if redressed by the government, would amount in his view to the concession of real independence. At first sight the eleven-point demand appeared far less dramatic and momentous than the Punjab and Khilafat 'wrongs' for which Gandhi had led his troops into non-violent battle in 1920, and a climb-down, even an irrelevance, after the resounding *purna swaraj* resolution a month earlier. The list consisted of several general demands – halving the cost of the army and civil service salaries, total prohibition, the release of political prisoners, reform of the CID (long a bugbear of nationalists weary of being spied on and watched), and liberalisation of the Arms Act of 1877 which controlled gun licenses (a seemingly un-Gandhian issue this perhaps but one which reflected longstanding resentment at restrictions on Indians' right to bear arms). Three further issues related directly to the interests of the commercial middle classes and industrialists – lowering the rupee–sterling exchange rate, protection for the Indian textile industry, and the reservation of coastal shipping for

Indians – while two others targeted the interests of the peasants and the poor – a 50 per cent reduction in the land revenue and the abolition of the salt tax and the state's salt monopoly. Gandhi's demands thus presented a broad, cross-class amalgam of national interests and grievances. When Irwin's government declined to respond, Gandhi, as if in a moment of pure inspiration, opted in early February to concentrate on only one of the eleven issues – the salt tax – as the focus of his civil disobedience campaign.

Salt duties had been a feature of government in India since Mughal times, but in 1878, as part of a series of measures to augment state revenues, a law was passed to create a uniform salt tax throughout British and princely India, prohibiting the private manufacture of salt and making the possession of salt not derived from government sources illegal. Along with similar taxes on alcohol and opium, the salt tax made a small, but not insignificant, contribution to government revenues. By 1880 it was bringing £7 million a year into the state's coffers, but in 1929–30 it amounted to less than 4 per cent of total revenues. But it was repeatedly criticised (not just by Indians) as an immoral tax on a basic human necessity and a 'cruel' imposition that fell with particular severity on India's poor – indeed, it was deeply ironic that the Salt Act was passed in 1878, one of the worst years of famine in nineteenth-century India. The issue of its repeal or reduction had been discussed for many years, not least in Imperial Legislative Council, where Gokhale had condemned it in 1902 and in the central Legislative Assembly during the 1920s (where many other of Gandhi's eleven points had also been debated). If this were a reminder of how constitutional and agitational issues intertwined, it was also an indication of how Gandhi was consciously striving for a wider national consensus than a series of Bardoli-style no-revenue campaigns was likely to generate. Gandhi twice referred to the salt tax in *Hind Swaraj*, noting in the tract's penultimate paragraph how this, along with other harmful consequences of British rule, needed to be removed if real swaraj were to be achieved.[9]

The tax was, as Judith Brown has remarked, 'a superbly ingenious choice' as the focus for the 1930 civil disobedience campaign.[10] Apart from its potential impact on government income, already clamped by the effects of the Bardoli Satyagraha on land revenue, the tax provided the kind of single-issue focus in which satyagraha excelled. It presented as a clear moral issue the need to wrest freedom from a foreign regime that was exploitative and unheeding. 'It was', Gandhi declared, 'the most inhuman poll tax that [the] ingenuity of man can devise.'[11] To American observers it might recall the Boston Tea Party that helped launch the career of their own war of independence, but for Gandhi it dramatised something more than a struggle over taxation and representation – the plight of the 'starving millions' to whom Gandhi repeatedly referred in 1930–1 as being the ultimate sanction for his campaign. Salt, like the flagging khadi campaign, had wider symbolic connotations. It was self-evidently swadeshi, a commodity accumulating with little human effort in vast glistening salt-pans along the coastline of India from the Rann of Cutch to Orissa (though with characteristic colonial disdain for local self-sufficiency, some parts of India received their salt from Britain). The 'illegality' of the salt tax, Gandhi explained in February 1930, was that the government 'steals the people's salt and makes them pay heavily for the stolen article'. Once they became 'conscious of their power', they would see that they had every right to 'take possession of what belongs to them'.[12] Salt also had connotations of loyalty: for sepoys of the old East India Company to be loyal was to be 'true to their salt'. If Indians were to demonstrate that the salt of India belonged to them, not to their foreign rulers, it was a symbolic way of declaring that they no longer owed them loyalty or recognised them as lawful rulers. Salt, like khadi, was non-sectarian: it offended no religion but provided a moral issue on which all classes and communities, women and men, could unite.

To Gandhi's ingenuity in selecting the salt issue as the focus for his campaign was added his brilliant orchestration of the resulting campaign. Having announced to the Government of India and to the world his intention to defy the salt law, on 12 March 1930 he set out, with 78 carefully chosen followers from Sabarmati Ashram, on a march that covered 241 miles and took 24 days, despite the summer heat, to complete. En route to Dandi, a small village just south of Surat, where Gandhi planned to break the salt law, he passed, in what increasingly appeared to be a triumphal procession, through the villages of rural Gujarat, stressing once more his ties to the peasantry and his native region. Between the villages, festooned in his honour, peasants sprinkled water on the roads to keep down the pre-monsoon dust, strewing them with fresh leaves and flower petals. The march caught the imagination of millions in India and abroad. A watching world was held in suspense while a 60-year-old man, clad in his loin cloth and bamboo staff in hand, marched briskly towards his goal. 'In nearly every settlement hundreds abandoned their work and joined the procession,' recalled William L. Shirer, an American journalist, 'until the original band of less than one hundred swelled to several thousand by the time the sea was reached.'[13]

The Salt March was not only 'one of the most dramatic events of modern Indian history',[14] but also one of the most stirring anywhere in the modern world. It echoed the march Gandhi had led from Natal into Transvaal in November 1913, and which had also involved a core of ashram disciples, but that had lasted only five days and attracted far less international publicity: Gandhi was now a saint, a 'Christ-like' figure,[15] taking on the might of the world's greatest empire armed with little more than his own determination to fight injustice. Of all the 'marches' by which a host of very different opposition movements in the 1920s and 30s drew attention to their cause and sought salvation or survival – from Mussolini's march on Rome in 1922, to the Long March of Mao Tse-tung and the Chinese communists in 1934–5, to the march of the unemployed from Jarrow to London in October 1936 – this was surely one of the most sensational and effective. With the government watching anxiously from the sidelines, Gandhi was able to win almost unfettered publicity for his cause, and, for all his personal aversion to modern technology, to exploit the vast potential of the media in India and abroad. Three Bombay cinema companies filmed the march, and newspaper reports, photographs and newsreels carried the story of his long march to freedom in words and pictures around the world. Ironically for the author of *Hind Swaraj*, Gandhi was as much a beneficiary as Hitler, Stalin and Mussolini of the rise of the mass media, of the new technologies of the radio and cinema, that enabled political leaders to appeal directly to the masses.

Gandhi arrived at Dandi, at the end of his 'pilgrimage', on the morning of 5 April and held prayers in honour of the 'goddess of swaraj'. The following morning, on the eleventh anniversary of the Rowlatt Satyagraha, he waded into the sea, declaring that 'This religious war of civil disobedience should be started only after purifying ourselves by bathing in the salt water'. He then stooped to pick up salt from the seashore and so formally broke the salt law. 'With this', he said, 'I am shaking the foundations of the British Empire',[16] and there were many who have seen that 'simple, poetic act' as not only uniting the Indian people as never before but also hastening the end of a still-mighty empire.[17] Once Gandhi had made his gesture of defiance, satyagraha moved into a different gear. Up until that moment the whole of India had waited for Gandhi: now other marches, other real or symbolic acts of salt-making, erupted across India, presenting the authorities with an unprecedentedly well-orchestrated and non-violent campaign. From the salt tax, the movement, increasingly 'an insurrection without arms',[18] widened to include, as in 1920–2, the boycott of foreign cloth and liquor. The British hesitated for a whole month, until 5 May, before arresting Gandhi. Using an old and obscure regulation, dating from 1827, he was held by the British without trial or sentence and for no fixed term of imprisonment. By this time India was 'seething in angry revolt' and tens of thousands of Indians had joined the civil disobedience campaign. By the end of the year an estimated 60,000 Indians had been imprisoned for their part in the movement.[19]

. . .

CIVIL DISOBEDIENCE

Unlike in 1921–2, the Congress forces seemed in 1930 to possess an unprecedented degree of self-discipline, even in the face of horrifying acts of police brutality. The worst of this state violence was exemplified by the response to Congress 'raids' on the Dharasana salt works, 150 miles north of Bombay, which began on 21 May 1930. Webb Miller, an American journalist, recorded in a despatch that was syndicated to more than a thousand newspapers around the world, how as each batch of unarmed satyagrahis advanced impassively to the gates of the salt works they were clubbed to the ground by *lathi*-wielding policemen, and beaten into 'a bloody pulp'. 'Not one of the marchers even raised an arm to fend off the blows. They went down like ten-pins,' Miller wrote. 'From where I stood I heard the sickening whack of the clubs on unprotected skulls. . . . Those struck down fell sprawling, unconscious or writhing with fractured skulls or broken shoulders. . . . The survivors, without breaking ranks, silently and doggedly marched on until struck down.'[20]

With the lessons of the Jallianwala Bagh massacre still in its mind, the government made a determined effort to minimise the use of force, by excluding troops as far as possible and even by equipping some policemen with canes instead of *lathis*. But it proved impossible for some 'atrocities' not to occur and the non-violent movement once again fed off public revulsion at the violence employed by the state and its subordinate agencies. The Liberal politicians, moderate nationalists and erstwhile Swarajists, who had defied the call early in

1930 to leave the legislatures, contributed their part by repeated criticism of government action and resolutions condemning police violence. The situation in 1930 was further intensified by the unprecedented participation of women, mostly from middle-class families. They, too, joined in protest marches, made illegal salt, picketed drink and foreign-cloth shops, faced police *lathis* and went to jail. In mid-November 1930 there were some 350 women in jail for civil disobedience offences. Their experiences, including being placed in cells with low-caste women, thieves, prostitutes and murderers, echoed the trauma of Gandhi's own initiation into prison life in South Africa twenty-five years earlier. But their presence also lent strength to the claim that this was a truly national campaign and heightened the contrast between the courage and self-sacrifice of the non-violent satyagrahis and the brutal and heavy-handed attempts of the state to crush the movement.

Gandhi's personal reputation had never been higher, though something of his millennarian aura had dissipated since the high expectations of his semi-divine or magical powers at Champaran in 1917 or on his visit to Gorakhpur in 1921. His popularity remained nonetheless enormous and the march to Dandi and breaking of the salt laws had deeply stirred the public's imagination. Many thousands of people turned out to hear, or at least to see, him. William Shirer, the American journalist who later reported for the *Chicago Tribune* on Hitler's speeches and the mass rallies at Nuremberg, was struck by the vast difference between the great crowds that spontaneously gathered around Gandhi when he toured India and the regimented ranks of the 200,000 assembled to hear Hitler's rants. The Indians, such as those who gathered, 150,000 strong, on the banks of the Sabarmati to welcome Gandhi back to Ahmedabad in March 1931, were 'unorganised and sometimes disorderly, milling about in their excitement at merely being in the presence of the Mahatma'. Many of the Nazis Shirer saw at Hitler's Nuremberg rallies were 'deeply moved' by the Führer's 'masterful oratory'. By contrast, 'Gandhi was no orator'. 'He scarcely raised his voice and made no gestures.' Although he began using a microphone at the Lahore Congress of 1929 to address his audiences, his voice was always 'rather thin' and 'small'. Shirer doubted whether the majority of the vast crowds heard most of what he said, but they were 'fulfilled by the sight of him and . . . by receiving his darshan'. They felt themselves to be in the presence of a great man and that 'something immense was suddenly happening in their drab lives', that this 'saintly man in a loincloth cared about them, understood their wretched plight and somehow had the power, even in the face of the great white sahibs in Delhi and the provincial capitals, to do something about it.'[21]

Continuing reverence for the Mahatma apart, the 1930–1 movement took on some characteristics that distinguished it from non-cooperation and civil disobedience in 1920–2. What the Congress had gained in discipline it had lost in spontaneity. Gandhi's tactics were better understood than they had been ten years earlier and seemed to hold less danger of spiralling out of control. Although he was imprisoned in May 1930 and could play no more direct part in the movement until his release the following January, the Congress party was better equipped to sustain the struggle than it had been ten years before. It had a more effective organisational network, a larger number of dedicated activists and supporters, and a more secure base among the middle classes and, especially in the aftermath of Bardoli, among at least the wealthier sections of the peasantry.

In 1921–2 there had been a whiff of revolution in the air, the possibility of peasant insurrection, and a growing fear of uncontrolled change among the propertied classes. In 1930–1 India seemed bent on a far less dangerous course. No one now called Gandhi a 'Bolshevik' as one British Governor had a decade earlier, and no Tagore-like Jeremiahs weighed in to warn against the Mahatma's misguided message. There was no radical peasant movement to match the Kisan Sabha agitation in the United Provinces in 1920–1, no Malabar Rebellion. There were some outbreaks of terrorist activity, notably in Bengal where revolutionaries carried out a sensational raid on a government armoury at Chittagong on 18 April 1930 and where new attempts were made to assassinate government officials. But these were seen as local episodes, not directly linked to Gandhi's movement. In the North-West Frontier Province Abdul Ghaffar Khan, a Pathan who had become a devoted follower of Gandhi and who defied the violent traditions of his community, led his 'Red Shirts' in non-violent support of the nationalist struggle. But in general in 1930–1, with no Khilafat cause to align them with a predominantly Hindu Congress party, Muslim support for the movement elsewhere was patchy. Of the 29,000 individuals in prison in connection with the movement in November 1930, only 1,500 were Muslims.[22]

Apart from a few local displays of solidarity, there was little active support from industrial workers either, in part because a wave of industrial unrest in the mid and late 1920s, marked by several major strikes, had already faded out by the start of the Salt Satyagraha.

By contrast, a number of businessmen and industrialists continued to support and help fund the Civil Disobedience Movement, with Gandhi's friend the Marwari businessman G. D. Birla alone contributing, according to British intelligence reports, half a million rupees. Aided by the onset of the world Depression, as well as by vigorous picketing, foreign cloth imports into India dwindled, nearly halving in value from £26 million to £13.7 million in 1930 and falling in volume from 1,248 million yards in 1929–30 to 523 million in 1930–1. This, coupled with the loss of land revenue and the reduced income from the salt tax and sales of alcohol, meant that the economic impact of the movement was beginning seriously to alarm the British and to increase the pressure for a more conciliatory approach to the nationalist campaign.

But, as in 1920–2, this initial high level of nationalist fervour could not be sustained indefinitely, and, beyond a dedicated core of hardened volunteers, those who had been imprisoned once were not necessarily willing to suffer so much again so soon. With some exceptions in Gujarat, the United Provinces and Bihar, by October 1930, with most of the Congress leadership in jail, the movement was starting to wane. In 1920–1 Gandhi had made the mistake of believing that he could secure swaraj in a single fight and, though the opportunity was slight, had lost the chance of a possible round table conference, which might have allowed him and his followers time to recuperate and squeeze some concessions from the government before renewing their campaign. By contrast, on his release from prison on 26 January 1931, Gandhi seemed willing to respond to Lord Irwin's overtures. On 14 February he wrote to the Viceroy seeking an interview. This marked the beginning of an important – and to some bewildering – new phase in the struggle.

·   ·   ·

THE GANDHI-IRWIN PACT

Although he may have forgotten it in his eager search for swaraj in 1921, compromise was for Gandhi an essential part of satyagraha. Just as he had sought to resolve conflict over Indian rights in South Africa in 1908 and 1914 through direct negotiation with Smuts, so now in 1931 in India he seized the chance to build on the political successes of the Salt Satyagraha to open a dialogue with the British in India. Discussions between Gandhi and Irwin continued intermittently at the newly built viceregal palace in Delhi from 17 February until on 5 March an agreement was reached, thereafter known as the Gandhi-Irwin Pact. The manner of these discussions was as significant as the 'pact' itself. Although there were advisers on both sides – government officials and members of the Congress Working Committee – they remained in the background. Gandhi met the Viceroy, face-to-face, as the sole representative of the Congress, and carried on discussions as if they were the commanders of two opposing but unbeaten armies agreeing a truce. This was a remarkable expression of Gandhi's ascendency over the Congress and his personal authority within the country, and it is hard not to see this moment as having 'marked the peak of Gandhi's political influence and prestige in India'.[23]

Irwin provided the almost perfect foil for Gandhi's satyagraha. He was courteous and humane, even writing to express his personal condolences to Gandhi when his much-loved nephew Maganlal died in 1928.[24] He was moral-minded, devoutly Christian, and disposed by temperament and conviction to favour negotiation and compromise over confrontation. Despite opposition in London, he had been willing in October 1929 to promise India a place among the Dominions in order to forestall the threat of Congress civil disobedience, and he remained anxious to repair the damage done by the Simon Commission report, published in June 1930, which promised responsible government in place of dyarchy in the provinces but made no commitment to Dominion Status. It is not without significance that seven years after his meetings with Gandhi, as Lord Halifax and Foreign Secretary in Neville Chamberlain's government, Irwin was one of the 'arch-appeasers' of Hitler's increasingly bellicose expansionism, and in November 1937, as Lord President of the Council, had flown to Berchtesgaden to meet the Führer. It can be argued that he misjudged Gandhi and the 'revolutionary' nature of the movement he led as badly as he misunderstood the founder of the Third Reich.[25] But Irwin's correspondence with the British government at the time gives no indication of any 'susceptibility to the hypnotic appeal of Gandhi's saintliness or the compulsions of his religious ideas'.[26] He was sufficiently astute and statesmanly to see the importance to Britain of bringing civil disobedience to an end and using Gandhi as a means to draw the Congress back from confrontation to constitutional action. A round table conference to unlock India's constitutional impasse had long been the Viceroy's goal and, though the first such conference had opened in London in

November 1930, it had been a lacklustre affair and Irwin well knew that the process would not succeed if the Congress continued to boycott it.

The negotiations between the Viceroy and the Mahatma were not, however, to the liking of many British civil servants in India. Nor were they to Winston Churchill, who had served in his youth on India's North-West Frontier and who met Gandhi for the first and only time in London as Under-Secretary for the Colonies in November 1906 as conflict over Indian rights in South Africa began to erupt. In the early 1930s Churchill turned opposition to Indian nationalist demands into as virulent a crusade as his campaign against Hitler and German rearmament. Believing that the loss of India would 'mark and consummate the downfall of the British Empire', he fulminated against British 'weakness' in India, condemned the 1919 constitution as a failure, and wanted the Congress leaders deported. 'Gandhi-ism', he warned, 'will have to be grappled with and finally crushed'. 'It is no use trying to satisfy a tiger by feeding him with cat's meat.'[27] In late February 1931 news of the Gandhi-Irwin negotiations in Delhi threw Churchill into fresh paroxysms:

> It is alarming and also nauseating [he declared] to see Mr. Gandhi, a seditious Middle Temple lawyer, now posing as a fakir of a type well-known in the East, striding half-naked up the steps of the Viceregal palace, while he is still organising and conducting a defiant campaign of civil disobedience, to parley on equal terms with the representative of the King-Emperor.[28]

Churchill's rhetoric, as it often did, got the better of him, and to call Gandhi a 'fakir', a Muslim ascetic, was derogatory but not very appropriate. (Gandhi, characteristically, took it as a kind of compliment.) But Churchill's remarks bore a deeper significance. They signalled his own almost fanatical determination to resist constitutional change in India, a position he maintained, to considerable effect, until Independence in August 1947. They were indicative, too, of the deep and bitter antagonism Gandhi could inspire in his opponents and the prominence his activities had begun to acquire in the perceived fate not just of India but the British Empire as a whole. Despite the recognition that India, in Churchill's words, was 'the most truly bright and precious jewel in the crown of the King',[29] it had seldom enjoyed the place in British politics to which its importance seemed to entitle it. Except for times of extreme crisis (like the rising of 1857) or moments of imperial pomp and pageantry (like the imperial durbar of 1911 at which George V was crowned King-Emperor), India was largely taken for granted in British political circles, and parliamentary debates, even on constitutional issues, were poorly attended. It was significant that as part of Gandhi's reform of the Congress in 1920, the party had abandoned its attempt to maintain a London-based British Committee to lobby Parliament and woo the British public. But what Gandhi achieved through non-cooperation in 1920–2 and more especially the Salt March and civil disobedience in 1930 was the political authority to force British politicians of all parties to take Indian demands far more seriously than they had in the days of petitions and deputations. Before the Salt Satyagraha had commenced, in January 1930, Gandhi had observed that 'The British people must realise that the Empire is to come to an end. This they will not realise unless we in India have generated power within to enforce our will.'[30] Churchill's angry words a year later were, paradoxically, a tribute to Gandhi's growing power and personal achievement.

But, in the short term, Churchill need not have been too alarmed. The contents of the Pact were, from a nationalist perspective, extremely disappointing. The salt tax was not abolished and, indeed, the salt law remained on India's statute books until Nehru had it removed in October 1946. In return for the Congress 'discontinuing' civil disobedience, Irwin agreed only to allow local inhabitants the right to gather salt for their own needs. Nor, despite vociferous Congress demands, was permission given for police officers accused of 'atrocities' during the Civil Disobedience Movement to be prosecuted. The government did agree to release all political prisoners held in connection with the movement, but it refused to reinstate village officers who had resigned, as a number had in Gujarat during the Salt March, in support of Gandhi's campaign. Gandhi also agreed, rather surprisingly, to one of Irwin's principal objectives – to go to London to participate in the second Round Table Conference. As if to deny the nationalist polemics of the past two years, the Pact even talked about 'reservations' and 'safeguards' and made no significant gesture towards *purna swaraj*. Among many of Gandhi's most ardent and loyal supporters (including the Patidars of Gujarat) there was a feeling of intense frustration and disappointment that, after so many months of struggle and the hardships and sacrifices of repeated jail-going, Gandhi had settled for so little.[31] Jawaharlal Nehru, who had been in the thick of the fight since 1927, later remarked that the terms on which civil disobedience was suspended left him with a 'great emptiness as of something precious gone, almost beyond recall'.[32] Echoing this view, and comparing Gandhi's tactics in 1931 with his apparent climb-down with Smuts in 1908, Sumit Sarkar has described the Pact as 'perhaps the greatest anti-climax of them all'.[33] Even the loyal editor of Gandhi's *Collected Works* conceded that the Gandhi-Irwin negotiations 'yielded no tangible gains to the nationalist cause'.[34]

Why then did Gandhi agree to such an unpromising agreement and such 'paltry' concessions? It may be that Gandhi was less concerned with the contents of the Pact than with its symbolic importance, seeing his single-handed negotiations, as if on equal terms, as a victory in itself, marking a shift of power from the viceregal representative of the King-Emperor to the khadi-clad forces of nationalism. And, indeed, for the remaining months of 1931, the Congress did assume (to the intense annoyance of civil servants) something of the character of a parallel government, constantly bringing grievances arising from the Pact before harassed local officials and demanding for party workers a co-equal status in the resolution of disputes.[35] Perhaps, too, Gandhi felt it was better to reach an agreement, on almost any terms, while the Congress was still in a relatively strong agitational position and before its support slipped away, as it did so rapidly in 1922, and had taken years to rebuild.

Sumit Sarkar goes further and argues that around the middle of February 1931 Gandhi was pushed in the direction of compromise by the more moderate politicians, T. B. Sapru, M. R. Jayakar and V. S. Srinivasa Sastri (themselves recently returned from London and keen, as constitutionalists, for the round table talks to succeed). Even more influentially, Sarkar suggests, given the nature of Gandhi's financial and political backing, he was being nudged towards negotiations by the Indian business community, concerned at the growing loss of trade caused by Congress boycotts and agitation at a time when the Depression was beginning to bite on the Indian economy.[36] Such a line of argument reinforces the idea that 1930–1 was all along a more measured campaign than 1920–2 and that Gandhi, while appearing publicly as a peasant leader and constantly repeating his opposition to the salt tax as a struggle on behalf of India's 'starving millions', also remained in many respects attached to, or influenced by, business interests. The commercial middle classes while wanting to utilise mass discontent to secure concessions from the British were anxious at the same time to keep it within measured bounds and secure 'an honourable settlement'.[37]

. . .

LONDON AND THE ROUND TABLE CONFERENCE

Gandhi's decision to go to the Round Table Conference in London was one of the most striking consequences of his negotiations with Lord Irwin. It raises once again the issue of the complex intermingling of agitational and constitutional politics in the interwar period and Gandhi's ambiguous part in it. Even before the Simon Commission had delivered its report in June 1930, the Labour government in Britain had decided to summon a Round Table Conference to discuss India's future constitution. The first conference, which opened on 13 November 1930 and concluded on 19 January 1931, was dominated by moderate politicians like Sapru and Sastri, by Hindu nationalists like Jayakar, Muslims like Jinnah and Muhammad Ali, and representatives of the princely states, whom the British were anxious to draw into the discussions as a counterweight to the nationalists and as part of a projected all-India federation. Neither the constitutional objectives of the conference, nor the nature of its participants, could be expected to appeal to Gandhi and in many ways it seemed a throwback to the durbar politics and Moderate Congress of the pre-Gandhian era.

Until the end of August 1931, despite his agreement with Irwin, Gandhi's willingness to go to London remained uncertain and he seemed to have had doubts, after all, about the value of attending the second Round Table Conference. He tried to use his attendance as a bargaining chip in his on-going negotiations with the Government of India over the implementation of the March Pact. Having won some last-minute assurances and the approval of the Congress itself, Gandhi finally decided to go, though even on the train carrying him to Bombay he remarked that 'There is every chance of my returning empty-handed'.[38] Again, shortly before he left India by steamer on 29 August 1931, he said that his 'expectations of the Conference' were 'zero', but added that 'being an optimist I am hoping that something will turn up to make the Conference a success from the national Indian standpoint'.[39]

For all his apparently negative attitude, Gandhi often responded to crises by identifying himself with precisely those causes that seemed most distant from, even diametrically opposed to, his own – his decision to hand over control of the Congress Party to the Swarajists in 1925 or his offer to Jinnah shortly before Partition to place the entire Government of India in the hands of the Muslim League. Such startling moves cannot be put down to sheer perversity on Gandhi's part. They were a part of Gandhi's satyagraha, a technique for disarming his opponents, shaming or persuading them with love and self-sacrifice to see his perspective or recognise an overriding need for unity and consensus. Just as he was prepared to support the British war effort in 1918 by encouraging recruitment as a token of India's loyalty to Britain, so in 1931 Gandhi may have seen his participation in the constitutional conference as a way of showing his 'love' for Irwin and his desire to go to an untypical and self-sacrificing extreme to win over even the Indian moderates. He was forgoing his own distaste for constitution-making in order to show his determination to make their way work, while in actually demon-strating, precisely through its failure, the emptiness and divisiveness of constitutional politics. From such a situation civil disobedience might yet again gain moral ascendency and strength.

There was a further reason. Gandhi had not been to London, or indeed, outside India (apart from a visit to Ceylon in 1927) since 1915. He had, nonetheless, retained a number of valuable friendships with Britons (including, since their first meeting in South Africa in 1914, the Anglican clergyman C. F. Andrews)[40] and acquired many new correspondents and admirers from Britain and elsewhere in Europe. A few, like Madeleine Slade, had journeyed to India to join him; others, like Muriel Lester, a Christian pacifist, temperance advocate, and co-founder of the Kingsley Hall community settlement in the East End of London, had visited Sabarmati Ashram and thought highly of Gandhi and his work. As Lord Halifax later ob-served, Gandhi did not care much about constitutions, but he was 'interested in the human approaches' offered by the prospect of a visit to London and Europe.[41] In an age increasingly drawn to the extremes of communism and fascism on the one hand and to pacifism and a revulsion against war, imperialism and capitalism on the other, Gandhi could see the opportunity to project his ecumenical message of non-violence and social harmony. As he remarked in a radio broadcast to the United States from London in September 1931, Gandhi saw a world 'sick unto death of blood-spilling' and seeking a way out of its misery. 'I flatter myself', he continued, 'with the belief that perhaps it will be the privilege of the ancient land of India to show that way out to the hungering world.'[42]

From the start of the Salt Satyagraha, Gandhi had been intent on showing that this was a struggle against foreign rule, not a demonstration of hatred against the British, among whom he counted many of his 'dearest friends'. 'My ambition', he announced in his letter to Irwin on 2 March 1930, 'is no less than to convert the British people through non-violence, and thus make them see the wrong they have done to India.'[43] To symbolise this intention he sent this message to the Viceroy through a young English Quaker and pacifist, Reginald Reynolds. While he forbade both Reynolds and Mirabehn to court arrest during the civil disobedience campaign, Mirabehn brought Gandhi his food during the subsequent negotiations with Irwin at the viceregal palace in Delhi and, dressed in her coarse khadi robes, accompanied Gandhi to London, where she was frequently to be seen at the Mahatma's side. Churchill might rant at the 'half-naked fakir', but Gandhi knew, especially in the wake of the much-publicised Salt Satyagraha, the powerful impression he made in London and during his visit to the depressed mill districts of Lanca-shire and the positive reputation he had among the more progressive sections of the British public. Going to London might not win any constitutional victories but it might recapture the easy intercourse with radicals and non-conformists he had enjoyed in his student days and, in bypassing obstructive officialdom in India, create a more intimate means of resolving imperial differences. His aim was 'win their hearts' in England, and, by speaking what he understood to be the truth, 'melt the icy mountain of suspicion and distrust'.[44]

Gandhi arrived in London on 12 September. As well as Mirabehn, he was accompanied by his son Devadas, his secretaries Mahadev Desai and Pyarelal Nayar, his businessman friend G. D. Birla, the Hindu nationalist Malaviya, and Sarojini Naidu, who had succeeded him as Congress President in 1925 and played a leading part in organising the 'raids' by Congress volunteers on the Dharasana salt works. But if Gandhi had any lingering hopes for the Round Table Conference, and for his ability to represent there the 'dumb, semi-starved millions' and to be the single voice of his country, they were soon dashed. In mid-1931 Britain was swept by a series of political and economic crises. With the fall of the Labour government and its replacement on 24 August by a National Government, still under the premiership of Ramsay MacDonald, the political mood had changed and made any prospect of substantial concessions unlikely. With the Depression deepening and MacDonald dependent on Conservative support for his survival, the government was unwilling to allow any initiatives that would rock the political boat or reduce the value of India as a market for British textiles and other manufactured goods. Until the end of October Britain was in the grip of a bitter general election campaign and its politicians had little time to ponder India's constitutional future. The National Government was returned to power with a massive majority.

Inside the conference hall, Gandhi found himself only one of the 112 delegates, 23 of whom represented the princely states, 69 British India and 20 the British government. In claiming to represent all Indians and asking for full control of the army, finance, foreign affairs and an impartial tribunal to resolve the question of India's sterling debts, Gandhi was virtually drowned out by the talk of federation and 'safeguards' and the clamour for special rights and concessions, including separate electorates to protect 'minority' interests. An obituary published in *The Times* in January 1948 and evidently by a British insider, remarked somewhat caustically of Gandhi's part in the conference:

> The expectation formed in many quarters here of seeing a man of commanding gifts was not fulfilled. He had no mastery of details; constitutional problems did not interest him. He was no orator; his speeches were made seated and delivered in low level tones, which did not vary whatever his theme might be. His interventions in discussion were mainly propagandist, and often had little real connexion with the matter at hand. He made no real constructive contribution to the work of the Conference.[45]

One thing that Gandhi did, in dismay, take away from the meetings was the strength of the demand for separate electorates for untouchables, articulated by B. R. Ambedkar, a lawyer who claimed that he, and not Gandhi, represented India's most downtrodden people. This, as we will see in the next chapter, laid the basis for his 'epic fast' in Yeravda jail in 1932 and the launch of his Harijan campaign. Gandhi was clearly ill at ease and out of place in a gathering where 'every divisive tendency in India was encouraged'.[46] The personal stature and authority he had enjoyed during his negotiations with Irwin only months earlier seemed now to have evaporated. By 8 October, when the conference still had two more months to run, in the face of repeated demands from the Muslims, Anglo-Indians and other 'minorities' demanding constitutional 'safeguards' for their communities, Gandhi was driven to confess he felt close to 'utter failure' in his attempt to resolve the communal deadlock and put across the simple demand for Indian independence.[47]

However, in his personal campaign to win hearts and minds, Gandhi had much greater success. He stayed at Kingsley Hall, a 'veritable Christian ashram' of pacifists and volunteer social workers,[48] at Bow in London's East End, close to where Annie Besant had led a strike of match-girls in 1888 and socially far from the boarding houses of Bayswater in which Gandhi had spent his early years in London. He also had a much-publicised tea with King George and was introduced to Charlie Chaplin. Gandhi had never seen any of his films and did not care for the cinema, but there was something akin to his own identification with the poor and downtrodden in Chaplin's 'little man' screen persona, as there was later in the engagement with soulless machinery in *Modern Times* and the delusions of tyranny in *The Great Dictator*. In a rare foray into industrial Britain, in late September Gandhi visited the textile towns of Lancashire to show his solidarity with the mill-workers, despite the hardship India's boycott of British cloth was causing them. Gandhi emerged from this episode at least as something of a popular hero. Although the political situation in India was deteriorating rapidly, on leaving London he travelled back through Europe. He conversed with Romain Rolland, his biographer and Mirabehn's other idol, at his villa outside Geneva, and in a meeting more portentous of the coming decade, had an awkward, ten-minute audience with Mussolini in Rome. The Pope declined to see him. Gandhi appears to have been far more impressed by the Sistine Chapel than by the Duce, and in an emotional response rare for him was moved to tears by a crucifix on the high altar, as if foreseeing in it a portent of his own martyrdom.[49] On 14 December he sailed from Brindisi for Bombay. He never left India again.

He arrived back to find India much changed. Irwin had left office the previous April to be replaced as Viceroy by the hardline Lord Willingdon, a former Governor of both Bombay and Madras. Tired of the niggardly British approach to even the limited concessions of the Gandhi-Irwin Pact and frustrated by the lack of progress in London, the Congress had swung back to civil disobedience. This time, however, the new Viceroy was in no mood to be cautious or conciliatory, and ordered the immediate arrest of all leading Congressmen, including Jawaharlal Nehru and Abdul Ghaffar Khan. Willingdon bluntly rejected Gandhi's request for an interview and ordered the implementation of a battery of wide-ranging ordinances, covering such matters as 'unlawful association', 'unlawful instigation', 'molestation' and boycotting, and cumulatively designed to prevent the movement from regaining its former momentum. Gandhi was arrested on 4 January on his arrival at Bombay and dispatched, without trial, to prison at Yeravda once more. Across the country, tens of thousands of Congress activists and supporters were arrested and imprisoned in one of the biggest political clampdowns India had yet seen: an estimated 120,000 men and women were arrested between January 1932 and March 1933. Despite the repression, continuing efforts were made to defy the government, but by the second half of 1932 the movement had virtually come to a standstill. It was formally called off on 7 April 1934. Gandhi, however, was not so easily defeated.

. . .

NOTES AND REFERENCES

1. Romain Rolland, *Mahatma Gandhi*, London, 1924, p. 117.
2. Judith M. Brown, *Modern India: The Origins of an Asian Democracy*, Oxford, 1985, pp. 223–40.
3. Robin Jeffrey, 'Travancore: Status, Class and the Growth of Radical Politics, 1860–1940: The Temple-Entry Movement', in Robin Jeffrey (ed.), *People, Princes and Paramount Power: Society and Politics in the Indian Princely States*, Delhi, 1978, pp. 151–5.
4. David Arnold, 'Industrial Violence in Colonial India', *Comparative Studies in Society and History*, 22 (1980), p. 242.
5. Dennis Dalton, *Mahatma Gandhi: Nonviolent Power in Action*, New York, 1993, p. 92; George Woodcock, *Gandhi*, London, 1972, p. 71,
6. *CWMG* XLI, p. 209.
7. Sumit Sarkar, *Modern India, 1885–1947*, Basingstoke, 1989, pp. 247–52, 267–74.
8. Ibid., p. 283.
9. M. K. Gandhi, *Hind Swaraj or Indian Home Rule*, Ahmedabad, 1938, p. 92.
10. Judith M. Brown, *Gandhi and Civil Disobedience*, London, 1977, pp. 92–4.
11. *CWMG* XLII, p. 501.
12. Ibid.
13. William L. Shirer, *Gandhi: A Memoir*, New York, 1979, p. 95.
14. Dalton, *Gandhi*, p. 91.
15. In New York in 1930, the Reverend John Haynes Holmes remarked that in Gandhi 'we see the Christ alive again': Francis Watson, *The Trial of Mr Gandhi*, London, 1969, p. 188.
16. Ibid., p. 115.
17. Woodcock, *Gandhi*, p. 10.

18. Louis Fischer, *The Life of Mahatma Gandhi*, New York, 1962, p. 273.
19. Ibid., p. 275.
20. Shirer, *Gandhi*, p. 98.
21. Ibid., pp. 76, 132.
22. Brown, *Modern India*, p. 270.
23. Brown, *Gandhi and Civil Disobedience*, p. xiii.
24. Dalton, *Gandhi*, p. 105.
25. Shirer, *Gandhi*, p. 70.
26. Watson, *Gandhi*, p. 198.
27. Carl Bridge, *Holding India to the Empire: The British Conservative Party and the 1935 Constitution*, New Delhi, 1986, pp. 61–2.
28. James D. Hunt, *Gandhi in London*, New Delhi, 1993, p. 176.
29. Bridge, *Holding India*, p. 62.
30. *CWMG* XLII, p. 422.
31. David Hardiman, *Peasant Nationalists of Gujarat: Kheda District, 1917–1934*, Delhi, 1981, pp. 234–9.
32. Jawaharlal Nehru, *An Autobiography*, London, 1936, p. 259.
33. Sumit Sarkar, 'The Logic of Gandhian Nationalism', *Indian Historical Review*, 3 (1976), p. 114.
34. *CWMG* XLV, pp. vi–vii.
35. David Arnold, *The Congress in Tamilnad: Nationalist Politics in South India, 1919–1937*, New Delhi, 1977, pp. 133–7.
36. Sarkar, 'Gandhian Nationalism', pp. 136–41.
37. Sarkar, *Modern India*, p. 311.
38. *CWMG* XLVII, p. 369.
39. Brown, *Gandhi and Civil Disobedience*, p. 245.
40. Hugh Tinker, *The Ordeal of Love: C. F. Andrews and India*, Delhi, 1979.
41. Watson, *Gandhi*, p. 211.
42. *CWMG* XLVIII, p. 9.
43. *CWMG* XLIII, p. 6.
44. *CWMG* XLVII, p. 120.
45. Hunt, *Gandhi in London*, p. 183.
46. Fischer, *Gandhi*, p. 292.
47. Hunt, *Gandhi in London*, p. 194.
48. Ibid., p. 181.
49. Mirabehn, *The Spirit's Pilgrimage*, London, 1960, p. 293.

Chapter 7

THE LONE SATYAGRAHI: GANDHI, RELIGION AND SOCIETY

Gandhi was never solely a political leader. He was obsessed, appalled and fascinated by power, but not just the power wielded, or aspired to, by conventional politicians. The experience of colonialism and the stark contrasts it threw up between a *diwan*'s household in Kathiawar, his student life and English friends in London, his years in white-dominated, racially divided South Africa, his discovery of the Indian peasants, their backwardness and poverty – all these made Gandhi aware that power did not alone reside in political parties, in ballot boxes, armies and constitutions. Power in a colonial world, especially for the colonised, manifested itself in almost every aspect of society and the self, but in India under the British was added the further complexity of Hindu society with its own elaborate notions of status, purity and pollution. It was not, therefore, surprising that Gandhi sought power in a number of different ways, some Indian, others Western, that constantly overlapped and interacted with one another. Power resided in what people ate, how they dressed, in the language they spoke, in the roles they ascribed to women. Gandhi found power in sex and even more in abstention from it, in silence, as on the many Mondays when he denied himself the power of speech, or in fasting, when he used the threat to his life as a means of asserting control not only over himself but also over others.

Some Indians sought to deal with the problem of power in a colonial situation through compartmentalisation – by being an English-speaking, Western-style Liberal in public and a socially conservative, ritually devout Brahmin at home, or by making a distinction between political progress and social reform. But Gandhi rejected this duality. In his mature life (dating, in effect, from his vow of celibacy in 1906) he claimed to recognise no clear distinction between politics and religion, morality and economics, nor between public and private life. If his 'experiments' in one field of power were thwarted, as often they were, Gandhi could switch with remarkable ingenuity and resilience to some other task, which in its way was no less moral or political, no less about the exercise or constraint of power. Swaraj for Gandhi did not simply mean freedom from British rule, but the creation of a society worthy of that freedom. In seeking to overturn the colonial status quo he identified an equal need to change society as well, or else, in his view, freedom would be empty of real meaning. Since in India social organisation was closely bound up with religious beliefs and identities, Gandhi's religious ideas greatly affected his thinking about politics and society just as the religious beliefs and attitudes of others influenced how they perceived and responded to him.

. . .

GANDHI'S RELIGION

Wrestling in prison in the mid-1930s with his own ambivalent attitudes to Gandhi, Jawaharlal Nehru paid tribute to his personal warmth and vitality. His writings, Nehru observed, did not do justice to the man: 'he is far greater than what he writes'. And, despite his emphasis upon religion and morality, he was far from being of the 'Calvinistic priestly type'. 'His smile is delightful, his laughter infectious, and he radiates light-heartedness. There is something childlike about him which is full of charm. When he enters a room he brings a breath of fresh air with him which lightens the atmosphere.'[1] But Nehru also acknowledged what 'a problem and a puzzle' Gandhi was 'to his own people' as well as to his British adversaries. In most modern countries Gandhi would have appeared out of place, Nehru observed, as anachronistic as the medieval Christian saints to whom he was often compared. But India still seemed to 'understand or at least appreciate, the prophetic-religious type of man', who talked of 'sin and salvation and non-violence'.

> Indian mythology [he continued] is full of stories of great ascetics, who, by the rigour of their sacrifices and self-imposed penance, built up a 'mountain of merit' which threatened the dominion of some of the lesser gods and upset the established order. These myths often come to my mind when I have watched the amazing energy and inner power of Gandhiji, coming out of some inexhaustible spiritual reservoir.[2]

While Nehru could acknowledge the popularity Gandhi possessed by virtue of being one of India's 'great ascetics', there was more than a little annoyance in this recognition. For Nehru, as for many of his other associates and adversaries, Gandhi had a disturbing habit of mixing up religion and politics, obscuring what should have been arrived at logically or through open debate. Instead, his claim that 'my politics are derived from my religion',[3] gave him free rein to follow his instincts and the licence to make pronouncements or take decisions on the basis of his conscience or 'inner voice' alone. This forestalled collective decision-making among the Congress leaders and frequently infuriated men like Nehru who wanted the Mahatma's mass appeal without the burden of his religiosity.

Religion, nonetheless, was one of the principal bases of Gandhi's power, one of the main sources of his authority over India and for his struggle against British imperialism. Gandhi's deeply held religious beliefs gave him great moral strength and physical courage, enabling him to endure long years of struggle, defeat and imprisonment. They also helped inspire in others that rare combination of bravery, commitment and self-sacrifice that characterised the nationalist movement under Gandhi. Equally, his use of religious ideas and images, drawn largely from popular Hinduism, did much to establish and sustain his national leadership after 1915. He adopted the cow as one of the most potent symbols of Hinduism and of India, and when referring to the India that was to result from the ending of British rule he frequently spoke of Ram Rajya, with its evocation of a restored (and explicitly Hindu) golden age. Gandhi had little interest in the outer forms and conventions of the Hindu religion, its rituals, shrines and pilgrimages, except when he could use them as symbols or metaphors – his prison cell became a 'temple', his Salt March a 'pilgrimage'. Although Gandhi drew heavily on Hindu mythology, it was largely in pursuit of allegories of suffering and renunciation, or figures of whose dedication, non-violence and self-sacrifice he approved – such as Harishchandra, the virtuous Sita, wife of Ram, and the faithful Draupadi of the *Mahabharata*. Women figured prominently in this canon, including the *bhakti* saint Mira, who gave up her life as a Rajput princess to follow a life of piety and poverty.

Gandhi has been seen as one of the seminal figures of modern Hinduism and even 'the greatest representative' of the renaissance of Hinduism that occurred in reaction to Christianity and the West during the nineteenth and early twentieth centuries.[4] It must be said, though, that Gandhi's Hinduism was of a highly idiosyncratic and eclectic kind. It spawned no reforming sect of its own, and many Hindus found difficulty in understanding or identifying with it. Gandhi 'made up his brand of Hinduism as he went along.'[5] To his upbringing in Kathiawar, where he was exposed to Jainism as well as Vaishnavite Hinduism, Gandhi acquired in London and South Africa a knowledge of Christianity and Theosophy and developed a largely self-taught understanding of Hindu concepts and classical texts, particularly through his study of the *Bhagavad Gita*. In the mid-1890s he corresponded with the devout Bombay jeweller Raychandbhai, thereby strengthening his acquaintance with Jainism, and, the better to understand his Muslim fellow-Gujaratis, he began to read the Koran. But Gandhi appears to have drawn relatively little from Islam, either in South Africa or during the Khilafat movement of the early 1920s. Perhaps he found the idea of a holy war or *jihad* against non-believers too much at variance with his own belief in ahimsa and the truth to be found in all regions, or considered *sufi* mysticism too remote from his this-worldly concerns. Like Christianity, Gandhi considered Islam a young religion, 'still . . . in the making' and 'still groping for its great secret'.[6]

Midway through his South African years, Gandhi began to deepen his commitment to Hinduism. He drew increasingly on Sanskrit terms and concepts to inform his political and moral philosophy and to generate an alternative vocabulary to that of Western politics and religion. While the substitution of swaraj for 'Home Rule' or 'independence' was not his work alone, he invested the term with a broader meaning and more religious tone than Naoroji and Tilak had given it. The invention of the word satyagraha in place of 'passive resistance' was similarly indicative of Gandhi's determination to find a more assertive term, one that shed suggestions of 'passivity', but it was also expressive of his determination to ground the concept in Indian rather than Western tradition. From Sanskrit, too, Gandhi drew other terms that were central to his emerging ideology – notably *ahimsa* (non-violence), *brahmacharya* (celibacy), *tapasya* (self-suffering) and *moksha* (salvation). He found in *dharma* (duty or right action) a concept that lay at the heart of Hinduism (and of the *Gita*) as he understood it. By contrast, Gandhi remained indifferent to many other aspects of Hinduism, from the folk beliefs and village deities of the Indian peasantry to the militant Hindu nationalism of Tilak and his Maharashtrian followers. For Gandhi religion formed the basis for everyday life, shaping every activity and belief. It was not something to be observed by retreating from everyday life, confined to holy days or relegated to contemplation of the afterlife. His ashrams in South Africa and India were an embodiment of his belief that religion and work should function side by side, not in isolation from each other. Gandhi's Hinduism was a moralistic, almost theistic, faith in which 'truth' was synonymous with God. 'My uniform experience has convinced me', he wrote in his autobiography, 'that there is no other God than Truth.'[7] And, on many other occasions throughout his adult life, Gandhi repeated the equation of Hinduism with non-violence and the restless pursuit of truth.

But Hinduism was not the only source of Gandhi's religious ideas and vocabulary. If he found it necessary to speak to India through the language and idioms of Hinduism, so he felt able to speak to the world through those of the Christian faith. The South African years brought Gandhi particularly close to Christianity.[8] It was not just that he was befriended and courted as a possible convert by Christians like Albert Baker, an attorney and lay preacher, and the Reverend Joseph Doke, his first biographer. He also found in a strain of Christianity, as represented by the Sermon on the Mount and Tolstoy's *The Kingdom of God is Within You*, something deeply moving and spiritually appealing, and certainly far less abrasive and intolerant than the Christianity propagated by missionaries on the streets of Rajkot in his youth. The early ashram communities he developed in South Africa, beginning with Phoenix Settlement in 1904, owed something to his visit to a Trappist community near Durban he visited in 1895 and which greatly impressed him. He also developed an abiding affection for Christian hymns – 'Lead, Kindly Light' and 'When I Survey the Wondrous Cross' – which he incorporated into his ashram prayer meetings in India.

But Gandhi did not accept Christianity uncritically. Before he had been in South Africa for very long, he had rejected any idea of converting to Christianity. 'I could accept Jesus as a martyr,' he wrote in his autobiography, 'an embodiment of sacrifice, and a divine teacher, but not as the most perfect man ever born.' The 'pious lives of Christians' did not seem superior to those of other faiths, philosophically 'there was nothing extraordinary in Christian principles', and, 'from the point of view of sacrifice', Hindus 'greatly surpassed the Christians'. It was, therefore, impossible to regard Christianity 'as a perfect religion or the greatest of all religions'.[9] But the issue may have been as much racial as theological. Gandhi may have resisted conversion because he could see that, as an Indian in a racially divided world, becoming a Christian would be neither liberating nor empowering. It would not remove the barriers of racial discrimination, or bring greater status and self-respect. Conversion might, even in matters of dress, diet and speech, signal the loss of his Indianness and deprive him of the strength to be derived from belonging to his own religious tradition. It was, after all, possible to borrow from Christian beliefs and practices, and build a 'creative synthesis' between faiths, without actually becoming a Christian. In a speech to Christian missionaries in Madras in February 1916, Gandhi explained that he had studied the Bible and considered it a part of his scriptures. 'The spirit of the Sermon on the Mount competes almost on equal terms with the *Bhagavad Gita* for the domination of my heart.' But, as a Hindu and despite his 'great leanings towards Christianity', he urged the missionaries to give up their attempts to proselytise and concentrate on philanthropic work in India.[10] For all its flaws, Hinduism was his swadeshi religion, and to abandon it would be to jettison a central part of his spiritual identity and inheritance. As Gandhi once remarked, 'I have been born a Hindu and I shall die a Hindu. . . . If there is salvation for me, it must be as a Hindu. Hinduism absorbs the best in other religions and there is scope for expansion in it.'[11]

Gandhi could, nonetheless, recognise that Christianity was a world religion in a way that Hinduism was not (at least, not then) and, moreover, that it was the religion of the British and their empire. To fail to engage with Christianity would be to ignore an essential element of Britons' self-belief and self-legitimation, a critical ingredient in their self-proclaimed 'civilising mission' in India. As a satyagrahi, it was important to him to probe their inner contradictions, and, rather than inflame their moral indignation and self-righteousness, try to appeal through their religion to their own better selves. Christianity, Gandhi learned in London and South Africa, was one of the most effective ways of developing a constructive dialogue with the West. If the ideals of satyagraha were to work and the British were to be won over to seeing the immorality of their empire, it could best be done by appealing to the finer aspects of their own Christian traditions. Gandhi's Christian friends, men like C. F. Andrews, were very important to him personally and politically, for they helped to bridge the moral as well as racial divide between the colonisers and the colonised. Gandhi's familiarity with Christianity helped to facilitate dialogue with the ruling representatives of the West, as shown by his negotiations with Lord Irwin in 1931, and it was as important internationally for Gandhi to be called 'Christ-like' and his Salt March to be compared with Jesus's triumphal entry into Jerusalem as it was for him to be hailed in India as the Mahatma. It was no accident that Gandhi found solid support among the Quakers, who also had a strong tradition of pacifism. His visit to London in 1931, with his timely denunciation of violence, seemed to confirm the view of Gandhi in Western eyes as a Quaker in a loin cloth. And yet it is as well to remember the confusion and the antagonism Gandhi's closeness to Christianity could create in the minds of many fellow-Indians. There was more alienation than admiration in the observation made in 1933 by a leading Bengali Congressman, Sarat Chandra Bose, that Gandhi was 'undoubtedly the greatest Christian in the world', adding 'I wish he had been, at the same time, a great Hindu. Had he been so', Bose averred, 'he would not have committed the blunders he has committed in the fields of religion and politics.'[12]

. . .

CASTE AND UNTOUCHABILITY

While Gandhi remained, in his own eyes at least, a devout Hindu, his approach to Hinduism, especially to its social organisation, was highly critical. After the passage in his autobiography quoted earlier in which he explained his reasons for not converting to Christianity, Gandhi added that the 'defects' of Hinduism were also 'pressingly visible' to him. If untouchability could be a part of Hinduism, it could only be 'a rotten part or an excrescence'. Nor could he see any justification for 'a multitude of sects and castes'.[13] The true nature of caste and the need to remove from it the 'blight' of untouchability were issues central to Gandhi in his attempts to revitalise Hindu society. While in his attack on 'modern civilisation' in *Hind Swaraj* Gandhi appeared to take the position of a social conservative and an upholder of Indian tradition, in many other respects he belonged to a long line of social reformers who, since the days of Rammohun Roy and Ishwarchandra Vidyasagar early in the nineteenth century, had campaigned to transform Hindu society from within and to remove some of its most grievous injustices.[14] But Gandhi, typically, brought to this legacy of social reform his own eclectic views and an idiosyncratic mixture of conservatism and change.

What caste is and how it affects the lives and identity of Indians, is a matter much debated in the scholarship of modern India. It has often been pointed out that the word 'caste' is of foreign (Portuguese) origin and so inevitably distorts the true nature of Indian social organisation, and that although caste is a characteristic primarily attributed to Hindu society, it also influences the perception, status and social interaction of other religious communities, including Muslims, Christians and Sikhs, in South Asia. *Varna*, the theoretical four-fold division of Hindu society described in Chapter 2, or *jati*, a word often employed to describe the locally operative sub-divisions of castes (but also, confusingly, used to identify an entire people or nation) might be better terms to use. But it was largely in terms of 'caste' that the structure of Hindu society was debated in the nineteenth and early twentieth centuries and hence in the social and political milieu in which Gandhi operated.

In taking up the idea of caste in the second half of the nineteenth century, the British gave it a more precise ethnographical, statistical and political meaning than it had previously possessed. From the time of the first all-India census in 1871–2, shortly after Gandhi's birth, caste became one of the principal criteria by which British officialdom categorised and enumerated the Indian population. By the late nineteenth century, scores of official manuals and handbooks had been produced which set out systematically to identify each caste, its supposedly distinctive social and physical characteristics, its religious practices and occupational status, and its seemingly immutable place in the social hierarchy. Such categories were not in themselves new, but by applying a seemingly scientific precision to caste across India the British helped to transform what had previously been a set of rather fuzzy, localised identities into far more strictly defined and tightly enumerated notions of community. In the army and other branches of the colonial administration, such as the police and the subordinate civil service, as well as among plantation managers and other employers of Indian labour, caste, alongside religion and region of origin, became a key factor in recruitment policies. It was assumed that by knowing an individual's caste it was possible to know his or her true identity, their capacity to be a good soldier, a tough or trustworthy policeman, an efficient clerk, or a hardworking 'coolie'. Caste was thus seen to be the distinctive and inescapable foundation of Indian society and to inhibit or preclude the possibility of a supra-caste, national, identity. When Gandhi and others claimed that India was and had always been a nation, Europeans replied that it was merely a loose confederation of castes and communities, so divided off from one another that they virtually constituted small nations in themselves.[15]

The colonial emphasis upon caste as the 'natural' constituent of Indian society encouraged or cajoled Indians to work within the designated parameters of caste, and to seek to use it as a vehicle for social change or political representation. In Gandhi's youth, and more especially during his South African years, a host of 'caste associations' sprang up in India, some responding directly to the census categories (contesting, for instance, the demeaning designation given to them or challenging the census commissioners to recognise their higher status and superior occupational pursuits).[16] As the administration grew and the constitutional system evolved, caste and community began to be built into the political process, and seats in municipal councils, district boards, even in the provincial legislatures themselves were allocated or sought after on the basis of caste and community. The British, in part responding to what they saw as meaningful divisions in Indian society, in part playing a manipulative game of 'divide and rule', supported separate representation for Muslims in the legislative councils under the Morley-Minto reforms of 1909. Separate representation meant that a certain number of seats in the legislature (based on their share of the population) were set aside for Muslims. Only Muslim voters were eligible to vote in these constituencies; only Muslims could be elected. This cut at the heart of Indian nationalism and offered a highly significant precedent for others. By 1918–19 other religious or caste communities – Christians, Anglo-Indians (Eurasians), Sikhs in Punjab, 'non-Brahmins' in Madras and Bombay, low-caste communities of various descriptions, and the untouchables or 'Depressed Classes' – were all seeking separate representation for themselves. Gandhi was growing up in, and more especially in 1915 returning to, an India in which caste and community had begun to assume a host of new meanings and an unprecedented political importance.

At first Gandhi appeared little troubled by these developments. In the peculiar conditions of South Africa, he identified himself without contradiction as a Bania, a Gujarati, a Hindu and an Indian. Only gradually, as he began to associate himself with Indians from other backgrounds, did the idea of caste begin to raise serious moral and political issues for him. In some ways Gandhi was strongly attracted to the principle of caste, though not of a rigidly hierarchical 'caste system'. Caste represented a vernacular alternative to Western society, ruined by 'life-corroding competition' and divided by the savage wars of class against class. It offered instead, at least in theory, a society of interdependent occupational groups, living and working harmoniously together for their mutual benefit. Members of the carpenter or potter caste could work amicably alongside those of peasant or weaver castes: each needed the other and could exchange their different skills and products within the self-sufficient confines of the Indian village.[17] Caste was a swadeshi institution, much as Hinduism was a swadeshi faith, and one did not lightly abandon time-tested traditions, sanctioned by the wisdom of past ages. As a means of preserving social order within and between different occupational and social groups, caste was also for Gandhi a mechanism which made the oppressive structure of the state almost irrelevant. Caste held village society together and historically, Gandhi believed (taking a leaf out of the Orientalist history books), it had enabled Indian society to remain virtually intact and locally self-governing, despite successive tides of foreign invaders. Speaking in 1916 Gandhi declared that the 'vast organisation of caste' not only served the religious needs of the community: 'it answered too its political needs. The villagers managed their internal affairs through the caste system, and through it they dealt with any oppression from the ruling power or powers.'[18] He similarly claimed in 1920–1 that caste had saved Hinduism from disintegration in the past, and though there were too many sub-castes, he was against any destruction of its fundamental constituents. Castes should not be about inferiority or superiority: they should 'define a man's calling' rather than enforce social hier-archy. In what might appear a backhanded tribute to the reforming tide of modernity, Gandhi added that the 'spirit of democracy', which was fast spreading throughout India and the rest of world, 'will, without a shadow of doubt, purge the institution of the idea of predominance and subordination.'[19]

On a more practical level, caste was a crucial element in the Gandhian campaigns of the 1917–32 period. Like many other politi-cians of his day, Gandhi addressed a large number of meetings organised by caste associations and appealed to their members for political support and for funds, partly on the basis of their traditional occupations and identity. If they were weavers by caste, he asked them to be true to their traditions and support khadi; if they were Kshatriyas, he called on them to show the warrior-spirit of the ancestors, only now in the service of satyagraha. Similarly, the at-traction of Gandhi's wider social programme, particularly abstention from alcohol, helped attract many upwardly aspiring castes and their leaders to his 1920–2 political campaign. Appeals to caste solidarity could, Gandhi more cautiously suggested, be supported by the sanction of social boycotts ('an age-old institution . . . coeval with caste'), so long as these were non-violent and used to encourage 'discipline', and not impose 'punishment'.[20] Scholars have noted the importance of such caste-based tactics in several satyagraha movements, including Kheda in 1918 and Bardoli ten years later.[21]

But, as Dennis Dalton has pointed out, Gandhi's ideas on caste and untouchability changed dramatically over time, from a position of relative conservatism to one far more radical and extreme.[22] Having dissolved his own sense of class in South Africa, it was hard for Gandhi to uphold a similar system of hierarchy and discrimination in India, and during the 1920s his ideas began to assume a more radical complexion. In a series of speeches in south India in September–October 1927, he attacked the idea of caste as inherited superiority and called for equality between castes. He argued that what he called *varna* or *varnashrama dharma* (the duty or right conduct appropriate to each *varna*) had 'nothing to do with caste' as currently understood, a 'monster', an 'excrescence', a 'travesty of *varna*' that was degrading both Hinduism and India.[23] Instead by *varnashrama dharma* he envisaged a return to broad *varna* categories. Indians belonged not to a myriad of individual castes and sub-castes, jostling for privilege and prestige, but to four broadly defined estates, as Brahmins, Kshatriyas, Vaishyas and Shudras. These were not arranged hierarchically, nor were they necessarily even hereditary categories, but represented different kinds of occupations, skills and abilities. All those who served society by imparting knowledge were in effect Brahmins, whether they were born into that caste or not, and their contribution to society was not, in Gandhi's view, superior to any other form of service such as manual labour. Each *varna* had its own *dharma*, its own rightful modes of livelihood, conduct and service.

Hence Gandhi was able, in theory at least, to synthesise East and West, to overturn the hereditary, hierarchical principle that appeared central to Hindu society and replace it with a society that was democratic and egalitarian but still recognised the different contributions each *varna* made to society as a whole. But in his latter years Gandhi seemed increasingly impatient for change. By the mid-1930s he was urging the removal of all restrictions on inter-dining and intermarriage. By 1946 he had taken his views on intermarriage a stage further, announcing that in future he would not be prepared to bless any marriage unless one of the partners was a Harijan or untouchable.[24]

From his South African days Gandhi's critical attitude to caste had also been informed by his deep-seated opposition to the 'crime' of untouchability. The issue assumed crisis proportions for him in 1915 with the admission of an untouchable and his family to the Sabarmati Ashram soon after its founding. In addition to the hostility of those who had hitherto been helping the ashram, Gandhi also had to face the dissatisfaction of Kasturba and his nephew Maganlal, on whom much of the running of the ashram depended. Helped by a timely donation, Gandhi managed to weather the storm without sacrificing his principles, proclaiming to the world that the ashram 'would not countenance untouchability'. He also persuaded himself, improbably, that because orthodox Hindus continued to provide financial support for the ashram, untouchability had been 'shaken to its foundations'.[25] Thereafter Gandhi became more open and resolute in his opposition to untouchability, denouncing it in his 'Ashram vows and rules' in 1916, as an 'ineffaceable blot' on Hinduism. While Gandhi often used the past as the authority for his beliefs, in this instance he refused to believe that 'this miserable, wretched, enslaving spirit' of untouchability could have been 'handed down to us from immemorial times'. 'That any person should be considered untouchable because of his calling passes one's comprehension.'[26]

Although untouchability had long concerned other Hindu social and religious reformers, such as Swami Vivekananda, Gandhi gave the issue a new political prominence. With his triumph over the Congress organisation in 1920 its removal became part of the Congress creed and enshrined in the Constructive Programme.[27] But, in certain respects, Gandhi's attitude to untouchability remained cautious: as with caste itself, he was eager as far as possible to encourage a consensus for change rather than openly antagonise Hindu orthodoxy. This was reflected in his partial support for the Vaikam Satyagraha of 1924–5 (referred to in Chapter 5), which concerned the right of untouchables to pass along a road in front of a caste-Hindu temple. Gandhi visited the area in April 1925 and helped persuade the state authorities in Travancore to remove the police barricade which had prevented untouchables from using the road. In the autumn of that year the local Brahmins gave in and a new road was later opened to allow untouchables to pass by the temple. But Gandhi opposed any extension of the campaign to press for the entry of untouchables into temples reserved for caste Hindus, and not until the late 1930s was a successful temple-entry campaign mounted.

. . .

THE 'EPIC FAST' AND HARIJAN CAMPAIGN

Gandhi was no conventional traditionalist, intent simply on preserving Hinduism as he found it, though he was guided by what he understood to be the original 'truth' or purity of his religion. This became especially clear in 1932–4 when he embarked on a campaign against untouchability. As he himself remarked at this time, 'It is the whole of Hinduism that has to be purified and purged. What I am aiming at . . . is the greatest reform of the age.'[28] While Gandhi's opposition to untouchability was longstanding, he was impelled towards a more radical public stance by several developments in the late 1920s and early 1930s. For a while, as Gandhi was drawn back into nationalist politics and took charge of the Salt Satyagraha of 1930, the question of caste reform and untouchability slipped into the background. He was better able to build consensus around his political leadership than in his role as a Hindu social reformer. But, as already noted in connection with his participation in the Round Table Conference in London in 1931, the discussion of India's constitutional future was closely bound up with the issue of 'minorities', variously defined by caste, race and religion, and the 'safeguards' they demanded.

One of the virtues that could be claimed for the Gandhian programme of boycotting the legislative councils and turning to direct action instead (in 1920 and again in 1930) was that this drew attention away from the incessant squabbling over communal representation and focused nationwide concern instead on the central issue of attaining swaraj. In London in 1931, however, Gandhi was forced to recognise that these issues, far from withering away, were gaining momentum as the prospect of a new constitution and an enlarged franchise drew nearer. The widening political participation that the Congress had contributed to over several decades did not merely aid the nationalist cause. It also gave rise to new demands and new forms of leadership among castes and communities that had previously been excluded from the arenas of formal political activity. These ranged from low-ranking Shudra communities, including peasant and artisan castes, to the untouchables, who from the late nineteenth and early twentieth century had been mobilising them-selves through caste associations and other organisations to press the colonial government and Indian political parties for recognition of their demands.

One of the most influential and articulate of the new untouchable leaders was Bhimrao Ramji Ambedkar. Born in 1891, Ambedkar came from the Mahar caste in Maharashtra, but was educated in the United States and London, and became a lawyer in the Bombay High Court. In 1919 he presented the case for a separate electorate for untouchables (along similar lines to that granted to Muslims in the reforms of 1909) to the Southborough Committee, appointed to prepare the detailed arrangements for the franchise under the new Government of India Act. His arguments were not accepted then, but Ambedkar, nominated to the Bombay Legislative Council in 1927 to represent the Mahar community, was not easily dissuaded from his faith in communal representation and separate electorates. In London in 1931, he skilfully allied himself with the Muslims, Indian Christians and others in a 'Minorities Pact' to press their joint demand for separate electorates. If accepted, untouchables would not form part of the 'Hindu' constituencies, but be able to elect members of their own communities for constituencies reserved for untouchables alone. At the time the Depressed Classes numbered some 50 million people, nearly 15 per cent of the population of India, and though relatively few of them would have a vote even under an enlarged franchise, the effect of separate representation, as with the Muslims, would be to harden their sense of separate identity.

For Gandhi, who claimed to 'represent the vast majority of the Untouchables', this was complete anathema. He could understand the arguments advanced by other minorities, but the claim advanced on behalf of the untouchables was 'the unkindest cut of all'.[29] It would signal the dismemberment of the Hindu community and leave it for ever divided between caste Hindus and untouchables, whereas Gandhi's aim had been to integrate the two and remove the artificial barriers that kept them apart. The conference broke up in bitter disagreement, and Gandhi returned to India to face the renewed civil disobedience and imprisonment. However, on 16 August 1932 the British Prime Minister Ramsay MacDonald announced the 'Com-munal Award' by which a total of seventy-one seats in the Indian legislatures were to be set aside for untouchables (though he promised to respect any alternative arrangement the communities themselves might agree to).

Apart from this, there were other factors driving Gandhi towards a fresh engagement with the untouchability question. Since the late nineteenth century there had been strong pressure to preserve the numerical and social strength of the Hindu community by trying to reconvert to Hinduism those who had become Muslims or Christians. This movement was particularly associated with the Arya Samaj, founded in 1875 by Dayananda Saraswati, a Gujarati Brahmin who wanted to restore Hinduism to what he understood to be its ancient Aryan heritage and Vedic purity. The reconversion movement grew in strength in the 1920s and 30s, aided on the one hand by the rise of new and overtly Hindu communal organisations – the Hindu Mahasabha, dating from 1907 but revived in 1923, and the shadowy and conspiratorial Rashtriya Swayamsevak Sangh (RSS), set up in 1925 – and, on the other, by the substantial number of untouchables who continued to convert to Islam or Christianity, thus stimulating Hindu fears that they were becoming a 'dying community', weakened and outstripped by other, proselytising, religions.

While Gandhi did not favour constitutional politics, and the communal arithmetic that accompanied it in colonial India, he did regard the untouchables as an essential and integral part of the Hindu community and indeed, along with the peasantry, one of the principal responsibilities of its educated and reforming leaders. To lose such a large part of the Hindu constituency, whether through separate electorates or religious conversion, was, for him, deeply perturbing. This is one illustration, among many (such as his attitude to the Vaikam Satyagraha and his response to the publication in 1927 of the American journalist Katherine Mayo's highly critical book *Mother India*),[30] of Gandhi's increasingly defensive and proprietorial attitude towards the Hindu community and its leaders' 'civilising mission'. The issue of the untouchables and their possible loss, like Mayo's book, touched the raw nerve that he had first felt in South Africa – Hindus' claim to be accepted as 'civilised'. With separate electorates, Gandhi believed, caste Hindus would feel denied, or absolved from, responsibility for the 'uplift' of the untouchables, whereas one of his concerns since 1915 had been to elevate them to a position of moral respectability within Hindu society, and through education and sanitation, by the abjuring of meat and alcohol and the rejection of impure lifestyles and livelihoods, enable them to become worthy members of Hindu civilisation. There was also a more pragmatic consideration. Back in prison and with the civil disobedience movement faltering in mid-1932, Gandhi could hope to use the issue of the

Communal Award to keep himself and his programme in the public limelight. In prison in 1922–4 Gandhi had been denied the 'oxygen of publicity': he was anxious not to be stifled again.

Having previously written to warn the Secretary of State for India and the Prime Minister, on 20 September 1932 Gandhi began a 'fast unto death' to protest against the Communal Award and to persuade untouchables and caste Hindus to unite in rejecting it. 'All eyes were now turned to Yeravda.'[31] Ambedkar at first opposed any concessions. 'I do not care for political stunts,' he remarked defiantly. 'My decision stands. If Mr Gandhi wants to fight with his life for the interest of the Hindu community the Depressed Classes will also be forced to fight for their lives to safeguard their interests.'[32] But the pressure on Ambedkar and other untouchable leaders steadily mounted as Sapru, Birla and other prominent public figures rallied to Gandhi's cause. Ambedkar, like the British before him, did not want to take on the awesome responsibility for Gandhi's death, and his position was further undermined by the willingness of another untouchable leader, M. C. Rajah, to support joint rather than separate electorates. Within five days of the fast's commencement, Ambedkar gave in and the 'Poona Pact' (echoing the Gandhi-Irwin agreement eighteen months earlier) was approved at Gandhi's prison bedside on 24 September, though he continued his fast two days longer, until 26 September. As a result of the Pact, subsequently accepted by the British government, there were to be joint electorates, shared by caste Hindus and untouchables, but with 18 per cent of seats reserved for untouchables. Although an element of special representation for the Depressed Classes remained, the separate electorate for which Ambedkar had so long campaigned was jettisoned.

The 'epic fast' and the Poona Pact were significant – and highly controversial – for several reasons. Supporters and admirers of Gandhi have often seen the fast as a major breakthrough. While conceding that the fast could not by itself 'kill the curse of untouchability' and that the 'Harijans remained the dregs of Indian society', Louis Fischer nonetheless claimed that it had 'snapped a long chain that stretched back into antiquity and . . . enslaved tens of millions'. After the fast, 'untouchability forfeited its public approval; the belief in it was destroyed.'[33] What is more certain is that the fast and the pact established Gandhi as a leading defender and reformer of Hindu society, and seemed to uphold the claim that he, not Ambedkar, represented India's untouchables. He followed up the fast by adopting the term 'Harijan' or 'children of god' to describe them. In February 1933 he formed a Harijan Sevak Sangh or 'service society' to undertake work on their behalf and in the same month launched a new weekly, the *Harijan*, to support his campaign. Freed from jail in May 1933, he was re-arrested in August for disobeying a restraint order. But a fortnight later, when he felt that the British were unreasonably obstructing his Harijan work while he was in prison, he embarked on a further (eight-day) fast and was released unconditionally. Between November 1933 and June 1934 Gandhi undertook an all-India 'Harijan tour', in the course of which he campaigned for the opening of wells, roads and temples to untouchables, for education and temperance, and for funds and other support from caste Hindus to help their 'uplift'. The temple-entry campaign gained momentum, and though the British blocked a bill in the Legislative Assembly in August 1934, an increasing number of temples, formerly confined to the higher castes, began to admit worshippers from the Depressed Classes for the first time.

In some respects, then, the fast and the launching of the Harijan movement were means by which Gandhi could revive his leadership and tactically outmanoeuvre the British during a phase of otherwise intense political repression. Like the Salt March three years before, the fast showed Gandhi's extraordinary capacity for capturing public attention, and for several days, during the tension and high drama of the fast and the accompanying negotiations, he was able to make his prison cell the centre of national and even international attention. This was a kind of revenge for the isolation and powerlessness he had been forced into during his 1922–4 prison term at Yeravda. Although Gandhi's approach to the Harijan issue has been called 'insensitive and demeaning',[34] there is little reason to doubt that his fast and subsequent campaign did help to highlight the plight of the untouchables, to set in train some ameliorative measures and draw several Depressed Classes leaders into the nationalist struggle, even if it failed to achieve a fundamental change in their social and political position.

But this was undoubtedly one of the most contentious phases of Gandhi's entire career. Like his fast during the 1918 Ahmedabad mill strike, the Yeravda fast and Ambedkar's capitulation raised troubling questions about the way in which Gandhi used this technique, strengthened, in this instance, by the novel tactic of threatening to fast 'unto death'. The result was virtually to blackmail Ambedkar into submission rather than to use fasting as a genuine means of persuasion and conversion as the rules of satyagraha would seem to have required.

For many commentators, the threat to kill onself, for whatever reason, 'can be nothing else but coercion'.[35] Recalling his own earlier confrontations with Gandhi in South Africa, J. C. Smuts in 1939 expressed his relief at not having had to deal with Gandhi's new-found technique of 'persuasion by semi-starvation', and saw similarities between this and the ways in which the dictators of the age also sought to overwhelm 'the public mind, not by reason but by play on the emotions, many of them of an irrational character'. He conceded, though, that fasting had 'worked wonders in India' and carried Gandhi to 'heights of achievement which would probably have been unattainable otherwise'.[36] Even more bluntly, it has been suggested that Gandhi's emphasis upon suffering and endurance, exemplified by his threatened 'fasts unto death', 'points to a strong sado-masochistic streak in his character'.[37]

Certainly, Ambedkar was far from persuaded by Gandhi's antics. In the years following the fast he wrote vitriolically (to quote the title of his 1945 book) about *What Gandhi and the Congress Have Done to the Untouchables*, and after Independence tried to lead the Depressed Classes, or Dalits as they have come to be called, out of Hinduism and into the Buddhist faith. For many of Gandhi's critics the very term 'Harijan' is patronising and condescending, reinforcing and rationalising the hegemony of the upper castes over God's 'children'. The Harijan movement was seen as a political gimmick which did not seriously address, let alone resolve, the real social and economic issues that lay behind their continuing oppression. Not surprisingly, therefore, among many Dalit organisations Gandhi is remembered with neither affection nor respect. A manifesto issued in 1973 by the Dalit Panthers of Maharashtra (who took their name from the Black Panthers in the United States but drew much of their ideology from Ambedkar) accused Gandhi of being 'deceitful, cunning, an orthodox caste-ist', who 'flirted' with the Dalit problem simply in order to 'preserve unity in the Independence struggle'. For them Gandhism signified the 'preservation of religion authority', 'casteism', upholding 'traditional divisions of labour', and 'an unscientific outlook'.[38] Nor did Gandhi's fast and the Poona Pact succeed in winning support from the Hindu Mahasabha, the RSS and Hindu communalists in general. Indeed, Gandhi now found his own weapons of protest turned against him. Orthodox Hindus blocked moves for Harijan temple entry and picketed his meetings with black flags, the treatment once meted out to the Simon Commission. In 1934 three attempts were made on his life, the most serious a bomb explosion at Poona on 25 June. He undertook a twenty-one-day purificatory fast, begun on 8 May 1933 while he was still in jail, but this failed to dissolve the hatred. Fifteen years before his eventual assassination, the opposition to Gandhi was beginning to mount and to cast a menacing shadow over his life.

.   .   .   .

GANDHI ADRIFT

For Gandhi, the 'epic fast' represented a significant turning point. This was true not just in terms of his public stance on untouchability, but also the evolution of his techniques. As Table 1 shows, Gandhi had used fasting for various purposes since his first major experiment with this technique at the Phoenix Settlement in South Africa 1914. These included the use of fasting as a way of expressing his deep sense of sorrow and hurt at the conduct of those he professed to love; to atone for the misdeeds of those for whom he felt responsible; as an 'intense spiritual effort' to stir other people's 'sluggish consciences' and 'sting them into action'; and to bring quarrelling parties together and encourage them to resolve their differences. There were elements in Gandhi's fasting of both a Hindu idea of penance and a Christian notion of suffering love. The aim of the fast was 'to purify oneself, to generate moral energy within oneself, and to appeal to the consciences and mobilise the moral energies of its intended constituency.'[39] Recognising that fasting could easily be misused, he imposed conditions on himself, including that it should be directed only at those with whom he had ties of love, that it should have clear and specific goals, and that it should not in any way serve his own ends. But it is questionable whether Gandhi actually observed his own guidelines.

From 1932 fasting became a frequent weapon in Gandhi's armoury, as he moved away from satyagraha as a form of collective protest and non-violent resistance to a highly personalised (and coercive) use of fasting. In particular, the threat of fasting 'unto death', first used in 1932 and repeated on two subsequent occasions (in 1939 and 1947), called into question the extent to which such extreme forms of fasting remained within the bounds of non-violent action. Gandhi became the lone satyagrahi, answerable to nobody, relying on his personal prestige and moral power to 'move the whole world'.[40] But when he succeeded it was not from the 'power of truth' but

Table 1 **Gandhi's principal fasts**[41]

Date	Place	Reason	Duration and type
February 1914	Phoenix Settlement	Misbehaviour of young ashramites (also 14 days in May 1914 for same reason)	7 days
March 1918	Ahmedabad	To strengthen resolve of strikers	3 days
April 1919	Ahmedabad	Penance for violence in Rowlatt Satyagraha	3 days
November 1921	Bombay	To stop violence during visit of Prince of Wales	5 days
February 1922	Delhi	Penance for death of police at Chauri Chaura	5 days
September–October 1924	Delhi	Penance for Hindu-Muslim violence	21 days
November 1925	Sabarmati Ashram	Misbehaviour of ashramites (also three days in mid-1928 for similar 'moral lapses')	7 days
September 1932	Yeravda Jail	To oppose Communal Award	'to death', but lasted 6 days
May 1933	Yeravda Jail	To 'purify' self and associates	21 days
August 1933	Yeravda Jail	To protest against British restrictions on Harijan work	8 days
July 1934	Wardha	Penance for violence against opponent	7 days
March 1939	Rajkot	To protest against ruler's conduct	'to death', but lasted 5 days
February–March 1943	Poona	To protest against British blaming Gandhi for Quit India violence	21 days
September 1947	Calcutta	To stop Hindu-Muslim violence	'to death', but lasted 4 days
January 1948	Delhi	To stop Hindu-Muslim violence	6 days

because Indians could not bear the guilt of his death and the British feared the public disorder that would erupt if they did not give in.

Gandhi's fasts and his espousal of the Harijan cause aroused further doubts about his leadership in the mid-1930s. Jawaharlal Nehru, one of those closest to Gandhi, was dismayed by his decision to fast 'to death' over the Communal Award. It seemed to Nehru that this was a 'side-issue', a constitutional distraction from the civil disobedience movement and the quest for independence, for which it was pointless to risk Gandhi's life. Nehru was angry at 'his religious and sentimental approach to a political question, and his frequent references to God in connection with it.' Gandhi even seemed to suggest that God had set the date for the Yeravda fast. 'What a terrible example to set!'[42] Nehru's anger and dismay were even greater when on 15 January 1934 a devastating earthquake struck Bihar, killing 15,000 people and injuring thousands more. Gandhi declared that this was a divine judgement, a 'chastisement' for the continuing 'sin of untouchability'. Nehru was 'staggered' by this remark, commenting that, 'Anything more opposed to the scientific outlook it would be difficult to imagine.'[43] Rabindranath Tagore, who had become reconciled to Gandhi in recent years and had even rushed to his bedside during the 'epic fast' in Poona, was also outraged: 'this kind of unscientific view of things is too readily accepted by a large section of our countrymen,' he warned. But Gandhi was unrepentant, insisting that while earthquakes, floods and droughts seemed to have only physical causes, he 'instinctively' felt that they were 'somehow connected with man's morals'.[44]

In the early 1920s Gandhi's rise to all-India leadership had profited not merely from an upsurge of nationalist fervour and bitter frustration with the constitutional process, but also from a mood of disenchantment among many of India's intellectuals with modernity itself. For some the mechanised mass-destruction of the First World War epitomised the waste and folly of the modern West; for others there was a feeling that India had been weakened and corrupted by the changing lifestyles that had flowed from British rule and a blind following of Western fashions – in diet, in dress, in the obsession with speed, with motor cars and 'fast' city living. Gandhi appealed to those who wanted to reject this delusory modernity and go back to India's simpler past, revive its ailing villages, return to wholesome food and drink and homespun clothing. But by the mid-1930s the mood had begun to shift once more, and India's scientific community, which had struggled for more than a decade with the taint of being unpatriotic, began to reassert itself and to question the wisdom of Gandhi's policies and pronouncements.[45] His remarks on the Bihar earthquake signalled the emergence of a new critique of Gandhi as 'superstitious', 'unscientific', out of touch with the realities of the modern world.

While Gandhi clung to ideas he had enunciated in *Hind Swaraj* thirty years earlier, younger Congress leaders like Nehru and Subhas Chandra Bose began to be attracted by the possibilities of using state power to effect much-needed social and economic change and of employing science and technology in the service of the nation. An editorial by the physicist Meghnad Saha in the first issue of the journal *Science and Culture* in 1935 captured this new mood. It criti-cised those among India's leaders who were incapable of seeing the 'great and inevitable part' which 'the new age of technic' would play in India's destiny and 'the lasting contribution' it was 'likely to make to the future of India's civilisation'. There was nothing to be gained by looking back to an imaginary golden age, 'when nobody is sup-posed to have had anything to complain of', or blaming science for all society's current ills. The editorial deplored the view that 'better and happier conditions' could be created by 'discarding modern scientific technic and reverting back to the spinning-wheel, the loin cloth and the bullock cart'. Properly used, science could provide 'far better solutions to our bewildering economic, social and even political problems'.[46]

Gandhi, it should be noted, was not entirely anti-science. He read fairly widely on scientific topics, his personal interest in dietetics leading him, for example, to study some of the recent literature on nutrition. But he remained sceptical of formal systems of science and medicine (including those belonging to the Hindu tradition), preferring to regard satyagraha as a science in its own right and his significantly named '*experiments* with truth', especially the effects of diet, celibacy, hydrotherapy and nature cures, as being for him far more meaningful and reliable.[47] In the aftermath of the Civil Dis-obedience Movement and his Harijan tour, Gandhi's 'experiments' seemed to take him further and further away from the Congress and nationalist leadership. Disappointed at the lack of active interest in the Constructive Programme and dismayed by the renewed gravita-tional pull of constitutional politics, in October 1934 Gandhi resigned from the Congress to devote himself to the regeneration of India's villages, work which he saw as closely linked to Harijan social ser-vice. If Congressmen forgot the Constructive Programme, Gandhi remarked with some bitterness, and confined themselves to winning elections and participating in 'fruitless debates' in the legislatures, 'they will soon find that I have taken with me the kernel of politics and they have kept for themselves only the outermost husk, without even the vitamins'.[48]

On 26 October 1934, before leaving the Congress, Gandhi set up yet another organisation, the All-India Village Industries Association. Having made a vow in 1931 that he would not return to Sabarmati Ashram until India gained its freedom, in April 1936, at the age of 66, he settled at the village of Segaon, near Wardha in the Central Provinces. Renamed Sevagram ('service village'), this became the last of Gandhi's four ashrams, and, apart from his imprisonment during the Second World War, he spent most of his time there until August 1946. The settlement grew out of work previously done in the area by his disciples Vinoba Bhave and Mirabehn and provided a new base for experimental work on education, sanitation, diet and Harijan uplift. Located close to the geographical heart of India, this was one of the poorest and most backward areas of rural India, Champaran with a vengeance. Sevagram was notoriously unhealthy. It was parched for most of the year, malnutrition was rife, as was malaria, to which Gandhi and his followers frequently succumbed.[49] Gandhi was forced, as never before, to grapple with the misery and hardship of village life; but, if he had genuinely hoped for seclusion away from the political limelight, he did not find it. Sevagram was within relatively easy reach of the railway junctions at Wardha and Nagpur, and as well as politicians seeking his advice and blessings, a stream of welfare workers and social activists, Indian and foreign, came to see him. The Mahatma had become the sage of Sevagram.

. . .

WOMEN AND GENDERED POLITICS

Along with caste and untouchability, one of the most vexed and widely debated issues of social reform in India under colonial rule was the role and status of women. From early in the nineteenth century, beginning with the controversy over *sati*, the immolation of Hindu widows on their husbands' funeral pyres, the treatment of India's women was used by European critics to judge the strengths, and more especially the weaknesses, of Hindu society and the worthiness of Indian civilisation. During the course of the century women's signifying role was kept alive among Indians as well as Europeans as they debated such contentious topics as widow remarriage, the age of consent, and women's rights to education and health. With respect to the 'women's question', as with caste reform or the removal of untouchability, Gandhi was heir to a long history of agitation and public debate.[50] Nonetheless, Gandhi has often been seen as a pioneer and an innovator in this as in so many other fields. He has been praised for his 'revolutionary approach to women in society' and for anticipating views later held by the feminist movement. He has been credited, particularly on the basis of their participation in the Salt Satyagraha, with having drawn women out of seclusion and into public life. In him, to quote Judith Brown, 'the women of India found a very considerable champion.'[51] But of late Gandhi's attitudes to women and the claims made for his role in their liberation have begun to be looked at as critically as the claims made for his role as a leader and emancipator of peasants and untouchables.[52] Gandhi's treatment of his own wife, Kasturba, has been called 'notorious' and, despite his large female following and many female associates, his influence on women 'both personally and politically' has been described as 'largely malign'.[53]

In London in 1906 and 1909, Gandhi heard and read about the activities of the Suffragettes and their campaign for the women's vote. As with Indian terrorists, he professed admiration for their bravery and their willingness to face imprisonment and physical hardship for their cause. But he was clearly unhappy about the Suffragettes' methods, especially their recourse to violence (such as smashing Prime Minister Asquith's windows) and their use of hunger-strikes. Gandhi also seemed to feel that the 'manly strength' they brought to their campaign was inappropriate for women.[54] Although in India Gandhi frequently commented on issues relating to women and saw himself as having a special relationship with them (he saw himself as a kind of honorary woman much as he portrayed himself as an honorary Harijan), he never undertook a satyagraha on their behalf. Indeed, the participation of Indian women in the 1913–14 campaign in South Africa (including Kasturba's arrest and imprisonment) and in the Salt Satyagraha (after women had been excluded from the Salt March) took Gandhi by surprise. Although he was forced to admire the courage showed by women in these movements, he was uneasy about their assuming such a high-profile public role and preferred them to engage in activities like picketing drink and foreign-cloth shops, forms of protest he considered far more suited to their feminine nature.[55]

There were many contradictions, and much condescension, in Gandhi's attitudes to women. He claimed to look upon women as 'equal partners in the fight for swaraj', and was critical of men who saw themselves as the 'lords and masters of women instead of considering them as their friends and co-workers'. But at the same time he identified a woman as 'the true helpmate of man in the mission of service' and as being, 'like the slave of old', unaware of her own right to equal status with men.[56] Although he worked alongside women in a number of his campaigns, such as Anasuya Sarabhai during the Ahmedabad mill strike or with Sarojini Naidu who succeeded him as Congress President in 1925 and helped orchestrate the 'raids' on the Dharasana salt works in 1930, in the main Gandhi regarded women as more potent as political and moral symbols than as real-life activists. He idealised women, including his mother, as models of non-violence, purity and self-sacrifice and contrasted this favourable imagery, as in the account in his autobiography of his 'carnal' father and his own conduct at the time of Karamchand's death, with male lust and selfishness. He looked to women in Hindu mythology as the embodiment of feminine ideals and believed that women's suffering and quiet patience was something that men should learn from and emulate. In this latter, Gandhi was to some extent engaged in a characteristic exercise in inversion. For more than a century the 'manly' British had criticised Indians (the 'martial races' apart) for being physically weak and morally soft, childlike and, above all, 'effeminate'.[57] Gandhi tried to turn this around by making the weak into the strong, praising precisely those aspects of Indian tradition and identity that reflected female strengths and virtues. Satyagraha itself was a kind of feminine power deployed against the brutal masculinity of colonial rule. But at the same time Gandhi fiercely and repeatedly – in South Africa in his fight against racism, in *Hind Swaraj*, in his response to the Jallianwala Bagh massacre, in the Non-Cooperation Movement of 1920–2 and on the eve of the Quit India Movement in 1942 – denounced colonialism for having robbed Indians of their manhood and appealed to them to be 'manful' in their defiance of injustice. To take but one of many examples, in the course of his trial in March 1922, he claimed that Indians had been 'emasculated' and India had become 'less manly under the British rule than she ever was before'.[58] Colonialism was a kind of castration, and, while at one level praising and identifying with what he saw to be feminine virtues and values, Gandhi (colonial subject as well as political leader and social reformer) was impelled by deep anger at this 'emasculation'.

Perhaps the language and imagery of gender was so powerful to Gandhi because at a personal level he was plagued throughout his adult life by his sexual drives and an obsessive struggle to control them. His own experience of marrying at 13 left him with an abiding sense of guilt about his adolescent sexuality and anxiety about the 'shackles of lust'. As a student in London he kept quiet about having a wife and son in India, and in later life was severely critical of the 'cruel custom' of child marriages, as he was more generally of dowries and expensive weddings.[59] His relations with the young Kasturbai seem to have oscillated between bursts of intense sexual desire and frustrated fury at his failure to educate her and reform her attitudes (as towards untouchability). From this there emerged a grudging admiration for her stubbornness, which Gandhi in retrospect chose to interpret as one of the routes by which he learned about satyagraha. Despite the idea of purity that framed Gandhi's general understanding of women, there are, to the contrary, several references to (unconsummated) encounters with prostitutes in his autobiography and in *Hind Swaraj* there is a tasteless denunciation of the British Parliament as a 'sterile woman' and a 'prostitute'. Elsewhere Gandhi's writing also suggests that he saw women as temptresses as well as saints and hence as a challenge to his quest for control over his own sexual desires. The need to control, or at least to sublimate, his troubling sexuality and direct that energy to what he understood to be nobler ends dominated Gandhi's attitude to women and their place in society at large.

Gandhi began to experiment with sexual abstinence around 1901, following the birth of his fourth son, and in 1906 took a vow of *brahmacharya*. While this meant self-denial and self-control in many different respects – indulgence in food, for instance – for Gandhi it primarily meant sexual abstinence. While extremely diverse attitudes to male and female sexuality are to be found within Hinduism, Gandhi was drawn to the idea that for men emission of semen represented a loss of spiritual as well as physical strength. In a passage that Gandhi may have read around 1903, Vivekananda observed:

> The chaste brain has tremendous energy and gigantic will power. Without chastity there can be no spiritual strength. Continence gives

wonderful control over mankind. The spiritual leaders of men have been very continent, and this is what gave them the power.[60]

At the time of the Zulu rebellion and his vow of *brahmacharya*, Gandhi felt unable to devote himself to his wife and immediate family at the same time as finding the physical and psychic energy needed to serve the Indian community and the satyagraha campaign.[61] The founding of Phoenix Settlement and Tolstoy Farm further illustrate his shift away from personal intimacy and the family to presiding over a wider collectivity. Gandhi was on his way from being 'Bhai' (brother) to his Indian associates to becoming 'Bapu' (father), as he began to be known in South Africa by 1914 and as Nehru, Mirabehn and others were to call him later in India. Gandhi came to see sexual attraction as unnatural and, even in the most loving relationship, as a form of violence and a cause for self-loathing. There could be no joy in sex, no fulfilment of human emotional and physical needs. At best it served the sordid needs of procreation. Otherwise, like other manifestations of violence, it needed to be vigorously controlled and if possible suppressed entirely.[62] The inmates of his ashrams in South Africa and in India, even when living alongside their wives and husbands, were expected to give up sexual relations and become sexless brothers and sisters. For many of them it was a severe trial and a cause of much underlying tension and conflict.

Gandhi believed, nonetheless, that ashram life was particularly conducive to women's education and advancement. In a programme of 'Ashram Observances' he drew up in 1932 he supported equal educational opportunities for women. There was to be coeducation for girls and boys up to the age of 8 and, as far as possible, to the age of 16; both were to learn how to cook, spin and sew.[63] Gandhi claimed that his ashram experiments with education achieved 'the largest measure of success with women', who thereby 'imbibed the spirit of freedom and self-confidence' as no other class of women had done. Ashram women were 'not subject to any restraint which is not imposed on the men as well. They are placed on a footing of absolute equality with the men in all activities. Not a single Ashram task is assigned to the women to the exclusion of the men.' Women were 'exempted from work which is beyond their strength'; but otherwise 'men and women worked together everywhere.' Gandhi saw the observance of *brahmacharya* as making 'a big contribution to this state of things. Adult girls live in the Ashram as virgins. We are aware that this experiment is fraught with risk but feel that no awakening among women is possible without incurring it.'[64]

Gandhi saw women as the embodiments of service – whether to the family or to the nation – and in ways that were, despite his claims for the ashram environment, almost entirely traditional. Gandhi had little interest in the way in which women were joining such professions as medicine and education or entering public life and forming their own welfare organisations.[65] Nor, from his disinterest in the constitutional process, was he much concerned with the struggle for women's right to vote, partly conceded for women with property and educational qualifications in the 1920s. At its session at Karachi in March 1931 the Congress passed a resolution on fundamental rights, in which women were promised political equality regardless of their social status and qualifications. But the impetus for this resolution came from Jawaharlal Nehru, not from Gandhi. As with the four *varnas* and their distinctive roles and duties, Gandhi saw men and women as equal but intrinsically different, with different contributions to make to the overall pattern of society. Indeed rather than advancing the women's movement in the 1920s and 30s, Gandhi seemed intent on imposing on women a new regime of moral obligations and social constraints. In particular he appealed to middle-class women to give up their finery, foreign cloth and jewellery and to spin and wear khadi instead. Spinning was one of the few economic activities Gandhi approved of for women: it kept them at home or in the villages and saved them from going to work in evil factories. Women's primary role was to manage the domestic environment, to be 'the queens of households', and nurture swadeshi in the home.[66] Except as servants of the nation, they were not encouraged to venture much beyond the home.

One of the striking aspects of Gandhi's attitudes to women was the extent to which he operated almost exclusively within the conventions and idioms of Hindu society. Few non-Hindu women figured among his favoured icons, and, while he acknowledged many imperfections in the treatment of Hindu women, he also saw many virtues in them not evident in other religions and societies. Thus he remarked in 1926 that 'a real Hindu widow is a treasure. She is one of the gifts of Hinduism to humanity.'[67] Conversely, he found little to praise or admire in Western women. He seems to have been baffled and perturbed by those he did encounter who had strong personalities or forthright convictions of their own – such as Annie Besant or Margaret Sanger, the American birth-control advocate who visited Gandhi at Wardha in January 1936 and who, with 'dreadful earnestness', tried to convince him that artificial contraception, not celibacy, was the best means to stop having too many children.[68] Gandhi found it easier to assimilate Madeleine Slade, giving her a suitably devout Hindu name, Mirabehn (after the *bhakti* saint Mira), though it was her decision, not his, that she adopt Indian dress, and the sexual chemistry between them became so intense that Gandhi had to send her elsewhere rather than succumb to temptation.[69]

In his later life Gandhi clearly enjoyed the physical presence of women and was photographed on a number of occasions supported under each arm by young female relatives and followers. At Sevagram in the late 1930s he began the practice of sleeping next to women at the ashram, including his physician Sushila Nayar. In February 1944, Kasturba died. On his release from imprisonment, and at a particularly difficult moment in his life, when he felt alone and comfortless, politically marginalised and failing in physical strength, Gandhi resumed his 'experiments' with sex. In one of the most notorious episodes in his highly controversial life, in December 1946, when he was 77, he shared his bed with his 19-year-old grandniece Manu, believing that in proving he could still control his sexual impulses he would regain his moral strength. According to one source, he even remarked 'If I can master this, I can still beat Jinnah', the Muslim League leader who by then, to Gandhi's deep dismay, was intent on Partition.[70] Many even of his closest associates were shocked by Gandhi's conduct and, though the episode was hushed up at the time, it ultimately contributed to the view in the West that Gandhi's ideas about sex were 'outlandish and almost inhuman'.[71] Gandhi seems to have thought only of testing his self-control, his *brahmacharya*, not of what the episode might mean to Manu or reveal about his instrumentalist view of women as a whole.

. . .

NOTES AND REFERENCES

1. Jawaharlal Nehru, *An Autobiography*, London, 1936, p. 515.
2. Ibid., pp. 253–4.
3. William L. Shirer, *Gandhi: A Memoir*, New York, 1979, p. 205.
4: William Theodore de Bary, *Sources of Indian Tradition*, II, New York, 1968, p. 250.
5. Bhikhu Parekh, *Gandhi*, Oxford, 1997, p. 5.

6. Rudrangshu Mukherjee (ed.), *The Penguin Gandhi Reader*, New Delhi, 1993, p. 211.

7. M. K. Gandhi, *An Autobiography, Or The Story of My Experiments with Truth*, Ahmedabad, 1940, p. 382.

8. Margaret Chatterjee, *Gandhi's Religious Thought*, London, 1983, ch. 3.

9. Gandhi, *Autobiography*, p. 101.

10. *CWMG* XIII, p. 220.

11. Antony Copley, *Gandhi: Against the Tide*, Oxford, 1987, p. 65.

12. Leonard A. Gordon, *Brothers Against the Raj: A Biography of Indian Nationalists Sarat and Subhas Chandra Bose*, New York, 1990, p. 264.

13. Gandhi, *Autobiography*, pp. 101–2.

14. C. H. Heimsath, *Indian Nationalism and Hindu Social Reform*, Princeton, 1964.

15. H. H. Risley, *The People of India*, Calcutta, 1908.

16. David Washbrook, 'The Development of Caste Organisation in South India, 1880–1925', in C. J. Baker and D. A. Washbrook, *South India: Political Institutions and Political Change, 1880–1940*, Delhi, 1975, pp. 150–203; Sekhar Bandyopadhyay, *Caste, Protest and Identity in Colonial India: The Namasudras of Bengal, 1872–1947*, Richmond, 1997.

17. M. K. Gandhi, *Hind Swaraj or Indian Home Rule*, Ahmedabad, 1939, p. 55.

18. Raghavan Iyer, *The Moral and Political Writings of Mahatma Gandhi*, III, Oxford, 1987, pp. 328–9.

19. *CWMG* XXI, p. 247; XIX, p. 84.

20. *CWMG* XIX, p. 368.

21. Ghanshyam Shah, 'Traditional Society and Political Mobilization: The Experience of Bardoli Satyagraha (1920–28)', *Contributions to Indian Sociology*, 8 (1974), pp. 93–101.

22. Dennis Dalton, 'The Gandhian View of Caste, and Caste after Gandhi', in Philip Mason (ed.), *India and Ceylon: Unity and Diversity*, London, 1967, pp. 159–81.

23. *CWMG* XXXV, p. 519.

24. *CWMG* LXXXII, p. 326.

25. Gandhi, *Autobiography*, pp. 299–301.

26. *CWMG* XIII, p. 232–3.

27. Eleanor Zelliot, 'Congress and the Untouchables, 1917–1950', in Richard Sisson and Stanley Wolpert (eds), *Congress and Indian Nationalism: The Pre-Independence Phase*, Berkeley, 1988, pp. 182–8.

28. *CWMG* L, p. 352.

29. Oliver Mendelsohn and Marika Vicziany, *The Untouchables: Subordination, Poverty and the State in Modern India*, Cambridge, 1998, pp. 104–5.

30. Katherine Mayo, *Mother India*, London, 1927. Although Mayo quoted his critical views on sanitation and untouchability extensively and with approval, Gandhi damned the book as 'slanderous' and a 'drain inspector's report': *CWMG* XXXIV, pp. 539–47.

31. Pyarelal, *The Epic Fast*, Ahmedabad, 1932, p. 22.
32. Ravinder Kumar, 'Gandhi, Ambedkar and the Poona Pact, 1932', in Jim Masselos (ed.), *Struggling and Ruling: The Indian National Congress, 1885–1985*, London, 1987, p. 95.
33. Louis Fischer, *The Life of Mahatma Gandhi*, New York, 1962, p. 323.
34. Burton Stein, *A History of India*, Oxford, 1998, p. 300.
35. Mark Jurgensmeyer, 'Shoring Up the Saint: Some Suggestions for Improving Satyagraha', in John Hick and Lamont C. Hempel (eds), *Gandhi's Significance for Today: The Elusive Legacy*, Basingstoke, 1989, p. 42.
36. J. C. Smuts, 'Gandhi's Political Method', in S. Radhakrishnan (ed.), *Mahatma Gandhi: Essays and Reflections on His Life and Work*, London, 1939, pp. 278–9.
37. Stein, *India*, p. 301.
38. Lata Murugkar, *Dalit Panther Movement in Maharashtra: A Sociological Appraisal*, London, 1991, pp. 234–5.
39. Parekh, *Gandhi*, pp. 11, 57–8.
40. George Woodcock, *Gandhi*, London, 1972, p. 90.
41. Based on J. T. F. Jordens, *Gandhi's Religion: A Homespun Shawl*, Basingstoke, 1998, pp. 259–60.
42. Nehru, *Autobiography*, p. 370.
43. Ibid., p. 490.
44. Sabyasachi Bhattacharya (ed.), *The Mahatma and the Poet: Letters and Debates between Gandhi and Tagore, 1915–1941*, New Delhi, 1997, pp. 158–60.
45. David Arnold, *Science, Technology and Medicine in Colonial India*, Cambridge, 2000, pp. 189–90, 205–9.
46. *Science and Culture*, 1 (1935), pp. 3–4.
47. Joseph S. Alter, *Gandhi's Body: Sex, Diet and the Politics of Nationalism*, Philadelphia, 2000, esp. pp. 21–7.
48. Mark Thomson, *Gandhi and his Ashrams*, London, 1993, p. 179.
49. Pyarelal and Sushila Nayar, *In Gandhiji's Mirror*, Delhi, 1991, pp. 34–43.
50. Kumkum Sangari and Sudesh Vaid (eds), *Recasting Women: Essays in Colonial History*, New Delhi, 1989.
51. Vina Mazumdar, 'The Social Reform Movement in India: From Ranade to Nehru', in B. R. Nanda (ed.), *Indian Women: From Purdah to Modernity*, New Delhi, 1976, pp. 41–66; Judith M. Brown, *Gandhi: Prisoner of Hope*, New Haven 1989, p. 209.
52. Madhu Kishwar, 'Gandhi on Women', *Economic and Political Weekly*, 5 October 1985, pp. 1691–702 and 12 October 1985, pp.1753–8; Sujata Patel, 'Construction and Reconstruction of Woman in Gandhi', ibid., 20 February 1988, pp. 377–86.
53. Stein, *India*, pp. 300–1.
54. James D. Hunt, *Gandhi in London*, New Delhi, 1993, pp. 95–6, 127–32.

55. Radha Kumar, *The History of Doing: An Illustrated Account of Movements for Women's Rights and Feminism in India, 1800–1990*, London, 1993, ch. 5.
56. *CWMG* LXXV, p. 155.
57. Mrinalini Sinha, *Colonial Masculinity: The 'Manly Englishman' and the 'Effeminate Bengali' in the Late Nineteenth Century*, Manchester, 1995.
58. *CWMG* XXIII, p. 118.
59. Fischer, *Gandhi*, p. 24.
60. Jordens, *Gandhi's Religion*, p. 26.
61. Gandhi, *Autobiography*, pp. 154–8.
62. See Gandhi's advice to his son Manilal on the eve of his marriage in March 1922: *CWMG* XXIII, pp. 101–2.
63. Raghavan Iyer, *The Moral and Political Writings of Mahatma Gandhi*, II, Oxford, 1986, p. 609.
64. Ibid., p. 610.
65. Kumar, *History of Doing*.
66. Gandhi, *Hind Swaraj*, pp. 33–4.
67. *CWMG* XXI, p. 314.
68. Yogesh Chadha, *Rediscovering Gandhi*, London, 1997, pp. 337–9.
69. Martin Green, *Gandhi: Voice of a New Age Revolution*, New York, 1993, pp. 304–6.
70. Erik H. Erikson, *Gandhi's Truth: On the Origins of Militant Nonviolence*, London, 1970, p. 404.
71. Shirer, *Gandhi* pp. 234–8; Bhikhu Parekh, *Colonialism, Tradition and Reform: An Analysis of Gandhi's Political Discourse*, New Delhi, 1989, ch. 6.

Chapter 8

GANDHI IN OLD AGE:
TRIUMPH OR NEMESIS?

Already 60 years old when he launched the Salt Satyagraha in 1930, Gandhi was nearing 70 when India was plunged into the Second World War in 1939. In 1919–22 and again in 1930–3 he had been the dominant figure in the nationalist movement, but by the mid-1930s younger leaders were coming to the fore, including Jawaharlal Nehru and Subhas Chandra Bose. In 1934, as the country's appetite for direct action waned once more and there was a new shift back to constitutionalism, Gandhi formally suspended civil disobedience, resigned from the Congress and devoted his time to the Harijan movement and village reform. With his retreat to Sevagram in April 1936, it might appear that Gandhi had nothing more to contribute to the struggle for Indian independence.

And yet, even from semi-exile in Sevagram, Gandhi continued to exercise a powerful influence on the course of nationalist politics. The outbreak of the Second World War brought him once more into the forefront of political leadership, culminating in August 1942 in the 'Quit India' Movement, Gandhi's last nationwide satyagraha campaign and his final term of imprisonment, lasting until May 1944. Just over three years later, after more than thirty years of struggle, in August 1947 Gandhi was witness to what might have seemed his greatest triumph – freedom from colonial rule – but it was independence attained amidst the bloodbath of Partition and swaraj in a form that disappointed and frustrated Gandhi's deepest hopes. He was assassinated by a Hindu extremist six months later on 30 January 1948. Thus the last fifteen years of Gandhi's life were marked by a kind of victory for Gandhi and the movement he led, but also defeat at the hands of all those violent and avenging forces – including a deepening communal divide – that he had hoped to have exorcised for ever.

. . .

GANDHI, NEHRU AND BOSE

Gandhi's peculiar position in the late 1930s and early 1940s can best be understood in relation to two of the younger nationalist leaders – Jawaharlal Nehru and Subhas Chandra Bose. Born into a family of Kashmiri Brahmins in Allahabad in November 1889, and educated in Britain at Harrow and Cambridge, Nehru returned to India in 1912 to join his father Motilal as a lawyer. But in 1920, in the wake of the Amritsar massacre, and having fallen under Gandhi's spell, he threw himself into the Non-Cooperation Movement and in 1921 suffered the first of his many terms of imprisonment. In 1926–7, as his interest in socialism grew, Nehru made an extended visit to Europe. He attended the Congress of Oppressed Nationalities in Brussels in February 1927 and in November visited the Soviet Union. He returned to India in December to move the 'Independence Resolution' at the Madras Congress session and was General Secretary of the Congress from 1927–9. Nehru grew close politically and personally to Gandhi, and it was evident even in the late 1920s that Gandhi was grooming Nehru, twenty years his junior, as his principal deputy, and, despite the reservations of the party's 'Old Guard' (which included Patel, Prasad and Rajagopalachari) as his ultimate heir and successor. But the tensions between the two men were also evident. Gandhi often found Nehru impetuous and his socialist rhetoric alarming, while Nehru, as we have seen, was frustrated by Gandhi's suspension of civil disobedience and the Gandhi-Irwin Pact in 1931 and by his apparent abandonment of civil disobedience in 1934.

In his autobiography, written during his time in jail and published in 1936, Nehru explained what it was that drew him to Gandhi in the first place, especially his powerful conviction that Gandhi represented the soul of India and had a unique ability to articulate the needs and sentiments of its oppressed masses. Nehru also believed that Gandhi's non-violence and satyagraha were essential for India to win swaraj, but he regarded the 'non-violent method' pragmatically, as a policy that promised certain results but not as 'a religion or an unchallengeable creed or dogma'.[1] In his presidential address to the Congress at Lahore in December 1929, Nehru stated that he rejected violence 'not on moral but on practical grounds'. Armed rebellion was out of the question under British rule, but if India rejected 'the way of violence' it was because 'it promises no substantial results'.[2] But Nehru was also deeply unhappy about the way in which Gandhi brought religion into the heart of Indian politics and his reactionary ideas of Ram Rajya. There was an air of religious dogma and super-stition about Gandhi that Nehru, socialist, internationalist and mod-erniser, found hard to stomach. At his most radical in the mid-1930s, Nehru wanted India to follow quite a different path from Gandhi. When he posed the question in October 1933, 'Whither India?', his own answer was 'Surely to the great human goal of social and eco-nomic equality, to the ending of all exploitation of nation by nation, and class by class, to national freedom within the framework of an international cooperative socialist world federation.' He further claimed that 'India's struggle today is part of the great struggle . . . all over the world for the emancipation of the oppressed.'[3] Nehru, now calling for a 'new social order', never accepted Gandhi's idyllic rural vision, outlined in *Hind Swaraj*, as a desirable or realistic objective, and as late as 1945 the two remained strongly divided in their view of society and the state.[4]

Although Nehru did not join the Congress Socialist Party when it was set up by Jayaprakash Narayan and others on the left of the Congress party in 1934, he broadly shared its Marxist rhetoric and its goal of winning over the Congress to a socialist agenda, though without wishing to sacrifice Gandhi's leadership, which he regarded as vital to maintaining the party's mass base and in securing independ-ence from the British. But by the mid-1930s, Gandhi seemed increas-ingly conservative and out of touch with the Congress left wing. Along with his ageing associates, like Vallabhbhai Patel and Rajendra Prasad, Gandhi was increasingly identified with the 'Old Guard' of the Congress in opposition to its socialist Young Turks. Despite the protracted struggle for the soul (and organisation) of the Congress, Nehru remained loyal to Gandhi and to the Congress, and Gandhi in turn was instrumental in Nehru keeping at the forefront of the Congress in these years (despite the death of his father, Motilal, in 1931 and of his wife, Kamala, in 1936), partly as a way of ensuring that the Congress did not split between left and right or between its older and younger generations. Nehru was elected Congress Pres-ident again in 1936 and 1937 and between July 1936 and February 1937 travelled over 50,000 miles to spread the Congress message and, despite his own distrust of constitutional politics while India remained under Britain rule, to support candidates for the reformed legislatures under the 1935 Government of India Act. Nehru thus took over from Gandhi much of the responsibility for leading and energising the Congress during these years, but he also seemed to represent a far more radical Congress, and one more in keeping with the times, than Gandhi now stood for. However, despite having formally resigned from the Congress in October 1934, Gandhi remained actively involved. His advice was constantly sought by other politicians, and, as he demonstrated in respect to Subhas Chandra Bose, he could still exercise real power within the party.

Bose was younger than either Gandhi or Nehru. Born in January 1897 into a Bengali middle-class family, he studied at Cambridge and sat the examinations for the prestigious Indian Civil Service, but abandoned all thoughts of joining the colonial administration in April 1921 for the Non-Cooperation Movement. The hero of his youth was not so much Gandhi as C. R. Das, the Bengali leader who sided with Gandhi and Motilal Nehru in 1920, thus allowing the Non-Cooperation and Khilafat faction to win control of the Congress, but who later (before his death in 1925) joined with Motilal Nehru to lead the move back to the legislatures and Swarajist politics in 1922–3. Imprisoned from 1924 to 1927, in the late 1920s Bose became Mayor of Calcutta and the pre-eminent youth leader in Bengal. He sought to build a wide basis of populist support, including industrial workers, students and women. But to many Gandhians he remained a suspect figure, with possible links to the terrorist movement in the province and a man whose personal loyalty to Gandhi was always uncertain. In 1928–9 Bose and Nehru tried to coax Gandhi and the Congress into a more radical programme of civil disobedience, but while Nehru, 'the good son', was rewarded with the Congress presidency in 1929, Bose, 'the bad son', was snubbed and understandably felt excluded from the party's high command.[5] Like Nehru, Bose was a moderniser, who recognised the remarkable hold Gandhi had over the Indian masses but who disliked the manner in which he mixed the roles of religious saint and political leader and seemed in terms of his social and economic attitudes to be tugging India backward rather than leading it forward. While Bose was seen by sceptics as unreliable and self-important, he also represented the underlying resentment felt by Bengal at its decline from all-India nationalist leadership following the rise of Gandhi and at the seemingly unsophisticated nature of the Mahatma's ideology and leadership.

Following further imprisonment during the Civil Disobedience Movement, Bose left for Europe in search of medical treatment and in order to avoid continual police harassment. Living mostly in Vienna, he kept a keen eye on political developments in Europe. He met Mussolini and, despite his concern at the growing race-hatred in Germany, which affected even 'Aryan' Indians, he established some tentative contacts with the Nazi leadership. He returned to India in April 1936 to endure a further bout of detention until finally released a year later. In February 1938 he succeeded Nehru as Congress President, alarming the old Gandhians by calling in his presidential address for 'a new industrial system', state planning and population control to address the problems of India's poverty.[6] Even so, membership of the Congress Working Committee for 1938–9 continued to favour the established (and largely pro-Gandhi) leadership. As President, however, Bose sought to steer the party in new directions, favouring more left-leaning policies while seemingly intent on turning it into a replica of the fascist parties of Europe. Believing that he alone could lead the party forward, he sought re-election for a second term in office in 1939.

Gandhi found Bose's policies and posturing increasingly unpalatable and blamed him for what he saw as the increasing indiscipline in the party and in the country at large. He was determined, despite his own formal withdrawal from Congress politics, to force a showdown with the socialists who were backing Bose and with the Bengali leader who seemed to be hijacking the party. The publication in 1938 of Bose's autobiographical narrative *The Indian Struggle*, in places highly critical of Gandhi and his associates, also helped to turn the tide against him. Late in 1938 Gandhi threw his immense political weight against Bose's bid for a second term as President. In an exceptionally fierce contest on 29 January 1939 Bose, with some left-wing support, held the presidency with 1,580 votes to the 1,375 polled for his opponent, Pattabhi Sitaramayya, a loyal, if lacklustre, Gandhian from Andhra. Gandhi saw Bose's re-election as a blow to his own authority, saying that Sitaramayya's defeat was 'more mine than his'. While he reluctantly acknowledged Bose's victory (remarking 'After all, Subhas Babu is not an enemy of his country'), he brushed aside all attempts at reconciliation and worked with single-minded determination to make the President's position untenable. On 22 February he was able to persuade 13 of the 15 members of the Congress Working Committee (all but Subhas and his brother Sarat) to resign rather than work with Bose. Nehru, to Bose's deep chagrin, was among those who (despite his own leftist leanings) sided with Gandhi and refused to support Bose. When the Congress met at Tripuri in the Central Provinces in early March 1939, it approved a resolution, moved by G. B. Pant, a leading Congressman from the United Provinces, reiterating faith in the Gandhian policies of the past two decades and asking Bose to constitute a new executive 'in accordance with the wishes of Gandhiji'.[7] With Gandhi thus reinstated as the supreme arbiter of nationalist politics, Bose found himself unable to form a Working Committee of his own. At the end of April he resigned and Rajendra Prasad, the obliging Gandhian, took over. The following month, on 3 May, he set up his own organisation, the Forward Bloc, initially as a pressure group within the Congress, aiming to rally 'all radical and anti-Imperialist progressive elements'.[8]

But Bose did not cease to be Gandhi's tormentor and antithesis. Kept under house arrest in Calcutta by the British for the first eighteen months of the Second World War, Bose effected a dramatic escape in January 1941 and eventually found his way via Moscow to Germany, where he hoped to enlist the support of the Axis powers in the fight for India's freedom. He formed an Indian Legion, 3,000 strong, from Indian prisoners of war, but the Nazi leadership was unenthusiastic about their fighting capacities and the Legion saw little action. At their only meeting, in May 1942, Hitler, who had formerly admired British rule in India and reviled the nationalist opposition, lectured Bose but offered little practical assistance. Bose, however, continued to believe, contrary to what Gandhi had held for more than thirty years, that India could only be liberated by military means and that the world war, now engulfing Asia as well as Europe and North Africa, was India's long-awaited opportunity. In another dramatic escapade, Bose was taken by German U-boat to the Indian Ocean where he was transferred, off the coast of Madagascar, to a Japanese submarine. He was taken first to Tokyo and then to Singapore in July 1943, where he took charge of the many thousands of Indian soldiers taken prisoner by the Japanese in their advance through South East Asia, who had been drafted into an Indian National Army under Captain Mohan Singh. Bose became the INA's supreme commander, and with the addition of civilian recruits, including women, the force eventually numbered nearly 50,000. As Bose set up a provisional Azad Hind (Free India) government in October 1943, his intentions were clear – to use Indian soldiers, with the backing of the Japanese, to invade India, march on Delhi, and establish an independent India.[9] His ambitious scheme for India's liberation through an armed struggle never materialised, and INA soldiers only briefly, in March–June 1944, fought on Indian soil, in eastern Assam in the battles for Kohima and Imphal.[10] Bose himself died in a plane crash in Taiwan on 18 August 1945, four days after Japan's capitulation had brought the war in Asia to an end. Nonetheless, Bose and the Indian National Army eloquently demonstrated that Gandhi did not have a monopoly of ideas as to how India might achieve its independence, nor was there universal acceptance either of his leadership or of his non-violent tactics. Gandhi in the later years of his life was under even more pressure than previously to show that non-violence worked and did indeed have the capacity to drive the British out of India.

· · ·

THE OFFICE QUESTION

Gandhi's strategy of attaining swaraj through non-violent non-cooperation and civil disobedience was under challenge from another quarter, too. With the collapse and abandonment of civil disobedience in 1933, the Congress began once again to drift back towards constitutional action. There was a limited attempt to return to the legislatures with elections to the central Legislative Assembly in 1934, in which Congressmen and their nationalist allies won half the seats open to election. Far more challenging was the passing of the Government of India Act in 1935 (despite years of stubborn opposition from Winston Churchill). The Act did not by any means give Indian politicians all they had worked for and demanded since the Montagu Declaration of 1917, or even since the appointment of the Simon Commission in 1927. It was transparently a British ploy to set up an all-India federation in which the princely states could be used at the centre as a counterweight to the largely nationalist provinces of British India and in which the granting of 'provincial autonomy' could be used to play off one province against another or to lure politicians further into the morass of local intrigue and machination, leaving the essentials of colonial rule (including the army and control of foreign policy) under the central government in New Delhi. Although Gandhi's 'epic fast' of September 1932 had frustrated the creation of separate electorates for untouchables, the constitution contained elaborate provisions for the representation of a host of different minorities and interest groups, including Muslims, Christian, Sikhs, Anglo-Indians and Europeans, women and industrial workers. But, on the other hand, the franchise had been significantly enlarged, from roughly 3 per cent of the population under the old constitution to 16 per cent under the new. Some 30 million Indians were now eligible to vote, roughly one-sixth of those who would have been eligible under universal suffrage.[11] For the first time it appeared as though ministers in the provinces could exercise real control over revenue policy, the police, and other areas of administrative importance.

As the experience of the fifteen years since the Congress boycott of 1920 had shown, there were always voters who would vote, candidates who would stand for election and members of the legislatures willing to take on the burden of being ministers. For all the Gandhian rhetoric of non-cooperation, the constitutional process had not ceased to function and even under the Swarajists in the 1920s it had only ever been marginally disrupted, never brought to a standstill. The Congress had to face the prospect in 1936–7 that if it did not contest the elections and take power in the provinces, then other political groups and factions would undoubtedly do so and to the detriment of the Congress. Conversely, a Congress party in office might thwart any further moves towards federation, punish those civil servants and police officers who had committed 'atrocities' against Congressmen and women during the Civil Disobedience Movement, and redirect the work of the government away from imperial interests and towards the needs of the people.

There was a further reservation about again boycotting the legislatures. Although Gandhi had honed civil disobedience into a powerful political weapon (as the Salt Satyagraha of 1930 had shown to India and the world), it remained a weapon of limited effectiveness. It had placed great pressure on the British but it had not, over more than a decade and a half, brought India swaraj or seriously deflected them from their constitutional path. If anything, its effect had been to strengthen the pressure on the British to make constitutional concessions in order to retain the support, if not the loyalty, of the more moderate politicians and voters. Moreover, Gandhi's hostility to the power of the state seemed an increasing anachronism in the 1930s and 40s. With few qualifications, he continued to see the state as innately repressive, coercive and remote from the needs of the people, and yet he offered India little practical alternative, apart from Ram Rajya and the dream of self-governing and self-sufficient village communities.[12] That seemed far removed from the increasingly violent and divided Indian countryside and the burgeoning industrial cities of India in the 1930s.

By contrast, in the Soviet Union under Lenin and Stalin, even in the United States of Roosevelt and the New Deal and in Britain's slow progress towards a welfare state, there was the idea of a state that could act as a powerful agent of social and economic change, boosting employment and providing incentives for new economic development, improving health, education and housing, and curbing the power of big landlords, business magnates and entrenched elites. This was a vision that tempted Nehru (even while he looked askance at the violent extremes of the Soviet system) to believe that there could be a good state – not all states were, or need necessarily be, the evil monster of Gandhi's imagining. And, for those who wanted real social and economic change, what alternative could there realist-ically be? Could satyagraha and trusteeship ever provide the essential impetus for change or a viable alternative to constitutional change and reforming laws? The Poona Pact, the Harijan campaign, the Constructive Programme and Gandhi's All-India Village Industries Association seemed to show the limits of Gandhian reformism. It might affect some local change and win some notable symbolic victories, but it had little capacity for the real transformation of society. For all Gandhi's personal efforts, even Sevagram remained impoverished, caste-ridden and insanitary. The idea of 'trusteeship', advanced by Gandhi with increasing fervour from the late 1920s onwards as the challenge of both socialism and the reforming state grew, seemed to all but the most dedicated Gandhians to offer little hope of resolving India's problems. To ask India's wealthy – its industrialists, merchant princes and *zamindars* – to 'serve the people' and voluntarily surrender part of their wealth to benefit the poor was for most people too idealistic to be a credible strategy and represented a naive and patronising attempt at class conciliation.[13] Increasingly, by the mid-1930s industrial workers looked to trade unions and strike action, peasants turned to the Kisan Sabhas, mass demonstrations and a radical manifesto of their own, in order to pursue their class objectives.[14] While Gandhi retained his old anti-pathy to constitutional participation and the constructive use of state power, many even among those closest to him saw no realistic altern-ative if India were to be spared bloodshed and revolution.

As a result of intense and carefully organised electioneering (in which ironically Gandhi's name was frequently invoked), the Congress won a landslide victory in the first elections held under the 1935 Government of India Act. The party took 716 of the 1,585 seats in the provincial legislative assemblies, and gained clear majorities in Madras, Bihar, Orissa, the Central Provinces and the United Provinces. It also held a commanding position in Bombay, Assam and the North-West Frontier Province, and in only 3 of the 11 provinces – Bengal, Punjab and Sind – did it hold a minority of seats.[15] In the first elections held under the formula agreed to in the Poona Pact, the Congress won just over half the seats set aside for the Scheduled Castes (79 out of 151). Although it won a small share of the Muslim seats (contesting only 58 out of 482 and winning a mere 26), the claims repeatedly made by Gandhi for the Congress as the only truly national party seemed to be substantially vindicated through success at the ballot box. Under intense pressure from the party and its backers, the Congress leadership decided to take office and formed ministries in seven provinces. These held office until the outbreak of the Second World War.

The twenty-seven months of Congress rule in the provinces made possible a partial implementation of the Gandhian programme by constitutional means. With control of land revenue for the first time in ministerial hands, it became possible to follow up the agitational achievements of Kheda and Bardoli and ensure that the revenue system operated more in favour of the peasants than formerly.[16] Some efforts were also made, particularly in the United Provinces and in response to mounting peasant discontent, to begin dismantling the *zamindari* system, but this was an objective more closely identified with the Nehruvian socialist wing of the Congress than with Gandhi who remained cautious about fuelling the agrarian class struggle. In Madras and Bombay, despite the loss of excise revenue involved, but in keeping with the prominence of anti-liquor agitation in the movements of 1919–22 and 1930–3, a start was made with prohibition through schemes that would in time have turned these into 'dry' provinces. Attempts were made, too, to promote khadi and village industries, and to encourage the use and teaching of Hindi, which Gandhi had long urged be taken up as India's national language. Temple entry for untouchables, an issue highlighted by the Vaikam Satyagraha in the mid-1920s and brought to national prominence by Gandhi's Harijan campaign in 1932–4, was also advanced by the Congress ministries, though little was otherwise done to address the needs and grievances of the Scheduled Castes.

Conversely, the years of Congress rule, in bringing new tensions and exacerbating old conflicts, helped fuel Gandhian arguments about the corrupting and divisive influence of the legislatures and the constraints of ministerial office under colonial rule. Congress membership swelled during these years and reached more than 4 million members in 1939 but, as Gandhi plainly saw, this was part of a 'bandwagon effect' in which office-seekers, without genuine loyalty to the Congress party or commitment to the struggle for swaraj, rushed to join the party in the hope of winning influence and material reward.[17] In the run-up to the 1937 elections relations between the Congress and the Muslim League had been relatively amicable, but once Congress ministers were ensconced in office the situation began to deteriorate rapidly. In the United Provinces the Muslim League had expected to be given a share of ministerial offices and was annoyed at its exclusion. In favouring Hindi, the ministers and their supporters seemed to discriminate against Urdu. The determination of Congress members to sing the nationalist anthem 'Bande Mataram' (Hail to the Motherland), seen by many Muslims as a Hindu song (or worse, as 'anti-Islamic and idolatrous'), further inflamed the discontent of Muslim League members who increasingly castigated the Congress ministries as harbingers of a 'Hindu Raj'.[18]

In several provinces Congress ministers behaved with an arrogance and self-importance that seemed at variance with the Gandhian programme. In Madras, Gandhi's long-time lieutenant, C. Rajagopalachari, was seen as being closer to the British Governor, Lord Erskine, and to British civil servants, than to his own party members and supporters. His autocratic attempt to 'impose' Hindi and make it the medium for instruction in all secondary schools in April 1938 led to fierce protests in Tamilnadu and to the arrest and imprisonment of more than a thousand protestors who sought to defend the interest of Tamil. On the labour front, too, the advent of the Congress ministries had given rise to hopes of a new deal for labour and trade union membership soared in the late 1930s, but the return of the Congress to the constitutional path, and more especially its assumption of ministerial office, had greatly strengthened its ties to the industrial and business classes. The ministries made some attempts to introduce new mechanisms for resolving industrial disputes through negotiation and arbitration, but on a number of occasions they fell back on the violent policing methods of their British predecessors. A resolution of the All-India Congress Committee in September 1938 gave its full support to any 'measures that may be undertaken by the Congress Government for the defence of life and property', and condemned 'people, including Congressmen . . . found in the name of civil liberty to advocate murder, arson, looting and class war by violent means'.[19]

During these years, Gandhi tried to keep alive an alternative sense of social service and to maintain public awareness of the value of satyagraha. In October 1937 he presided over an educational conference at Wardha at which he advanced his ideas for 'basic education' through vernacular languages and manual training. As discussions continued about the princes joining an all-India federation under the 1935 Government of India Act, the issue of the future of the princely states, which had previously been largely ignored, took on a new importance. Gandhi had hitherto sought to leave the states outside the nationalist movement and indeed viewed them as capable of a kind of reforming trusteeship. However, in 1938–9 he and Vallabhbhai Patel saw the opportunity of using the princely states to extend their political base, remind the public of the power of satyagraha and weaken Subhas Chandra Bose as he strove for a second term in the Congress presidency.

Patel took up the cause of constitutional reform in Rajkot and pressed the Thakur and his *diwan* to make significant concessions under threat of a satyagraha campaign. When in January 1938 the ruler appeared to renege on an agreement with Patel to end the satyagraha, Gandhi intervened in person. Having spent thirteen years of his early life in Rajkot, six of them with his father as the state's *diwan*, Gandhi could present himself as a 'son of Rajkot', enjoying a special relationship with its current ruler. In an extraordinary act of pointless melodrama, Gandhi declared on 3 March 1939 a 'fast unto death' unless the Thakur complied with his ultimatum, but at the same time he sought the intervention, through the British political agent, of the Viceroy of India. On 7 March the Viceroy, Lord Linlithgow, devised a solution to the apparent impasse and Gandhi promptly called off his fast. In the short term, the Rajkot Satyagraha seemed a tactical victory for Gandhi, not least in upstaging Bose three days before the start of the Tripuri Congress. But Gandhi later confessed that the fast had been coercive and was not governed by his own rules of ahimsa and the conversion of his opponent. In fact, the Thakur and his *diwan* proved too wily for Gandhi and his fast failed to deflect them from their original path. What had been intended as a showpiece satyagraha for princely India proved a damp squib. But, even though the satyagraha was in many respects a failure, it showed Gandhi's continuing determination not to be sidelined by the politics of constitutionalism and to keep himself and his methods before the public eye.[20]

His opportunity came around once more, with the outbreak of the Second World War. Gandhi's personal life and political strategy had already, over several decades, been profoundly influenced by war and the consequences of war on three continents – by the Anglo-Boer War and Zulu Rebellion in South Africa and by the impact of the First World War not only on Britain but also on India. Despite his adherence to ahimsa, Gandhi was a man for whom the stratagems and metaphors of war had deep resonances, and the Second World War was to have an even greater effect on him and on the struggle for swaraj than the First World War had done. On 3 September 1939, in a gesture that mirrored the one-sided presumptiveness of the appointment of the Simon Commission twelve years earlier, Lord Linlithgow unilaterally declared that, since Britain was now at war with Germany, this automatically meant that India was at war as well. Declaring that it could not identify itself with a war for democratic freedom when democracy was itself denied to India, the Congress, with evident reluctance in some cases, protested by resigning its ministerial offices in October 1939. Gandhi welcomed this as an opportunity to break away once more from constitutional action, but sensed that the country was not yet ready for a return to mass civil disobedience. The Congress held out for some concessions to be made in return for its support for the British war effort, but when this proved in vain, on 17 October 1940 Gandhi instigated a new campaign of 'individual satyagraha' by which nominated individuals were called on to defy the law and court imprisonment. The campaign began with the arrests of Vinoba Bhave and Jawaharlal Nehru, and by the end of 1941 more than 23,000 Congressmen and women had been sent to jail, but without either attracting popular support or significantly embarrassing the British. This was 'far and away the weakest and least effective of all the Gandhian national campaigns',[21] and in sharp contrast to what was to happen barely a year later.

. . .

'QUIT INDIA'

The Individual Satyagraha of 1940–1 brought few tangible results and the stalemate in Indian politics – between a still firmly entrenched British government and a Congress out of office but hungry for power – lingered on into 1942. But developments were starting to move with bewildering speed. On 7 December 1941 Japan declared war on Britain and began to advance rapidly through South East Asia. The invasion of Malaya, commenced on 8 December, concluded barely two months later with the fall of Singapore, once deemed impregnable, on 15 February 1942. Japanese forces overran Burma between January and May 1942, and occupied the Andaman islands – Indian territory – in the Bay of Bengal in March 1942. Bombing raids on the east-coast cities of Calcutta and Vishakhapatnam (Vizagapatam) seemed to threaten an imminent invasion of India itself. In 1914–18 India had known war mainly at a distance. Now in 1942 it was swelling over its doorstep. As in the previous war, India contributed massively to Allied manpower. During the course of the Second World War it contributed nearly 2.5 million men, a fifth of the entire fighting force of the British Empire. Indian industry and agriculture also made huge contributions to the war effort – in textiles, clothing, ordnance, food and medical supplies – and to support the large number of Allied troops stationed in India and on its borders.[22] The prospect of war had been evident to Nehru and a number of other Congress leaders for some time, and while Bose was to see it as an opportunity for India finally to wrest its freedom by aligning militarily with Britain's enemies, Germany and Japan, Nehru was more inclined to see the international struggle against fascism as the hour's greatest need, but he loyally supported a Congress policy of withholding support until India's nationalist demands were met.

In May 1940 Gandhi's old adversary Winston Churchill became head of the wartime coalition government in Britain. Despite Britain's desperate plight he remained determined not to make concessions to the Congress or weaken its hold on India: 'I have not become the King's First Minister in order to preside over the liquidation of the British Empire,' he later declared.[23] In August 1940 Linlithgow made a grudging offer (as much as Churchill would allow) of Dominion Status at some unspecified point in the future with a constituent assembly to devise a constitution and, in the interim, an increased Indian presence on the Viceroy's Executive Council. The 'August Offer' left the Congress leadership unmoved and little further happened on the constitutional front for more than a year. But, following Japanese successes in South East Asia, in early 1942 the British government became desperate to rally what was left of Indian loyalty and retain India as an invaluable recruiting ground and base for military operations. The loss of India would have been catastrophic for Britain's morale and its ability to continue the war in Asia, North Africa and Europe. The impact Gandhi had made on Britain and the United States in 1930–1 was now beginning to tell against Churchill's obduracy. Prodded by its own Labour members and worried by its American allies, the coalition government felt obliged to at least be seen to make a further effort to resolve the constitutional standoff. A maverick Labour politician, Sir Stafford Cripps, was despatched to India in March 1942 with a draft declaration that Britain would grant full independence after the war, including the eventual right to secede from the Commonwealth if that was agreed to by a post-war constituent assembly. But Cripps's scheme were hedged about with many conditions unacceptable to the Congress and fatally undermined by Churchill's determination not to grant any additional concessions. Talks collapsed on 10 April with both the Congress and the Muslim League rejecting the proposals as inadequate. Gandhi, whose role was still crucial, reputedly described the Cripps offer as a 'post-dated cheque on a failing bank'.[24]

While these fruitless discussions were taking place, the Japanese advance through Burma and into the Bay of Bengal continued at a ferocious pace. Reports were beginning to reach India with returning refugees that the British had simply abandoned Indians in South East Asia in order to save themselves. The prestige and credibility of the British rulers had never been at such a low ebb. It is customary to regard Gandhi as having lost faith in the British Empire at the close of the First World War and certainly with the Amritsar massacre of 13 April 1919. There is an obvious truth in this, but Gandhi continued to have a number of British friends, to deal with the British administration in India, as his face-to-face negotiations with Irwin showed, and, as demonstrated by his visit to London in 1931, to believe in the possibility of persuading the British public (if not crusty bureaucrats in India) to recognise India's legitimate demand for swaraj. But by 1942, with the Japanese apparently at India's gates and the power of the British seemingly gone for ever, but with nothing more to offer than the miserly Cripps mission, Gandhi seemed to have finally despaired of the Empire and all those who served it. India had now, more than ever, to make its own destiny.

The background to the Quit India Movement of August 1942 underscores another important point about Gandhi and the national-ist movement at this time. Gandhi partly rose to power in 1919–20 on the back of the Amritsar massacre and the revulsion it created throughout India. But, while not unique, that episode was somewhat exceptional in the history of British dealings with the Indian nationalist movement: on no other occasion in the following twenty years were so many slain at one time, nor was the army again allowed such unfettered freedom against unarmed civilians. The British acknowledged that the slaughter in Jallianwala Bagh had been a terrible mistake and sought to distance themselves from Dyer's impetuous action: they grew cautious about their use of force and anxious not to follow any course that might make Gandhi a martyr. Other regimes, colonial or otherwise, might not have given Gandhi so much licence, nor have served up constitutional concessions, however grudgingly, as a sop to nationalist demands. Gandhi, for his part, was confronted with a regime which, for all its moments of aggression and stark brutality and its continuing belief in the 'moral' value of periodic displays of force, recognised, as the novelist and historian Edward Thompson put it in the late 1930s, 'that the game of insurrection and repression had rules'. His enemy had 'streaks of humanity and liberalism' and so found itself 'ultimately helpless' when, as in the summer of 1930, 'line after line of nationalists stood up fearlessly, to be struck down by the *lathis* of the police'. This 'liberal' disposition on the part of the British should not be overstated but it certainly made satyagraha possible and contributed to its successes.[25]

However, even in the late 1930s there was a feeling that Gandhi was out of touch with the world of the 'new Caesars', the ruthless men who ran the fascist states in Europe and the military in imperial Japan and for whom violence was a *raison d'état*. How, it was asked with increasing anxiety of Gandhi, would he use satyagraha against the Italian gassing and bombing of Ethiopia or the German invasions of Czechoslovakia and Poland? When Gandhi was asked how the Jews should defend themselves against persecution and genocide at the hands of the Nazis, he proposed that they should use non-violent protest and be prepared to sacrifice their lives in the belief that even Hitler would be moved and shamed by their suffering. Perhaps Gandhi, who found it difficult to understand how a man as given to violence as Hitler could possibly be a vegetarian, was simply out of his depth, and recognised too little distinction between the plight of the Indian minority in South Africa in the 1890s and that of the Jews fifty years later, confronted by a Holocaust of almost unimaginable dimensions.[26] It should be noted, though, that Gandhi's non-violence was not unconditional and there were instances in which he believed that, as a last resort or as the only honourable option, violence should not be shied away from. Writing to Mirabehn in May 1942 at a time when an invasion of Orissa appeared imminent, he observed that the one thing the people of the province should never do was 'yield willing submission to the Japanese'. That would be a 'cowardly act, and unworthy of freedom-loving people. They must not escape from one fire only to fall into another and probably more terrible.' Their attitude must always be one of resistance to the Japanese, even, implicitly, if this meant recourse to violent action.[27]

Gandhi's decision to pursue non-violence in the depths of war reflected his continuing personal belief in the practical efficacy and moral superiority of satyagraha. And yet 'Quit India' of August 1942 was a Gandhian movement with a difference. While Gandhi had repeatedly stressed in his previous satyagraha campaigns the need for strict adherence to non-violence, and indeed called off civil disobedience in 1922 following the violence at Chauri Chaura, from time to time he suggested that non-violence might not be the only way to counter authoritarian intransigence and armed aggression. In a speech he made in London in 1931 Gandhi shocked his largely pacifist audience by remarking that Indians were willing to pay any price for their freedom and would not hesitate even 'to let the Ganges run red to obtain it'.[28] In mid-1942 Gandhi, in a 'strange and uniquely militant mood',[29] seemed to go as far as endorsing the need for violent resistance against the British Raj without explicitly advocating it. Reviving an old theme – the contrast between India's ancient civilisation and the 'slavery' of colonial rule – he expressed his growing exasperation and said that he could wait no longer for non-violence to be perfected:

> I have waited and waited, until the country should develop the non-violent strength necessary to throw off the foreign yoke. But my attitude has now undergone a change. I feel that I cannot afford to wait. If I continue to wait, I might have to wait till doomsday. . . . That is why I have decided that even at certain risks . . . I must ask the people to resist the slavery. . . . The people have not my ahimsa, but my ahimsa should help them.[30]

On 8 August 1942 the All-India Congress Committee, meeting at Bombay, passed a resolution demanding that the British finally 'quit India'. It was the Congress Party's own declaration of war, with Gandhi once more its supreme commander. Adapting to his own purposes Tennyson's 'Charge of the Light Brigade', Gandhi called on Indians to 'Do or die'. Either they would become free or die in the attempt, but they would not live to see the perpetuation of their 'slavery'.[31] Many nationalists interpreted this, rightly or wrongly, as a licence to use violence finally to wrest India from British rule. The so-called 'Andhra Circular' drew up a programme for disruptive action and sabotage, though it is unclear how far this represented the aims of the Congress High Command. Vallabhbhai Patel, one of those closest to Gandhi, was reported making during the course of July 1942 a series of speeches in which he appealed for all-out action and told people not to be 'too squeamish about non-violence'.[32] It is, however, also likely that, unlike the Individual Satyagraha of 1940–1, the call to 'Quit India' appealed to popular imagination and, in addition, gave a new generation of young nationalists and socialist militants within the Congress, led by Jayaprakash Narayan, the opportunity to push the movement in a more violent and revolutionary direction than Gandhi and his associates had originally intended.[33]

Given the wartime situation, the Government of India was not prepared to respond passively to this new declaration of civil war. Repeating the tactics of January 1932 and not allowing Gandhi any time to assert his leadership or parley with the Viceroy, it immediately declared the Congress an illegal organisation and early on the morning of 9 August 1942 all leading Congressmen and women were arrested and thrown into jail. Gandhi, once again denied a trial, was taken to the Aga Khan's palace at Poona and remained interned there with a small party of his associates until his release in May 1944. But the agitation was rapidly taken up by others, especially by young party workers and students, many of them frustrated by the limited results non-violence had yielded in the past. Across a large swathe of India official property, including railway stations, post and telegraph offices, police stations and government buildings were attacked: 332 railway stations and nearly 1,000 post and telegraph offices were severely damaged or destroyed. Railway lines were torn up and bridges wrecked. In an echo of Chauri Chaura, 208 police stations and outposts were besieged and heavy damage inflicted, and, in an important sign of weakening state authority, some 200 policemen fled or 'defected'. Two thousand police officers were wounded and a further 63 killed. In some areas, notably Midnapore in southwest Bengal, Satara in Maharashtra, and even in Ahmedabad, 'parallel governments' were set up to replace expelled officials and usher in popular Congress rule. In scenes that recalled the rebellion of 1857, parts of northern India passed for weeks out of British control. The government responded in a manner and on a scale rarely equalled since the Mutiny, using the full force of its armed might to suppress the uprising. Police and troops opened fire on demonstrators, individuals suspected of involvement were whipped, and on at least five occasions demonstrators were shot at from the air. Official statistics indicate that the police opened fire more than 600 times, resulting in 763 fatal casualties: the army fired 68 times, causing 297 deaths. Heavy fines as well as imprisonment were imposed in an attempt to dampen down the revolt.[34] In all about 92,000 arrests were made, especially in the movement's epicentres – Bombay, Bihar and the United Provinces.

Eventually repression took its toll and by the end of September 1942, six weeks after it had begun, most active signs of the movement had died away. So ended this seemingly most un-Gandhian of Gandhi's campaigns. In detention once more, and chafing at his political impotence, Gandhi tried to open up a dialogue with the Viceroy and, when that failed, to reassert himself by blaming the British for the 'Quit India' violence and denying his own responsibility. On 10 February 1943 he decided once more to 'crucify the flesh', embarking on a twenty-one-day fast, but he could not recapture the drama of Yeravda eleven years earlier and Linlithgow coolly dismissed it as 'political blackmail'. Churchill ordered that no concessions be made to Gandhi and if necessary he should be allowed to starve himself to death.[35] Apart from the bitter frustrations of his imprisonment in the early 1920s, this two-year period of detention in the Aga Khan's palace was Gandhi's most trying time in prison and, in personal terms, the most tragic. His long-serving secretary and companion, Mahadev Desai, succumbed to a heart attack on 15 August 1942, and his wife, Kasturba, died of chronic bronchitis on 22 February 1944. His release, on grounds of ill-health, came not long after, on 6 May that year.[36] Having first entered prison in South Africa in January 1908 when he was 38, Gandhi was an old man of 74 by the time he left the Aga Khan's palace in May 1944. He had spent in all nearly six and a half years in colonial prisons.

Did the Quit India Movement have much impact? Francis Hutchins has argued that this was 'India's revolution', the South Asian equivalent of the American War of Independence, the moment at which Indians united to throw off the colonial yoke, and though independence did not actually come until five years later, in the August of 1947, not 1942, it nonetheless set in train the inevitable process of India's decolonisation.[37] This interpretation would seem, however, to attach too much importance to a single episode. In the short term, the British appeared as determined as ever to hold on to India. On 10 November 1942 Churchill, in bombastic mood, declared: 'We mean to hold our own. We intend to remain the effective rulers of India for a long and indefinite period.'[38] In the short term at least, the British seemed determined to muzzle Gandhi and not to submit to nationalist demands. Other factors than Quit India contributed to the final demise of British rule five years later. The 'man-made' Bengal famine of 1943, in which an estimated 3 million people died, provided further evidence, if such were needed, of the callous disregard the colonial regime might have for the lives of its Indian subjects. Exhaustion from the war accelerated the British decision to leave India, coupled with the growing reluctance in Britain itself to commit more troops and money to holding on to India by force when the public was more interested in its own recovery from wartime hardship and austerity. Longer-term factors also played a significant part in unravelling British rule. It has been argued, with some justification, that the process of Indianisation, by which Indians replaced Europeans in the higher echelons of the administration, was one contributing factor. Slow though this process appeared to be, cumulatively and especially under the impetus of the Second World War and the accentuated European 'manpower shortage' it brought, the British presence in the Indian Civil Service (the 'steel frame' of the Indian Empire) was steadily reduced and a parallel trend was beginning by 1945 to transform the Indian Police Service and the Indian Army as well.[39] Alongside the grant of provincial autonomy in 1937 and the wartime expansion of the Viceroy's Executive Council to include more Indian members, this change ensured that India was arriving at a stage where it was already being governed at all but the highest level by Indians themselves

But Gandhi's share in the erosion of British power should not be underestimated. He had not succeeded, in 1920–2, in 1930–3, or (in circumstances over which he had far less control) in 1942, in bringing about the collapse of British rule or in winning swaraj at a single stroke. The strength and resolution of the Empire was too great for that and the forces of Indian opposition too weak and internally divided. But each successive campaign was a hammer-blow that further weakened British prestige and resolution. Many would-be civil servants were discouraged from going to serve in India; the idea of

India remaining under British tutelage indefinitely, so fundamental to the Victorian understanding of Empire, seemed increasingly untenable; and to all but a dwindling minority of British trading houses, entrepreneurs and industrialists the profits to be derived from a swadeshi-minded India seemed less and less assured. Gandhi was not alone responsible for these changes in imperial attitudes, but his political campaigns, his victories, real or merely symbolic, and his persistently anti-colonial stance and almost unshakeable moral stature contributed enormously to the sea-change that had taken place in Indian politics since the Rowlatt Satyagraha of 1919.

Among the Indian population, too, independence no longer appeared a distant prospect but an increasingly imminent one. Even without the urgency injected by the crises of the Second World War, many Indians were confident by the late 1930s that their country would be free of British rule within a decade or two. Although non-cooperation had been a limited success in 1920–2, a quarter-century later, by the end of the Second World War, there were few sections of the Indian population on whom the British any longer could unquestionably rely – the peasants, the businessmen and industrialists, the middle classes and the industrial workers had all to varying degrees become disenchanted with the British and had many good reasons to want to see them go. Perhaps only the princes remained as possible allies in adversity, but they too had declined to be drawn into federation and their very future now appeared shrouded in doubt. In the wake of Quit India and the Indian National Army, even the loyalty and obedience of the police and the army, on whom so much of British power in India had for so long ultimately rested, was no longer assured. Gandhi, not alone but in conjuncture with other nationalist elements in the legislatures and elsewhere, had exposed the frailty of British rule and robbed it of both the aura of legitimacy and the means to sustain it. By 1945–6 the British were well aware that if they were faced with yet another Gandhi-style mass campaign or, worse, something along the lines of Quit India, perhaps incorporating a left-led uprising of peasants and industrial workers, they would be hard pressed politically and militarily to hold on to India. 'Our time in India is limited', wrote Lord Wavell, the successor to Linlithgow as Viceroy, in October 1946, 'and our power to control events almost gone.'[40] It had taken a quarter of a century but in the end Gandhi had left the British with no alternative but to quit.

. . .

ONE NATION – OR TWO?

Consistently, and throughout his adult life, Gandhi had seen a need for Hindus and Muslims to work together in harmony in order for India to attain self-rule. He addressed the question in *Hind Swaraj*, arguing that nation and religion were not synonymous and that 'India cannot cease to be one nation because people belonging to different religions live in it.' Religions were, however, 'different roads converging to the same point' and the alleged 'enmity' between Hindus and Muslims was essentially an invention of the British.[41] In the Khilafat movement and through the Constructive Programme, he worked tirelessly for inter-communal harmony and in 1924 undertook his longest fast thus far to promote Hindu–Muslim trust and cooperation. And yet it could be argued that Gandhi failed to understand the depth of the growing Hindu–Muslim rift in India and through his 'saintly' approach to politics and his identification of Indian nationalism with Hinduism helped exacerbate that divide.

As A. B. Shah has remarked, 'Next to freedom, Hindu–Muslim unity and the liquidation of Untouchability were the two most important goals of Gandhi's public life in India.' But, while he had some success with the removal of untouchability, 'Hindu–Muslim unity evaded Gandhi throughout his active life except for a brief spell during the Khilafat agitation.' Even then the Khilafat movement was a 'unity born of expediency' and not a genuine basis for inter-communal understanding and harmony.[42] When that movement collapsed the rift between Hindus and Muslims grew ever greater. There were major communal riots on several occasions during the 1920s, and the Nehru Report and Round Table Conferences in London showed how far many Muslim leaders were from accepting that the interests of their community were safe in Congress hands. The period of the 1937–9 ministries brought a new intensity to disagreements between the Congress and the Muslim League. On 22 December 1939, following the resignation of the Congress ministers, the League called a 'Day of Deliverance' to demonstrate how oppressive and how overtly Hindu it regarded Congress rule as having been.

By this stage the Muslim League, after a long period of inaction, had been reinvigorated by the leadership of Mohammed Ali Jinnah, and on 23 March 1940 at the League's annual session at Lahore (with bitter irony the very city where the Congress had unfurled its demand for *purna swaraj* in 1929) a resolution was passed calling for the partition of India and the creation of a separate Muslim state. Although the term had not yet been taken up by Jinnah and the League, the idea of Pakistan (a name coined in 1933 by Choudhury Rahmat Ali while a student at Cambridge), carried the logic of the colonial census categories and separate electorates to its extreme. Pakistan was to bring together all the Muslim majority areas of north-west (including Baluchistan, Sind, Punjab and Kashmir) and northeast India (Bengal and Assam) into two 'autonomous and sovereign' states.[43] In advancing this claim, Jinnah directly contested the claim of the Congress to represent the entire Indian population. In his view there were two nations – one Hindu, the other Muslim – belonging to 'two different civilisations'. Their differences (in faith, in language, in historical traditions and social conventions) were deep and unbridgeable. They did not arise simply from British rule, as Gandhi claimed, but were ancient, profound and enduring.[44]

The rise of Muslim separatism had many causes, not a few of them predating Gandhi's rise to all-India leadership, but there is no doubting that, despite his inclusive understanding of Indian nationalism and his frequently professed faith in Hindu-Muslim unity, he unwittingly contributed to it. Gandhi appeared, in many eyes, an increasingly Hindu figure during the 1920s and 30s – in the manner of his speech and dress, in the religious symbolism he employed, and in the way in which, for example at the time of the 'epic fast' in 1932, he presented himself as a leader with a special responsibility for the Hindu community. Despite having many Muslim associates, and despite his evident differences with the Hindu right, he seemed to many Muslims to epitomise the Congress as an essentially Hindu organisation. Moreover, he could not shed his basic conviction, expressed in *Hind Swaraj* in 1909, that India was not just a nation but a civilisation, and that essentially an ancient Hindu civilisation, into which other religions and cultures had over time been assimilated. There was no room within this single civilisation for any other 'nation'.

Writing on 9 April 1940 in response to the League's resolution at Lahore and the prospect of India being divided up between Hindus and Muslims, Gandhi remarked:

> Partition means a patent untruth. My whole soul rebels against the idea that Hinduism and Islam represent two antagonistic cultures and doctrines. To assent to such a doctrine is for me denial of God. For

I believe with my whole soul that the God of the Koran is also the God of the *Gita*. . . . I must rebel against the idea that millions who were Hindus the other day changed their nationality on adopting Islam as their religion.[45]

This last sentence, in suggesting that India's Muslims were only converts from Hinduism (when not a few proudly traced their descent from Iran, Central Asia and Arabia) or despite their conversion remained essentially Hindus, showed how closely Gandhi's concept of national identity remained bound up with his wider notion of Hindu civilisation and its importance in providing the real basis for Indian nationalism. Gandhi repeated the same idea in a letter to Jinnah on 15 September 1944 when he remarked:

I find no parallel in history for a body of converts and their descendants claiming to be a nation apart from the parent stock. If India was one nation before the advent of Islam, it must remain one in spite of the change of faith of a very large body of her children.[46]

Quite apart from their political differences, which were profound, there was much personal rivalry and animosity between the two, which can be traced back to Gandhi's return from South Africa in 1915 and his first blundering forays into Indian politics. Gandhi had insensitively dismissed Jinnah, born in Karachi but the scion of another Gujarati trading community, the Khoja Muslims, and seven years younger than himself, as typical of the old Moderate elite, a highly Anglicised, English-speaking lawyer-politician, remote from the masses and the real needs of the Indian nation. Jinnah, in return, saw Gandhi's 'extreme programme' in 1920 as plunging India into 'disorganisation and chaos', and he could not abide Gandhi's 'Hindu fads'.[47] After the political setbacks of the 1920s, the death of his estranged wife in 1929 and a period of semi-exile in London in the early 1930s, Jinnah returned to India in 1935 with a new determination to make his mark on Indian politics and as the champion of Muslim separatism. When Jinnah made a speech at Lucknow in October 1937 denouncing the leadership of the Congress for alienating the Muslims of India and more and more 'pursuing a policy which is exclusively Hindu', Gandhi took this, not inappropriately, as a 'declaration of war', but, his eyes fixed on the struggle with the British, he was in no mood to negotiate with the League. Jinnah went on in December 1938 to denounce 'Mr Gandhi' (as he insisted on calling him) as the person primarily responsible for destroying 'the ideal with which the Congress was started', and for turning the party into 'an instrument for the revival of Hinduism'.[48] When Gandhi launched his 'Quit India' campaign in August 1942, Jinnah promptly condemned it as an attempt to blackmail the British into transferring power to a Hindu Raj. Despite what has often been seen as his aloof and haughty manner, in late 1937 Jinnah began to remodel himself as a popular leader (even putting aside his trademark Saville Row suits for a long black Punjabi coat and accompanying headgear) and to rebuild the League as a mass party to match the Congress. Like Gandhi (and many other politicians of the period), he acquired a popular title, becoming 'Quaid-i-Azam' (the Great Leader). For Jinnah, the quest for Pakistan was something of a personal vendetta, a test of wills against Gandhi and the rest of the Congress leadership.

On his release from jail on 6 May 1944, at a time when most other Congress leaders were still in prison, Gandhi was again plunged into the thick of political negotiations and was used by the British in an attempt to advance the settlement that had eluded them in 1940–2. In July and August 1944 he conducted a correspondence with the Viceroy, Lord Wavell, over India's political future, but there was a lack of respect and confidence between the two: Wavell, the blunt general, was no Irwin and found Gandhi an 'enigma' – or worse, a malevolent fraud.

Between 9 and 27 September 1944, Gandhi and Jinnah met in Bombay for a series of talks, Jinnah in the hope that this would lead to Congress recognition of Pakistan, Gandhi in the expectation that 'the whole of the Pakistan proposition' would be shown to be 'absurd'.[49] Gandhi, believing that such demands were primarily a reflection of British 'divide and rule' policies, asked that independence be given to India 'as it stands' and only then might some limited form of autonomy be given to Muslim majority areas, if the Muslims still felt it to be necessary. Jinnah, who had already rejected a similar proposal from the veteran Congress leader C. Rajagopalachari as amounting to a 'mutilated and moth-eaten Pakistan', repeated his demand for the creation of Pakistan at the same time as independence and consisting of the whole of six provinces – Punjab, Sind, Baluchistan, the North–West Frontier Province, Bengal and Assam. Gandhi again proposed a diluted version of Partition but without accepting the 'two nations' theory. Talks broke down on 27 September, with Jinnah declaring that he had evidently failed in his task of trying to 'convert Mr Gandhi'.[50]

. . .

INDEPENDENCE AND PARTITION

The period July–September 1944 effectively marked the end of Gandhi's single-handed attempts to negotiate on behalf of the Congress with the British and with the Muslim League. Thereafter, though he continued to play a significant part in the discussions that led up to the 'transfer of power' in India, he had, officially at least, a supporting role to Nehru, Patel and Maulana Azad (Congress President from 1940 to 1946). In a way this suited him. It left him free to pursue his own course, including individual forms of protest and direct action, rather than being caught up in constitutional wrangles, political deals and all the machinations involved in the 'end-game of empire'. But, even in old age and with no formal political authority, Gandhi, while ruing what he saw as his growing powerlessness, continued to have a significant impact on the course of the events.

On 7 May 1945 Germany surrendered to the Allied forces, followed on 14 August by Japan. On 14 June Wavell announced his intention to expand the Viceroy's Executive Council to include several Indian politicians, and the following day the remaining Congress leaders were released: most had been held in jail continuously since the Quit India Movement nearly three years earlier. Between 25 June and 14 July an all-parties conference was held at Simla (which Gandhi briefly attended) but it failed to agree even on Wavell's plan for an almost entirely Indian Executive Council, for Jinnah insisted on the League's right to nominate all its Muslim members and to enjoy parity with all other parties combined.[51] On 26 July the Labour Party under Clement Attlee won a landslide victory in Britain, thus ending Churchill's premiership (and sidelining his adamantine opposition to Indian independence) and increasing expectations that Britain was at last about to withdraw from an increasingly unmanageable India. The ill-judged attempt to put three officers of the former Indian National Army on trial in Delhi in late 1945 was soon abandoned, but it underscored the extent to which Britain was fast losing its grip on India. It was followed by a short-lived mutiny among ratings of the Royal Indian Navy in Bombay in February 1946 and a police strike in Bihar in April.

During December 1945 and January 1946 fresh elections were held in India, the first for nine years, but they seemed only to deepen communal divisions and the constitutional impasse. The

Congress won heavily in the main constituencies, but, unlike its poor performance in the 1937 elections, the Muslim League won all 30 of the Muslim seats in the central Legislative Assembly and 426 of the 509 seats reserved for Muslims in the provinces. The results appeared to confirm the nationwide strength of the Congress while endorsing Jinnah's claim that only the League could speak for India's Muslims, a quarter of the total population. The British made a further effort to resolve the Indian situation. A Cabinet Mission visited India in March–June 1946 under Lord Pethick-Lawrence, the Secretary of State for India (and with Sir Stafford Cripps and A. V. Alexander as its other members), but its compromise plan of dividing India into three zones (the Hindu-majority provinces plus the Muslim-majority provinces in the northwest and the northeast) linked by a weak federal government was wrecked by Jinnah's insistence on a separate state of Pakistan including the whole of Assam and Bengal. Treated by Pethick-Lawrence with a deference that dismayed Wavell, Gandhi's own demands to the Cabinet Mission were for the abolition of the salt tax, the release of political prisoners and the removal of Ambedkar from the Executive Council.[52] The Mission achieved little more than its predecessors, but the momentum for independence, even at the price of Partition, now appeared unstoppable.

On 2 September 1946 an Interim Government was formed with Nehru as Vice-President of the Viceroy's Executive Council and virtual Prime Minister. The League, having at first refused to participate, agreed to join the provisional government on 13 October. On 20 February 1947 Attlee announced that Britain would leave India by June 1948 and appointed Lord Louis Mountbatten, previously Supreme Allied Commander South-East Asia and a great grandson of Queen Victoria, to replace Wavell and oversee the last days of the Raj. Mountbatten arrived a month later and on 3 June brought forward the date of Britain's departure to 15 August 1947. At the same time he announced that India was to be partitioned between India and Pakistan, the latter divided into two wings, East and West Pakistan, separated by a thousand miles of Indian territory. By this time India was descending into a communal bloodbath. Following the failure of the Cabinet Mission, on 16 August 1946 the Muslim League, taking a leaf out of the Congress book, called for a 'Direct Action Day' to press its demands for Pakistan. In Calcutta this sparked three days of rioting and murder – 'the Great Calcutta Killing' – in which an estimated 4,000 people were killed and 15,000 injured. Violence erupted again in October, with Bengal and Bihar (where alone 7,000 Muslims were killed) the provinces worst affected, and in February 1947, this time particularly in Punjab, where within five months an estimated 5,000 Sikhs, Hindus and Muslims were slaughtered. India, a land of non-violence no longer, seemed to be slipping rapidly into bloodshed and chaos.[53]

Through all this Gandhi, now in his mid-70s, remained defiantly dedicated to non-violence. Rather than accept the 'two-nations' theory he proposed to both the Cabinet Mission and to the newly arrived Mountbatten that Jinnah be given complete control of the Interim Government, but Nehru and the other Congress leaders would not accept such an unwelcome and impractical suggestion.[54] Without the power to mount a new satyagraha, Gandhi set out to prove that the two communities could nonetheless be reconciled. In October 1946, with 'undiminished courage', he toured riot-torn Noakhali in east Bengal, walking more than a hundred miles and trying to restore peace to Hindus and Muslims. In November, to the alarm of Nehru and Patel, he threatened to fast to death if the Hindus of Bihar did not stop their killing. On 2 January 1947 Gandhi scrawled in his diary, 'All around me is utter darkness. When will God take me out of this darkness into His light?'[55] He set out, at great personal risk, on a pilgrimage for peace that lasted seven weeks, walking barefoot with a few companions through villages torn apart by communal violence. Sumit Sarkar has aptly seen this, rather than the Salt Satyagraha of 1930, as 'the Mahatma's finest hour', adding that 'Gandhi's unique personal qualities and true greatness [were] never more evident than in the last months of his life' as he displayed his 'passionate anti-communalism' and his 'total disdain for all conventional forms of political power'.[56] But Gandhi was in agony over the direction in which India appeared to be moving. On 31 May he remarked, 'My life's work seems to be over. I hope God will spare me further humiliation.'[57] When in June 1947 the Congress leadership reluctantly conceded the demand for Partition, Gandhi considered it a 'spiritual tragedy' and bitterly lamented that for him 'thirty-two years of work have come to an inglorious end'.[58]

At the stroke of midnight on 14 August 1947 India and Pakistan became independent states, and Nehru, India's Prime Minister, spoke eloquently of this as India's long-awaited 'tryst with destiny', awakening at last to 'life and freedom'.[59] It was, by any standard, an extraordinary historical moment. More than sixty years after the founding of the Indian National Congress had marked the start of an organised nationalist movement, and eighteen years after the party leadership had declared its goal to be 'complete independence', India had at last won its freedom from colonial rule. With a population of 400 million, more than two-thirds of the entire British Empire, India's departure represented the greatest loss – in prestige as well as territory – the Empire had known since the American colonies had won their independence in 1783 and brought the first British Empire to an end. With India's independence, Britain lost the 'jewel' in its imperial crown, and the decolonisation of its remaining territories in Asia and Africa became almost inevitable.

As Mountbatten, now Governor-General of India, remarked amidst the rejoicing in New Delhi on 15 August, 'At this historic moment, let us not forget all that India owes to Mahatma Gandhi – the architect of her freedom through non-violence.'[60] But for Gandhi, far away in Calcutta trying to quell communal rioting, this was not a moment to celebrate or savour. Independence also brought Partition, India's 'vivisection' as Gandhi repeatedly described it, and unleashed mass migration and communal violence on an unprecedented scale. An untold number of people – perhaps 6 million – were forced to flee their homes and possibly a million more died in India's holocaust.[61] For the apostle of non-violence, for the man who had hoped for more than forty years to lead India to swaraj, independence on 15 August 1947 came as a day not of victory but of mourning, disillusionment and despair. Gandhi reflected this in October 1947 when he remarked with deep bitterness: 'It is I who am to be blamed. There has been some flaw somewhere in my ahimsa.'[62]

. . .

THE ASSASSINATION

In the days and months that followed Gandhi did what he could to use his diminished influence and moral authority to restore peace and sanity. On 1 October 1947, on the eve of his 78th birthday, he began his third and final fast 'unto death' to try to bring communal violence in Calcutta to an end. He broke his fast four days later after local peace had been restored.[63] His immense personal efforts were acknowledged by Nehru, Mountbatten and others, but Gandhi did not conceal his anguish not just over Partition itself but with the suffering of the many thousands of refugees, huddled together in insanitary makeshift camps on the outskirts of Delhi and other cities, and by the parody of swaraj India's independence had brought. His erstwhile Congress colleagues, now ensconced in power, seemed either intent on maintaining the worst aspects of colonial rule or were blind to the misery all around them.

Even before independence, on 1 April 1947, at one of the daily prayer meetings in Delhi which had become the last vehicle for his innermost thoughts and frustrations, Gandhi had remarked of the Congress leadership:

> No one listens to me any more. I am a small man. True, there was a time when mine was a big voice. Then everyone obeyed what I said; now neither the Congress nor the Hindus nor the Muslims listen to me . . . I am crying in the wilderness.[64]

Nine months later, on 11 January 1948, he appealed in vain for the Congress to give up power and dissolve itself rather than continue as it had now become, full of 'decay and decline', a place of 'corruption' overrun by 'power politics'. Reiterating his longstanding belief in the importance of social action, he called for a new 'Lok Sevak Sangh' (a People's Service Society) to replace the Congress, which had 'outlived its use'. This was to be made up of dedicated self-sacrificing workers who would help to bring genuine swaraj, 'social, moral and economic independence' to India's villages.[65] Again on 27 January 1948 Gandhi observed that the Congress had 'won political freedom' but had yet to win 'economic freedom, social and moral freedom'. These freedoms were harder to attain than political freedom 'because they are constructive, less exciting and not spectacular'.[66]

Gandhi was dismayed at the policies followed by Nehru but even more by India's Home Minister, his old associate, Vallabhbhai Patel, who now appeared to be drifting close to right-wing Hindu communalism and insensitive to the needs of the large number of Muslim refugees in Delhi and elsewhere. Gandhi undertook a new fast, this time to protest against anti-Muslim violence in Delhi from 13 to 18 January, but it was also by implication a fast against Patel's apparent indifference to Muslim suffering and the Government of India's unwillingness to pay the Rs 550 million (equivalent to £40 million) promised to Pakistan under the Partition agreement. In a bitter conversation shortly before his death Gandhi remarked to Patel, 'You are not the Sardar I once knew.'[67]

Gandhi, no stranger to personal violence since his early years in South Africa, found his life increasingly under threat for his attempts to restore Hindu-Muslim harmony. On 16 September 1947 there were chants of 'death to Gandhi' when he insisted on using passages from the Koran in his prayers, and four days later a bomb exploded near one of his meetings. A further attempt was made on his life on 20 January 1948. Then, just after 5 o'clock on 30 January, on his way to his evening prayer meeting at Birla House in Delhi, a Hindu extremist, Nathuram Godse, shot Gandhi three times at close range. He muttered 'Hey Ram' (Oh, God) and fell to the ground, dead.

Gandhi had long anticipated such an end, perhaps even regarding it as the ultimate sacrifice he would need to make in the cause of peace and communal harmony. At his prayer meeting on 12 January 1948 he complained of his own powerlessness, the 'impotence' that had been 'gnawing' at him of late, adding, 'Death for me would be a glorious deliverance rather than that I should be a helpless witness of the destruction of India, Hinduism, Sikhism, and Islam.'[68] As one of his biographers remarked, Gandhi's willingness to sacrifice himself (through a Christian rather than Hindu preoccupation with martyrdom), ran 'like a dark streak through his thoughts' from his early manhood onwards. It merged at the end of his life 'with the sense that immolation might give back a meaning which his life seemed to have lost in this time of horror and disappointment'.[69]

Why was Gandhi killed? To Godse, who had connections to both the Hindu Mahasabha and the RSS, he was the 'Father of Pakistan', the man who had failed to save India from the humiliation of Partition and was actively encouraging Muslim demands. But the reasons for Gandhi's assassination went deeper than that. Godse was a Maharashtrian and a Chitpavan Brahmin, a member of the caste that had conspicuously identified itself with Shivaji and with the Hindu nationalism of Tilak. Godse shared the belief that India was essentially a Hindu nation, betrayed and oppressed by Muslims, and that India could only be truly liberated by force. Gandhi's death was a restatement of an old antipathy between neighbours, between the militant Brahmins of Maharashtra and the non-violent Banias of Gujarat. In his Hinduism Gandhi had sought to uncover and expound a tradition of ahimsa and a positive identification with feminine virtues. For Godse and other Hindu revolutionaries this spelled humiliation: for them India's real tradition was that of the Kshatriyas, not in the metaphorical way Gandhi employed it but as physical, not merely moral, force. Godse was greatly influenced by

V. D. Savarkar, the Maharashtrian militant and Hindu nationalist Gandhi had first encountered more than forty years earlier as an India House revolutionary in London, and the ghost of the old faith in assassination as a weapon of political action had come back to haunt Gandhi in his very last days. Ironically, while Godse and one of his co-conspirators, Narayan Apte, were sentenced to death, Savarkar escaped conviction and died of old age in 1966. Thus in Gandhi's violent death two conflicting traditions of religion and politics did battle for the soul of Hinduism and of India.

The Chitpavan Brahmins were also representative of India's old political elites, the kind who had lost out to Gandhi and his Congress supporters in the momentous changes of 1918–20 and, who, like Bose and his followers in Bengal, had never accepted this usurpation and demotion as final. Gandhi's 'epic fast' of 1932 and his espousal of the Harijan cause offended many high-caste Hindus and made him more than ever a threat to their high-caste status and privileged leadership. This was especially important as an issue in Maharashtra: Gandhi's fast had been conducted in Poona, the old Maratha capital, and in a province where low-caste movements and the assertiveness of castes like Ambedkar's Mahar community had aroused deep resentment.[70]

Gandhi's death – or martyrdom, as many contemporaries saw it – threw India into deep shock. Nehru, his political heir and successor, spoke desolately of a 'light' having gone out in the lives of millions of Indians, leaving 'darkness everywhere'. Echoing a poignant phrase he had used of his dead wife ten years earlier, Nehru lamented: 'Our beloved leader, Bapu as we called him, the Father of the Nation, is no more.' But, he added, 'the light that shone in this country was no ordinary light.' It represented 'something more than the immediate present' and would continue to 'illuminate this country for many more years', giving 'solace to innumerable hearts'. Gandhi's 'light' represented 'the living, the eternal truths, reminding us of the right path, drawing us from error, taking this ancient country to freedom.'[71] Far from Delhi, in her Himalayan ashram, Mirabehn mourned the Mahatma but recalled the crucifixion that had moved him years earlier in Rome. Now, she reflected on his martyrdom: 'The long-drawn-out crucifixion of Bapu's spirit was over, completed and consummated in the crucifixion of the flesh. It might take years, it might take centuries, but this last sacrifice, willingly given for the love of humanity, would conquer where all else might fail.'[72]

Biographers and historians have generally shared the view that Gandhi's assassination was not without effect and gave a final meaning to his life. More than any other single event, it has been said, his death served to stop the communal violence surrounding Partition: its 'cathartic effect' was felt throughout India and made men and women realise 'the depth to which hatred and discord had dragged them'.[73] In the words of Bhikhu Parekh, the assassination 'discredited Hindu extremists, chastened moderate Hindus, reassured the minorities, and pulled the mourning nation back from the brink of a disaster.'[74] Further, as Judith Brown has observed,

> Gandhi martyred proved even more powerful a bond for Indians than he had been alive, particularly in his last years when he had been isolated from the main stream of Congress politics and weakened by the escalation of Muslim nationalism. He became a national symbol, and in time almost a myth, his name invoked in times of national crisis and disunity.[75]

The 'light' that Nehru spoke of might still shine, but in future India would have to face times of crisis and disunity without the man who, over more than thirty years, had done so much to shape its identity and to fashion its destiny.

· · ·

NOTES AND REFERENCES

1. Jawaharlal Nehru, *An Autobiography*, London, 1936, p. 84.
2. *Selected Works of Jawaharlal Nehru*, IV, New Delhi, 1973, p. 192.
3. *Selected Works of Jawaharlal Nehru*, VI, New Delhi, 1974, p. 16.
4. Jawaharlal Nehru, *A Bunch of Old Letters*, London, 1958, pp. 507–10.
5. Leonard A. Gordon, *Brothers Against the Raj: A Biography of Indian Nationalists Sarat and Subhas Chandra Bose*, New York, 1990, pp. 218–20.
6. Ibid., pp. 350–2.
7. Ibid., p. 378.
8. Ibid., pp. 390–2.
9. Ibid., ch. 11.
10. Peter Ward Fay, *The Forgotten Army: India's Armed Struggle for Independence, 1942–1945*, Ann Arbor, 1995.
11. Judith M. Brown, *Modern India: The Origins of an Asian Democracy*, Oxford, 1985, pp. 275–305.
12. One partial exception was his willingness to assist the princely ruler of the tiny state of Aundh in 1938–9 to draw up a constitution embodying his ideas of village democracy: Joseph S. Alter, *Gandhi's Body: Sex, Diet and the Politics of Nationalism*, Philadelphia, 2000, ch. 4.

13. Rudrangshu Mukherjee, *The Penguin Gandhi Reader*, New Delhi, 1993, pp. 235–55.
14. Sumit Sarkar, *Modern India, 1885–1947*, Basingstoke, 1989, pp. 331–65.
15. Brown, *Modern India*, p. 287.
16. David Hardiman, 'The Crisis of the Lesser Patidars: Peasant Agitations in Kheda District, Gujarat, 1917–34', in D. A. Low (ed.), *Congress and the Raj: Facets of the Indian Struggle, 1917–47*, London, 1977, p. 71.
17. Louis Fischer, *The Life of Mahatma Gandhi*, New York, 1962, p. 344.
18. Anita Inder Singh, *The Origins of the Partition of India, 1936–1947*, Oxford, 1987, pp. 33–6.
19. Sarkar, *Modern India*, p. 352.
20. John R. Wood, 'Rajkot: Indian Nationalism in the Princely Context: The Rajkot Satyagraha of 1938–9', in Robin Jeffrey (ed.), *People, Princes and Paramount Power: Society and Politics in the Indian Princely States*, Delhi, 1978, pp. 240–74.
21. Sarkar, *Modern India*, p. 381.
22. Brown, *Modern India*, p. 309.
23. Fischer, *Gandhi*, p. 357.
24. Yogesh Chadha, *Rediscovering Gandhi*, London, 1997, p. 375.
25. Edward Thompson, 'Gandhi: A Character Study', in S. Radhakrishnan (ed.), *Mahatma Gandhi: Essays and Reflections on His Life and Work*, London, 1939, p. 285.
26. Dennis Dalton, *Mahatma Gandhi: Nonviolent Power in Action*, New York, 1993, pp. 134–7.
27. Mirabehn, *The Spirit's Pilgrimage*, London, 1960, p. 233.
28. William L. Shirer, *Gandhi: A Memoir*, New York, 1979, p. 190.
29. Sarkar, *Modern India*, p. 388.
30. D. G. Tendulkar, *Mahatma: Life of Mohandas Karamchand Gandhi*, VI, Bombay, 1953, p. 113.
31. *CWMG* LXXVI, pp. 389–92.
32. David Hardiman, 'The Quit India Movement in Gujarat', in Gyanendra Pandey (ed.), *The Indian Nation in 1942*, Calcutta, 1988, pp. 82–3.
33. Francine R. Frankel, *India's Political Economy, 1947–1977: The Gradual Revolution*, Princeton, 1978, pp. 52–3.
34. Francis G. Hutchins, *India's Revolution: Gandhi and the Quit India Movement*, Cambridge, Mass., 1973, pp. 230–2.
35. Fischer, *Gandhi*, pp. 388–91.
36. Sushila Nayar, *Mahatma Gandhi's Last Imprisonment: The Inside Story*, Delhi, 1996.
37. Hutchins, *India's Revolution*, ch. 3.
38. Chadha, *Gandhi*, p. 384.
39. David Potter, 'Manpower Shortage and the End of Colonialism: The Case of the Indian Civil Service', *Modern Asian Studies*, 7 (1973), pp. 47–73.

40. Penderel Moon (ed.), *Wavell: The Viceroy's Journal*, Oxford, 1973, p. 368.
41. M. K. Gandhi, *Hind Swaraj or Indian Home Rule*, Ahmedabad, 1939, pp. 44–5.
42. A. B. Shah, 'Gandhi and the Hindu-Muslim Question', in Sibnarayan Ray (ed.), *Gandhi, India and the World: An International Symposium*, Philadelphia, 1970, p. 188.
43. Singh, *Origins*, pp. 55–6.
44. M. H. Saiyid, *The Political Study of M. A. Jinnah*, Delhi, 1986, pp. 688–9.
45. *CWMG* LXXI, p. 412.
46. *CWMG* LXXVII, p. 101.
47. Shirer, *Gandhi*, p. 120.
48. *CWMG* LXVI, p. 257; Stanley Wolpert, *Jinnah of Pakistan*, New York, 1984, p. 166.
49. Singh, *Origins*, p. 112.
50. Ibid., pp. 109–12.
51. Ibid., pp. 121–3. For Jinnah's aims, see Ayesha Jalal, *The Sole Spokesman: Jinnah, the Muslim League and the Demand for Pakistan*, Cambridge, 1985.
52. Singh, *Origins*, pp. 153–6; Jalal, *Sole Spokesman*, ch. 5.
53. Singh, *Origins*, pp. 181–7.
54. Stanley Wolpert, *Nehru: A Tryst with Destiny*, New York, 1996, pp. 384–8.
55. Pyarelal, *Mahatma Gandhi The Last Phase*, I, Book 2, Ahmedabad, 1956, p. 115.
56. Sarkar, *Modern India*, p. 437.
57. *CWMG* LXXXVI, p. 302.
58. Fischer, *Gandhi*, p. 470.
59. *Selected Works of Jawaharlal Nehru*, III (second series), New Delhi, 1985, pp. 135–6.
60. Wolpert, *Nehru*, p. 406.
61. Brown, *Modern India*, p. 327.
62. Judith M. Brown, *Gandhi: Prisoner of Hope*, New Haven, 1989, p. 376.
63. Dalton, *Gandhi*, ch. 5.
64. *CWMG* LXXXVI, p. 187.
65. Pyarelal, *Mahatma Gandhi: The Last Phase*, II, Ahmedabad, 1958, p. 44.
66. *CWMG* XC, pp. 497–8.
67. Sarkar, *Modern India*, p. 438.
68. *CWMG* XC, pp. 408–10.
69. George Woodcock, *Gandhi*, London, 1972, p. 98.
70. Ashis Nandy, 'Final Encounter: The Politics of the Assassination of Gandhi', in his *At the Edge of Psychology: Essays in Politics and Culture*, Delhi, 1980, pp. 70–98; Chadha, *Gandhi*, pp. 469–503.

71. *Selected Works of Jawaharlal Nehru*, V (second series), New Delhi, 1987, p. 35.
72. Mirabehn, *Spirit's Pilgrimage*, p. 293.
73. Dalton, *Gandhi*, p. 167.
74. Bhikhu Parekh, *Gandhi*, Oxford, 1997, p. 25.
75. Brown, *Modern India*, p. 337.

CONCLUSION

Gandhi is one of the most immediately recognisable political leaders of modern times, but also one of the most elusive, complex and contradictory. The abundance of his own speeches and writings, spread over more than fifty years of active public life and covering an enormous range of topics, makes it virtually impossible to arrive at a definitive statement of exactly who Gandhi was and what he stood for. Almost any claim about Gandhi's motives and beliefs can be contradicted from one source or another, or confounded by the shift from one phase of his life to the next. The image of the Mahatma, in part self-generated, in part imposed by admirers and *darshan*-seekers, further stands in the way of an objective understanding. The determination in some quarters to see Gandhi as nothing less (and little more) than a saint – Hindu or Christian – obscures much of what made Gandhi both representative and unique.

There was not much in Gandhi's life, even in his beliefs and aspirations, that was particularly untypical of his age or of his reluctant status as a colonial subject. There were other Indians who came from small towns and became provincial lawyers, who studied abroad but found disappointment at home, who worked for at least part of their lives in Africa or elsewhere in the Empire, who lost their 'loyalty' and became nationalists, who 'discovered' the peasants and workers, or aspired to reform Hindu society and religion, or even who became swamis and saints, the revered 'servants' or 'leaders' of their chosen people. If Gandhi was unique it was because he combined *all* these (and many other) roles and identities. Growing up a *diwan*'s son in Kathiawar and London, coming to maturity in South Africa, learning from Champaran, Kheda and Ahmedabad, experimenting with *brahmacharya*, ahimsa and satyagraha, being a Bania by birth, but also a Kshatriya in spirit, a Shudra of sorts and a self-elected Harijan, espousing the cause of the 'poor, dumb millions' but consorting with capitalists, a man tormented by sex and taunted by India's 'emascula-tion', a devout Hindu profoundly influenced by Christianity, Gandhi acquired an exceptionally deep and wide-ranging awareness of the tensions and contradictions involved in being an Indian in a world full of white men's empires, of being caught between what was traditional and what was modern, between what was lauded as civilisation and lampooned as savagery. In picking his way through this minefield of paradox and adversity, Gandhi learned how to turn weakness into strength, fear into courage, and India, a place of 'slavery', into a society capable and worthy – or almost so – of his elevated conception of swaraj. While Gandhi spoke incessantly of 'truth', it was the extra-ordinary range and versatility of his understanding and use (or abuse) of power that was so remarkable and bordered on the unique.

There was, then, no single source for Gandhi's 'power'. Although scholars have found much of interest and importance in *Hind Swaraj* and *The Story of My Experiments with Truth*, Gandhi's writings were not themselves a major source of his political authority or social influence. Gandhi was not much of an orator, nor to judge by his dealings with Smuts, Irwin and Jinnah was he a particularly effective negotiator. He was clearly out of place in round table discussions like those held in London in 1931. He did not have a commanding physical presence, but he undoubtedly had great personal magnetism, which, coupled with his evident sincerity, patriotism, courage and capacity for self-suffering, helped him win the enduring loyalty of a large number of associates and followers, even when they disagreed with certain of his policies and practices. If he had the capacity to infuriate and antagonise – and a powerful authoritarian streak – he also had a 'child-like' sense of humour, with which he could win friends or puncture the pomposity of others. Beyond these personal qualities, Gandhi had the supreme asset of 'saintliness' and the au-thority this gave him not only with the masses of India but with the Indian middle classes and with a wider audience in Europe and beyond. This saintliness had many facets – from the Hindu avatar of Champaran and miraculous Mahatma of Gorakhpur to Romain Rolland's intimations of 'another Christ'. But, we should not forget that saintliness was a power that could repel as well as attract, and to many of his adversaries – to many Liberals, Marxists and Muslims, to the likes of Jinnah, Churchill and Ambedkar – it was precisely Gandhi's saintly attributes and presumptions, his 'Hindu fads', his 'inner voice', and the injection of 'superstition' into the rational discussion of political and social issues, that they found most infuriating and alienating (even while, often times, being forced to acknowledge the power this gave Gandhi over the masses of India).

But alongside the 'religious' Gandhi, and despite his frequent claim to recognise no meaningful distinction between religion and politics, Gandhi was a consummate politician. One part of this, which arguably owed something to his Bania background, was his seemingly tireless organisational ability, his unflagging attention to fund-raising, touring, pamphleteering, to making countless speeches and writing endless newspaper articles. This industriousness not only brought new life, unprecedented financial security and organisational strength to the Congress itself, but also helped spawn dozens of new societies and associations, some deservedly short-lived, others of more lasting importance like the Natal Indian Congress, the All-India Spinners' Association and the Harijan Sevak Sangh. Another element in his power was his un-saintly capacity, as he showed so deftly in his capture of the Congress in 1920 and so ruthlessly in his struggle against Subhas Chandra Bose in 1938–9, to outwit his opponents, to win, through sheer determination and the mobilising of personal allegiances and factional ties, the politics of committees, resolutions and organisational politics.

More important even than this organisational ability was satyagraha, the technique of non-violent civil disobedience which Gandhi developed well beyond the precedents of H. D. Thoreau, the Suffragettes and others and made uniquely and famously his own. Gandhi might not command armies or hold high office, but here was an instrument of proven efficacy, at least against the kinds of adversaries he encountered in South Africa and in British India, and Gandhi was the expert who knew best how to wield this remarkable weapon. It was this which made Gandhi's intervention seem potentially so attractive to the peasants of Champaran or the mill-hands of Ahmedabad but more especially to the Congress in 1920–2, 1930–3 and 1942. Like any weapon, however awesome, satyagraha had its limitations. Gandhi himself argued, sometimes to the bewilderment of supporters and opponents, that non-violence was not unconditional and that there were situations in which even a dedicated satyagrahi like himself might contemplate the necessity for violence. To be effective satyagraha also required a disciplined following, which Gandhi could not always command, and the kind of adversary who was prepared, when pushed hard enough, to make concessions and not merely dish out more coercion. It is ironic that in India civil disobedience had to contend with two other major strands of nationalist politics – the constitutionalism of the legislative arena and the violent strategies of the revolutionary terrorists and the Indian National Army. In this situation, even in India, satyagraha did not reign solitary or supreme, and the politics of constitutionalism and violence played no insignificant part in its eventual independence. The power of these alternative paths to freedom and political action plagued Gandhi throughout his adult life and pursued him, in the case of the cult of violence, to his very death. But, that said, Gandhi's technique did undoubtedly play a vital part in mobilising opposition against the British, in eroding their moral authority and political legitimacy, and in hastening the advent of independence and the dissolution of the Empire.

The last main element of Gandhi's power, not unrelated to the last, was his strategy of class conciliation. Although he repeatedly identified himself with the poor and oppressed, 'the dumb millions of India' as he chose to describe them, he was strongly opposed to class-based struggle and the war for social and economic justice that many in India were demanding. The benefit of this strategy from the Gandhian perspective was that it enabled the cross-class alliance of the nationalist movement to survive rather than fragment and it allied the wealth of India's merchants and industrialists to the jail-goers and the self-sacrificing activists involved in its freedom struggle. But in clinging to an impractical notion of trusteeship, and by assuming a somewhat patronising and moralistic attitude towards peasants, workers, untouchables and women, Gandhi failed to offer practical solutions to India's very real economic and social problems and to devise a form of executive agency or political action that could deliver the necessary reforms – a problem Jawaharlal Nehru was left to grapple with in the years after Independence. Gandhi had a remarkable political gift for dramatising issues and finding powerful symbols (more often than telling words) to express them – the salt tax and march of 1930 being striking examples. He was also prepared, to an extent unique among leaders of the modern world, to make his own body a battlefield, to put his life on the line and, through a succession of fasts, to use the power of his own self-suffering to win over the hearts and minds of others. But too often Gandhi was seduced by his own identification with the marginalised and the oppressed, by the warmth of personal contacts and exchanges, by symbols and gestures which did little to transform the reality he purported to address, or by alluring slogans and elusive concepts which mystified political objectives, obscured social goals and made him their sole arbiter and interpreter.

Over fifty years Gandhi won many seeming victories but most of them ended in unsatisfactory compromises and left issues unresolved. In all too few of these encounters were his opponents genuinely persuaded of the rightness of his cause or course of action. More often they were cowed or coerced by the power he had deployed against them. Gandhi, to his credit, often realised this weakness in himself, and even his greatest apparent triumph, India's independence in 1947, marred by violence and communalism, was, as he bitterly recognised, a kind of defeat. In a way, his death left the world free to determine for itself what Gandhi's legacy should be. He could be simultaneously, and without too much fear of contradiction, a Christian saint and upholder of Hindu tradition, the architect of Indian independence and father of the modern Indian nation, the inspiration for anti-colonial and nationalist movements around the world, a prophet of non-violence and world peace, an opponent of the machine age and modern civilisation, a virtual anarchist, a class conciliator and 'mascot of the bourgeoisie', a liberator of women, a saviour of peasants, untouchables, and all who find themselves oppressed. Gandhi was all (or nearly all) of these, but none of them in isolation does true justice to the complexity of the man and the contradictions of his life and legacy.

GLOSSARY

ahimsa	non-violence
ashram	spiritual community
Bania	caste from which Gandhi came; more generally, a moneylender and trader
Bapu	father; name affectionately given to Gandhi
bhakti	a devotional form of Hinduism
brahmacharya	celibacy
brahmachari	one who observes celibacy
Brahmin	the highest (priestly) caste and *varna*, representing spiritual authority
charkha	spinning-wheel
darshan	having sight of a holy person (or deity) and thereby receiving his blessings
dharma	religious and moral duty
diwan	chief minister in a princely state
Harijan	'Child of God', a term given by Gandhi to untouchables
hartal	cessation of work and closure of shops as a mark of protest
khadi	homespun, handwoven cloth
kisan	peasant
Kshatriya	member of a warrior caste, the second highest *varna* category, representing temporal power
lathi	a metal-tipped stave
Mahatma	'Great Soul'
moksha	spiritual liberation
Panchama	another term for an untouchable

236

panchayat	village or caste council
purna swaraj	complete independence
raiyat	peasant
Raj	government or rule, especially used to describe the British regime in India
Ram Rajya	'Rule of Ram', Hindu vision of idealised or ancient India
sadhu	a Hindu holy man
sannyasi	A Hindu mendicant, a renouncer
satyagraha	'truth-force', the struggle for truth (*satya*)
satyagrahi	one who practises satyagraha
Shudra	the lowest *varna* category, representing manual labour
swadeshi	goods made in one's own country; indigenous products or ideas
swaraj	'self-rule' or freedom: for Gandhi it also meant having control over oneself
taluk	sub-division of a district
Vaishya	the third *varna*, representing wealth and commerce
varna	the four orders of Hindu society (Brahmin, Kshatriya, Vaishya, Sudra)
varnashrama dharma	the theory and respective duties of the four *varnas*

GUIDE TO
FURTHER READING

GANDHI'S WRITINGS

Any worthwhile investigation of Gandhi's life and ideas must begin
with Gandhi's own writings. These are conveniently gathered together in the ninety volumes of *The Collected Works of Mahatma
Gandhi* (*CWMG*), (New Delhi, 1958–84). They include *Hind Swaraj*,
in *CWMG* X, pp. 6–68, which has also been issued separately by the
Navajivan Press in Ahmedabad, the principal publisher of Gandhi's
works, in various editions since 1938. Gandhi's other main work,
An Autobiography, Or the Story of My Experiments with Truth, first
published in two parts in 1927 and 1929, is also available in various
editions, including one published by Penguin Books. Useful thematic
selections from Gandhi's works include: Raghavan Iyer (ed.), *The
Moral and Political Writings of Mahatma Gandhi* in 3 volumes (Oxford,
1987); Rudrangshu Mukherjee (ed.), *The Penguin Gandhi Reader* (New
Delhi, 1993); and Dennis Dalton (ed.), *Mahatma Gandhi: Selected
Political Writings* (Indianapolis, 1996).

BIOGRAPHIES OF GANDHI

Biographies of Gandhi are legion, but disappointingly few are informed and critical or adequately locate Gandhi in his historical context. Among the more accessible are Geoffrey Ashe, *Gandhi: A Study in
Revolution* (London, 1968); Judith M. Brown, *Gandhi: Prisoner of Hope*
(New Haven, 1989); Yogesh Chadha, *Rediscovering Gandhi* (London,

1997), which incorporates extensive quotations from Gandhi; Louis Fischer, *The Life of Mahatma Gandhi* (New York, 1950), reissued 1962 and still a useful source; Penderel Moon, *Gandhi and Modern India* (London, 1968); B. R. Nanda, *Mahatma Gandhi* (Bombay, 1958), a rather sketchy introduction, and, more substantially, Robert Payne, *The Life and Death of Mahatma Gandhi* (London, 1969). Gandhi's writings and other useful materials are also brought together in the eight-volume biography by D. G. Tendulkar, *Mahatma: Life of Mohandas Karamchand Gandhi* (Bombay, 1951–4), which also contains a large number of photographs of Gandhi. Among the shorter introductions particularly helpful are Bhikhu Parekh, *Gandhi* (Oxford, 1997), and George Woodcock's concise and insightful, *Gandhi* (London, 1972). It is necessary, however, to look to recent monographs and articles for a more critical and scholarly understanding of Gandhi.

. . .

INTERPRETATIONS OF GANDHI

This is where some of the most challenging and insightful views of Gandhi are to be found. Margaret Chatterjee, *Gandhi's Religious Thought* (London, 1983) is a helpful introduction to its subject, especially Gandhi's complex relations with Christianity. His Hinduism and other aspects of his religious ideas receive consideration in J. T. F. Jordens, *Gandhi's Religion: A Homespun Shawl* (Basingstoke, 1998). Two original and exemplary studies of Gandhi's ideas and practices are Dennis Dalton, *Mahatma Gandhi: Nonviolent Power in Action* (New York, 1993) and Bhikhu Parekh, *Gandhi's Political Philosophy: A Critical Examination* (Basingstoke, 1989). Critical views of Gandhi are to be found in condensed form in M. D. Lewis (ed.), *Gandhi: Maker of Modern India* (Boston, 1965); see, too, Subayashi Bhattacharya (ed.), *The Mahatma and the Poet: Letters and Debates between Gandhi and Tagore, 1915–1941* (New Delhi, 1997), and B. R. Nanda, *Gandhi and His Critics* (New Delhi, 1985).

For the more general context of Gandhi, colonial India and the nationalist struggle, see: Sugata Bose and Ayesha Jalal, *Modern South Asia: History, Culture, Political Economy* (London, 1998); Judith M. Brown, *Modern India: The Origins of an Asian Democracy* (Oxford, 1985); Burton Stein, *A History of India* (Oxford, 1988); and especially Sumit Sarkar, *Modern India, 1885–1947*, first published in Delhi in 1983 and, in a revised edition, in 1989.

For other wide-ranging interpretations of Gandhi's personality, ideas and methods, see: Joan Bondurant, *Conquest of Violence* (Princeton, 1988); chapter 4 of Partha Chatterjee, *Nationalist Thought and the Colonial World: A Derivative Discourse?* (London, 1986); Michael Edwardes, *The Myth of the Mahatma* (a decidedly unsympathetic view of Gandhi); Erik H. Erikson, *Gandhi's Truth: On the Origins of Militant Nonviolence* (New York, 1969) for a psychoanalytical approach; Richard G. Fox, *Gandhian Utopia: Experiments with Culture* (Boston, 1989), a useful contextualising of Gandhi's ideas; Richard B. Gregg, *The Power of Non-Violence* (Philadelphia, 1934), an important American pioneering work on Gandhi; H. J. N. Horsburgh, *Non-Violence and Aggression* (London, 1968); Ashis Nandy, *The Intimate Enemy: Loss and Recovery of Self Under Colonialism* (Delhi, 1983), pp. 26–63; Bhikhu Parekh, *Colonialism, Tradition and Reform: An Analysis of Gandhi's Political Discourse* (New Delhi, 1989), which supplements but does not quite match the same author's *Gandhi's Political Philosophy*; and Lloyd I. Rudolph and Susanne Hoeber Rudolph, *Gandhi* (Chicago, 1983), which gives an interesting account of 'Gandhi's courage'.

· · ·

MEMOIRS OF GANDHI

There are a considerable number of these, of very mixed quality. Among the most useful are: G. D. Birla, *In the Shadow of the Mahatma* (Bombay, 1953); Nirmal Kumar Bose, *My Days with Gandhi* (Calcutta, 1953); Krishnadas, *Seven Months with Mahatma Gandhi* (Ahmedabad, 1951); Mirabehn, *The Spirit's Pilgrimage* (London, 1960); Pyarelal and Sushila Nayar, *In Gandhiji's Mirror* (Delhi, 1991); and, from an American's perspective, William L. Shirer, *Gandhi: A Memoir* (New York, 1979). In its wealth of ambiguity about Gandhi, Jawaharlal Nehru's *Autobiography* (London, 1936) remains one of the most revealing and challenging of all these accounts.

· · ·

GANDHI'S CHILDHOOD AND LONDON YEARS

In addition to his autobiography and the many biographies, the significance of Gandhi's early years is best gleaned from: A. L.

Basham, 'Traditional Influences on the Thought of Mahatma Gandhi', in R. Kumar (ed.), *Essays on Gandhian Politics: The Rowlatt Satyagraha of 1919* (Oxford, 1971), pp. 17–42; Stephen N. Hay, 'Jain Influences on Gandhi's Early Thought', in Sibnarayan Ray (ed.), *Gandhi, India and the World* (Philadelphia, 1970), pp. 29–38; and Howard Spodek, 'On the Origins of Gandhi's Political Methodology: The Heritage of Kathiawar and Gujarat', *Journal of Asian Studies*, 30 (1971), pp. 361–72. For the London years, see Stephen Hay's articles 'The Making of a Late-Victorian Hindu: Gandhi in London, 1888–91', *Victorian Studies*, 33 (1989), pp. 76–98, and 'Between Two Worlds: Gandhi's First Impressions of British Culture', *Modern Asian Studies*, 3 (1969), pp. 305–19, as well as James D. Hunt, *Gandhi in London*, an invaluable and wider ranging study than its title might suggest, first published in New Delhi in 1978 and in a revised edition in 1993.

. . .

GANDHI IN SOUTH AFRICA

Most of the standard biographies cover the South African period, notably Brown, *Gandhi: Prisoner of Hope* and Fischer's *Life of Mahatma Gandhi*. It is also worth turning directly to one of Gandhi's less considered works, *Satyagraha in South Africa* (*CWMG* XXIX, pp. 1–269), as well as to his autobiography, and to the essays in Judith M. Brown and Martin Prozesky (eds), *Gandhi and South Africa: Principles and Politics* (Pietermaritzburg, 1996). Chandran D. S. Devanesen, *The Making of the Mahatma* (Madras, 1969), which covers Gandhi's early years as well as South Africa, Robert A. Huttenback, *Gandhi in South Africa* (Ithaca, 1971), Huttenback's 'Some Fruits of Victorian Imperialism: Gandhi and the Indian Question in Natal, 1893–99', *Victorian Studies*, 11 (1967), pp. 153–80, and Martin Green's *Gandhi: Voice of a New Age Revolution* (New York, 1993), especially chapters 4 and 5, are all useful. A more provocative interpretation is to be found in Maureen Swan, *Gandhi: The South African Experience* (Johannesburg, 1985).

Hind Swaraj, one of the principal products of Gandhi's South African years and an essential source for his ideas, is reproduced in Mukherjee's *Penguin Gandhi Reader*, pp. 1–67; in Iyer's *Moral and Political Writings*, I, pp. 198–264, and, with a useful commentary and background notes, by Anthony J. Parel in *Gandhi: Hind Swaraj and Other Writings* (Cambridge, 1997). On Gandhi's 'critique of modern civilisation', see also Dalton, *Mahatma Gandhi*, Hunt, *Gandhi in London*, and Parekh, *Gandhi's Political Philosophy*.

. . .

GANDHI AND THE CONGRESS

For Gandhi's own writings, see his *Autobiography*, Mukherjee's *Penguin Gandhi Reader*, especially pp. 125–56 and Iyer's *Moral and Political Writings*, volume III. Gopal Krishna, 'The Development of Congress as a Mass Organization', *Journal of Asian Studies*, 25 (1966), pp. 413–30, and Judith M. Brown, *Gandhi's Rise to Power: Indian Politics, 1915–1922* (Cambridge, 1972), are valuable guides to the political developments of this period, but there are several important collections of articles worth consulting, including J. Gallagher, G. Johnson and A. Seal (eds), *Locality, Province and Nation: Essays on Indian Politics, 1870–1940* (Cambridge, 1973); Kumar (ed.), *Essays in Gandhian Politics*; D. A. Low (ed.), *Congress and the Raj: Facets of the Indian Struggle* (London, 1977); Ray (ed.), *Gandhi, India and the World*; Richard Sisson and Stanley Wolpert (eds), *Congress and Indian Nationalism: The Pre-Independence Phase* (Berkeley, 1988). Helpful, too, in tracing the course of the Non-Co-operation Movement and its significance are: H. F. Owen, 'Towards Nationwide Agitation', in D. A. Low (ed.), *Soundings in Modern South Asian History* (London, 1968), pp. 159–95; P. H. N. van den Dungen, 'Gandhi in 1919: Loyalist or Rebel?', in Kumar (ed.), *Essays in Gandhian Politics*, pp. 43–63; and Gail Minault, *The Khilafat Movement: Religious Symbolism and Political Mobilization in India* (Delhi, 1982).

New and more detailed interpretations of Gandhi's 'rise to power' are to be found in Shahid Amin, 'Gandhi as Mahatma: Gorakhpur District, Eastern U. P., 1921–22', in Ranajit Guha (ed.), *Subaltern Studies III* (Delhi, 1984), pp. 1–6; Kenneth L. Gillion, *Ahmedabad: A Study in Urban History* (Canberra, 1969), chapter 5; Rajat Ray, 'Masses in Politics: Non-Cooperation in Bengal, 1920–22', *Indian Economic and Social History Review*, 11 (1974), pp. 343–410; Stephen Henningham, 'The Social Setting of the Champaran Satyagraha: The Challenge of an Alien Elite', *Indian Economic and Social History Review*, 13 (1976), pp. 59–73; and Jacques Pouchepadass, 'Local Leaders and the Intelligentsia in the Champaran Satyagraha (1917): A Study in Peasant Mobilization', *Contributions to Indian Sociology*, 8

(1974), pp. 67–87. A more extended and revised discussion of this satyagraha is to be found in Pouchepadass's *Champaran and Gandhi: Planters, Peasants and Gandhian Politics* (New Delhi, 1999).

. . .

GANDHI AND THE PEASANTS

This topic obviously overlaps with the previous one, but see, too: Judith Brown, 'Gandhi and India's Peasants, 1917–22', *Journal of Peasant Studies*, 1 (1974), pp. 462–85; D. N. Dhanagare, *Peasant Movements in India, 1920–1950* (Delhi, 1983); A. R. Desai, *Peasant Struggles in India*, as well as Gail Omvedt 'Gandhi and the Pacification of the Indian National Revolution', *Bulletin of Concerned Asian Scholars*, 5 (1973), pp. 2–8, and Ranajit Guha, *Dominance Without Hegemony: History and Power in Colonial India* (Cambridge, Mass., 1997), chapter 2. There are a large number of significant regional studies, including: W. F. Crawley, 'Kisan Sabhas and Agrarian Revolt in the United Provinces', *Modern Asian Studies*, 5 (1971), pp. 95–109; David Hardiman, *Peasant Nationalists of Gujarat: Kheda District, 1917–34* (Delhi, 1981); Kapil Kumar, *Peasants in Revolt: Oudh, 1918–22* (Delhi, 1984); Gyan Pandey, 'Peasant Revolt and Indian Nationalism: The Peasant Movement in Awadh', in Ranajit Guha (ed.), *Subaltern Studies I* (Delhi, 1982), pp. 142–91; and Gyanshayam Shah, 'Traditional Society and Political Mobilization: The Experience of the Bardoli *Satyagraha* (1920–1928)', *Contributions to Indian Sociology*, 8 (1974), pp. 89–107.

. . .

GANDHIAN ECONOMICS

Among the most useful discussion of Gandhi's economic ideas, are: Ajit K. Dasgupta, 'Gandhian Economics', in his *A History of Indian Economic Thought* (London, 1993), pp. 131–62; Ira Klein, 'Indian Nationalism and Anti-Industrialization: The Roots of Gandhian Economics', *South Asia*, 3 (1973), pp. 193–204; J. C. Kumarappa, *Gandhian Economic Thought* (Benares, 1962); J. S. Mathur, *Essays on Gandhian Economics* (Allahabad, 1960); and Vivek Pinto, *Gandhi's Vision and Values: The Moral Quest for Change in Indian Agriculture* (New Delhi, 1998). For some aspects of khadi and the Constructive

Programme, see Emma Tarlo, *Clothing Matters: Dress and Identity in India* (London, 1996), chapter 3, and Mark Thomson, *Gandhi and his Ashrams* (London, 1993).

. . .

GANDHI, CAPITALISM AND THE WORKING CLASS

In addition to Sarkar, *Modern India*, see the selection in Mukherjee, *Penguin Gandhi Reader*, pp. 235–55, and Sabyasachi Bhattacharya, 'Cotton Mills and Spinning Wheels: Swadeshi and the Indian Capitalist Class, 1920–22', in K. N. Panikkar (ed.), *National and Left Movements in India* (New Delhi, 1980), pp. 27–44; Ravinder Kumar, 'From Swaraj to Purna Swaraj: Nationalist Politics in Bombay, 1920–32', in Low (ed.), *Congress and the Raj*, pp. 77–107; Claude Markovits, 'Congress Policy towards Business in the Pre-Independence Era', in Sisson and Wolpert (eds), *Congress and Indian Nationalism*, pp. 250–68; Jim Masselos, 'Some Aspects of Bombay City Politics in 1919', in Kumar (ed.), *Essays in Gandhian Politics*, pp. 145–88.

. . .

CIVIL DISOBEDIENCE AND AFTER

Judith M. Brown, *Gandhi and Civil Disobedience: The Mahatma in Indian Politics, 1928–1934* (Cambridge, 1977), and Dalton, *Mahatma Gandhi*, chapter 4, provide good introductions to the Civil Disobedience Movement of 1930–4, but important aspects of the movement and its wider historical context are discussed in Sumit Sarkar, 'The Logic of Gandhian Nationalism: Civil Disobedience and the Gandhi-Irwin Pact (1930–1931)', *Indian Historical Review*, 3 (1976), pp. 114–46; D. A. Low, 'Civil Martial Law: The Government of India and the Civil Disobedience Movement, 1930–34', in Low (ed.), *Congress and the Raj*, pp. 165–98; and Carl Bridge, *Holding India to the Empire: The British Conservative Party and the 1935 Constitution* (New Delhi, 1986). This movement, too, is covered in a number of regional studies, including: Leonard A. Gordon, *Bengal: The Nationalist Movement, 1876–1940* (New York, 1974); Hardiman, *Peasant Nationalists of Gujarat*, chapter 8; and Tanika Sarkar, *Bengal, 1928–34: The Politics of Protest* (Delhi, 1987). For Congress and

Gandhi in the mid- and late 1930s, see B. R. Tomlinson, *The Indian National Congress and the Raj, 1929–1942: The Penultimate Phase* (London, 1976); D. A. Low, *Britain and Indian Nationalism: The Imprint of Ambiguity, 1929–1942* (Cambridge, 1997); Judith Brown, 'The Mahatma in Old Age, 1935–42', in Sisson and Wolpert (eds), *Congress and Indian Nationalism*, pp. 271–304; and J. R. Wood, 'Rajkot: Indian Nationalism in the Princely Context: The Rajkot Satyagraha of 1938–9', in Robin Jeffrey (ed.), *People, Princes and Paramount Power* (Delhi, 1978), pp. 240–74. On the interesting question why Gandhi, despite his international reputation, did not receive the Nobel Prize for Peace in the late 1930s or shortly before his death, see Thomas Weber, 'Gandhi and the Nobel Peace Prize', *South Asia*, 12 (1989), pp. 29–47.

. . .

GANDHI, WOMEN AND SEX

For Gandhi's general views, see Mukherjee's *Penguin Gandhi Reader*, pp. 179–203; Brown, *Gandhi*; and Geraldine Forbes, *Women in Modern India* (Cambridge, 1996). For more detail and comment, see: Joseph S. Alter, *Gandhi's Body: Sex, Diet, and the Politics of Nationalism* (Philadelphia, 2000); Madhu Kishwar, 'Gandhi on Women', *Economic and Political Weekly*, 5 October 1985, pp. 1691–702 and 12 October 1985, pp. 1753–8; Sujata Patel, 'Construction and Reconstruction of Woman in Gandhi', *Economic and Political Weekly*, 20 February 1988, pp. 377–87; Radha Kumar, *The History of Doing: An Illustrated Account of Movements for Women's Rights and Feminism in India, 1800–1990* (London, 1993); U. Mazumdar, 'The Social Movement in India: From Ranade to Nehru', in B. R. Nanda (ed.), *Indian Women from Purdah to Modernity* (New Delhi, 1976) pp. 41–66; and Parekh, *Colonialism, Tradition and Reform*, chapter 6.

. . .

GANDHI, HINDUISM AND UNTOUCHABILITY

For Gandhi's own writings, see Mukherjee, *Penguin Gandhi Reader*, pp. 207–33; Iyer, *Moral and Political Writings*, I, as well as B. R. Ambedkar, *What Congress and Gandhi Have Done to the Untouchables* (Bombay, 1945), Chatterjee, *Gandhi's Religious Thought*, Dalton,

Mahatma Gandhi, Jordens, *Gandhi's Religion*, and Parekh, *Colonialism, Tradition and Reform*, chapter 7. More specifically, see: Ravinder Kumar, 'Gandhi, Ambedkar and the Poona Pact, 1932', *South Asia*, 8 (1985), pp. 87–101; Pyarelal, *The Epic Fast* (Ahmedabad, 1932); and Eleanor Zelliot, 'Congress and the Untouchables, 1917–1950', in Sisson and Wolpert (eds), *Congress and Indian Nationalism*, pp. 182–97.

. . .

'QUIT INDIA' AND THE SECOND WORLD WAR

On the Quit India Movement, apart from Gandhi's own writing, collected together as M. K. Gandhi, *Quit India*, the most authoritative source is Francis G. Hutchins, *India's Revolution: Gandhi and the Quit India Movement* (Cambridge, Mass., 1973), supplemented by Gyanendra Pandey, (ed.), *The Indian Nation in 1942* (Calcutta, 1988), which contains several regional studies of the movement. On Bose and the Indian National Army, see: Leonard A. Gordon, *Brothers Against the Raj* (New York, 1990); and Peter Ward Fay, *The Forgotten Army: India's Armed Struggle for Independence, 1942–45* (Ann Arbor, 1995).

. . .

GANDHI AND PARTITION

In addition to Mukherjee, *Penguin Gandhi Reader*, pp. 259–83, and Bose and Jalal, *Modern South Asia*, chapters 15–17, see: R. J. Moore, *Churchill, Cripps and India, 1939–45*, Oxford, 1979; David Page, *Prelude to Partition* (Oxford, 1982); as well as, in a more novelistic vein, Larry Collins and Dominique Lapierre, *Freedom at Midnight* (Delhi, 1976); Parekh, *Gandhi's Political Philosophy*; Bimal Prasad, 'Congress versus the Muslim League, 1935–1937', in Sisson and Wolpert (eds), *Congress and Indian Nationalism*, pp. 305–29; A. B. Shah, 'Gandhi and the Hindu-Muslim Question, in Ray (ed.), *Gandhi, India and the World*, pp. 188–208; and Anita Inder Singh, *The Origins of the Partition of India, 1936–1947* (Oxford, 1987). Mushirul Hasan (ed.), *India's Partition: Process, Strategy and Mobilization* (Delhi, 1993) contains a useful selection of historical sources and interpretive essays: C. H. Philips and M. D. Wainwright (eds), *The Partition of India: Policies and Perspectives, 1935–1947* (London, 1970) is now rather dated but covers some topics and lines of argument relating to Partition not found elsewhere. Stanley Wolpert's two studies, *Jinnah of Pakistan* (New York, 1984) and *Nehru: A Tryst with Destiny* (New York, 1996) add useful biographical perspectives on two of the principal participants. For a substantially different understanding of Jinnah's aims and motives, see Ayesha Jalal, *The Sole Spokesman: Jinnah, the Muslim League and the Demand for Pakistan* (Cambridge, 1985).

.   .   .

THE FINAL PHASE

Gandhi's final years and the assassination are covered in most biographies, including Payne, *Life and Death of Mahatma Gandhi*, pp. 637–41 and, more recently, Chadha, *Rediscovering Gandhi*, pp. 461–503, and at greater length and in loving detail in Pyarelal, *Mahatma Gandhi: The Last Phase*, 2 vols (Ahmedabad, 1956–58). See, too, Dalton, *Mahatma Gandhi*, chapter 5, for the Calcutta fast of September 1947, and Ashis Nandy, 'Final Encounter: The Politics of the Assassination of Gandhi' in his *At the Edge of Psychology: Essays in Politics and Culture* (Delhi, 1980), pp. 70–98.

.   .   .

GANDHI'S LEGACY

In addition to the biographies and interpretative works, see, for the assessment of a near contemporary, Frank Moraes, *India Today* (New York, 1960). One of the finest scholarly assessments of Gandhi's contribution to modern India is to be found in Francine R. Frankel, *India's Political Economy, 1947–1977: The Gradual Revolution* (Princeton, 1978), chapter 2. Fox, *Gandhian Utopia*, looks at some of the consequences of Gandhi's legacy for India, as does Geoffrey Ostergaard, from a more sympathetic perspective, in *Nonviolent Revolution in India* (New Delhi, 1985). Dalton, *Mahatma Gandhi*, chapter 6, discusses Gandhi's impact on Martin Luther King and the United States. Although their focus is more on Nehru, his principal heir, than on Gandhi, there are some useful ideas about his impact and legacy in Sunil Khilnani, *The Idea of India* (London, 1997), P. R. Brass, *The Politics of India since Independence* (Cambridge, 1990), and Judith M. Brown, *Nehru* (London, 1999), also published in this 'Profiles in Power' series.

· · · · · · ·

CHRONOLOGY

1869 born, 2 October, Porbandar, Gujarat
1882 marries Kasturbai Makanji
1885 death of his father, Karamchand Gandhi
1888 arrives in London (November); enrols as a law student
1890 joins the London Vegetarian Society
1891 returns to India from London (June)
1893 goes to South Africa as a legal adviser
1894 helps found the Natal Indian Congress
1896 return visit to India (June to November)
1899 Boer War: organises ambulance corps
1901 back to India, intending to stay, but returns to South Africa (1902)
1903 sets up legal practice in Johannesburg
1904 reads Ruskin's *Unto This Last*; establishes Phoenix Settlement near Durban
1906 ambulance work during Zulu Rebellion; takes vow of celibacy; visits London
1908 adopts term satyagraha; first imprisonment (January); second (October to December)
1909 third imprisonment (February to May); visits London (July-November); writes *Hind Swaraj*
1910 establishes Tolstoy Farm near Johannesburg
1913 renewed satyagraha and protest marches in South Africa; Kasturba imprisoned; fourth imprisonment (November-December)
1914 agreement with Smuts (January); leaves South Africa (July); visits London

1915   returns to India (January); starts Sabarmati Ashram at Ahmedabad (May)

1916   speech at Benares Hindu University (February)

1917   begins Champaran Satyagraha in Bihar (April)

1918   Ahmedabad mill strike (February); Kheda Satyagraha in Gujarat (March)

1919   6–18 April, Rowlatt Satyagraha; 13 April, Jallianwala Bagh massacre in Amritsar

1920   Non-Cooperation launched (August); Calcutta Special Congress approves non-cooperation programme (September); confirmed at Nagpur (December)

1921   Malabar Rebellion (August); civil disobedience started (December)

1922   4 February, Chauri Chaura; arrested 10 March; fifth imprisonment (March 1922 to February 1924) begins

1924   released from jail (February); becomes Congress President for 1925 (December)

1927   Statutory (Simon) Commission appointed; first volume of *The Story of My Experiments with Truth* published

1928   Nehru Committee report; Bardoli Satyagraha; *Satyagraha in South Africa* published

1929   second volume of autobiography published; complete independence resolution at Lahore (December)

1930   12 March–6 April, Salt March from Sabarmati to Dandi; arrested for breaking salt laws; sixth imprisonment, May 1930 to January 1931

1931   released from jail (January); 4 March, Gandhi–Irwin Pact agreed; September to December in London for Second Round Table Conference

1932   civil disobedience resumed; arrested 4 January; seventh imprisonment, January 1932 to May 1933; fast over separate electorates for untouchables; 25 September, Poona Pact

1933   released from jail (May); rearrested and released (eighth imprisonment, August 1933); begins Harijan tour (November 1933 to June 1934)

1934   civil disobedience formally suspended (May); bomb attempt on his life (June); resigns from Congress (October)

1935   Government of India Act

1936   establishes Sevagram Ashram near Wardha (April)

1937   presides over educational conference at Wardha

1939   3 to 7 March, Rajkot fast

1940   'Individual Satyagraha' (begins October)
1942   8 August, launches Quit India movement; arrested; ninth imprisonment, August 1942 to May 1944
1944   death of Kasturba (22 February); released from prison (May); talks with Jinnah (September)
1945   attends Simla Conference (June)
1946   meets Cabinet Mission (June); Calcutta riots (August); tours Bengal and Bihar over communal violence (for four months from November 1946)
1947   15 August, Independence Day and Partition; 1–5 September, Calcutta fast
1948   13–18 January, Delhi fast; assassinated 30 January

A fuller chronology can be found in each of the three volumes of Raghavan Iyer, *The Moral and Political Writings of Mahatma Gandhi*, Oxford, 1987.

. . . .

MAPS

SIND

THAR DESERT

RAJPUTANA

GREAT RANN OF CUTCH

GUJARAT

GULF OF CUTCH

Dwarka

Rajkot

Ahmedabad
Kaira
Nadiad
Cambay

KATHIAWAR

Baroda

Porbandar

Bhavnagar
Broach

Surat

ARABIAN
SEA

Diu
(Portuguese)

GULF OF CAMBAY

Daman
(Portuguese)

Nasik

Baroda
Other Princely States
British India

0   50   100 miles
0   75   150 km

Bombay

Poona

1.   Western India in the late nineteenth century

N

PORTUGUESE
EAST AFRICA

TRANSVAAL

Pretoria
Tolstoy Farm
Johannesburg

Delagoa Bay
Lourenço Marques

SWAZI-
LAND

Standerton
Volksrust
Charlestown
Newcastle
Ladysmith

ORANGE FREE
STATE

Bloemfontein

NATAL

ZULULAND

BASUTO-
LAND

Phoenix
Pietermaritzburg
Durban
Pinetown

*INDIAN
OCEAN*

CAPE COLONY

East London

Port Elizabeth

| 0 | 100 | 200 miles |
| 0 | 150 | 300 km |

2.   Southeast Africa in the 1890s

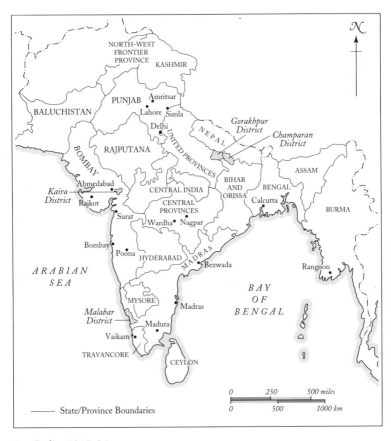

3. India, 1915–36

INDEX